The Golden Spurs of Kortrijk

The Golden Spurs of Kortrijk

*How the Knights of France
Fell to the Foot Soldiers
of Flanders in 1302*

RANDALL FEGLEY

McFarland & Company, Inc., Publishers
Jefferson, North Carolina, and London

Library of Congress Cataloguing-in-Publication Data

Fegley, Randall, 1955–
    The golden spurs of Kortrijk : how the knights of France
fell to the foot soldiers of Flanders in 1302 / Randall Fegley.
       p.   cm.
    Includes bibliographical references and index.
    ISBN 0-7864-1310-7 (softcover : 50# alkaline paper) ∞
    1. Kortrijk (Belgium), Battle of, 1302.   2. Flanders
(Belgium)— History.   3. France — History — Philip IV,
1285–1314.   I. Title.
DH801.F462F44   2002
949.3'01— dc21   2002000544

British Library cataloguing data are available

On the front cover: *"De Guldensporenslag" (the Golden Spurs
battle), an oil painting by* Nicaise de Keyser *(Collection of
Stedelijke Musea Kortrijk — City Museum of Kortrijk)*

Manufactured in the United States of America

McFarland & Company, Inc., Publishers
  Box 611, Jefferson, North Carolina 28640
   www.mcfarlandpub.com

Acknowledgments

Many people helped to complete this project and deserve recognition.

For illustrations, I am indebted to Sarah Bauwens, W. Rycquart and Griet Teetaert of the Stedelijke Musea Brugge, Bruges, Belgium; Catherine Rastgou and Tatiana Trusevitch of the Bibliothèque Nationale de France, Paris; Christina Ceulemans, Jaak Jansen and Dr. Liliane Masschelein-Kleiner of the Institut Royal du Patrimoine Artistique/Koninklijk Instituut voor het Kunstpatrimonium (IRPA/KIK), Brussels, Belgium; and David Plotkin of Corbis Images, New York. For illustrations, ideas and much useful information, my thanks go to Isabella De Jaegere and Greet Verschatse of the Stedelijke Musea Kortrijk, Kortrijk, Belgium; Joris De Sutter of De Liebaart; and the Bruges Tourist Office.

For proof-reading and many helpful suggestions, I would like to thank John Bambrick, Ann Leithiser, Dara McCue and Maggie Rice for reading parts of the manuscript and for numerous suggestions.

Most importantly, my wife and best friend Connie provided numerous ideas, much forbearance, and a hundred and one acts of encouragement and assistance. Without her presence, this work would have not been possible.

v

A Note on Language

Language is an issue of defining importance in Belgium. In naming places I have preferred to use the traditionally accepted English forms of well-known Belgium places (Ghent, Bruges, Antwerp, Brussels) rather than their local equivalents (Gent, Brugge, Antwerpen, Bruxelles/Brussel). One exception I have made to this rule is the use of Kortrijk, as opposed to its more familiar French form Courtrai. As the events recounted in this book are a source of great pride to the Flemings, it hardly seemed appropriate to use a French term. For lesser known places, the local name has been used. Personal names are based on the cultural identity of their owners, although this was not always easy to determine.

Contents

Acknowledgments   v

A Note on Language   vii

List of Maps   x

Introduction   1

Chapter 1 — Metropolis in the North   3

Chapter 2 — The Overlords   47

Chapter 3 — The Deadly Politics of Medieval Flanders   73

Chapter 4 — The Matins   103

Chapter 5 — The Battle   123

Chapter 6 — The Aftermath   145

Chapter 7 — The Legacy   169

Notes   195

Bibliography   215

Index   227

List of Maps

Medieval Flanders   4
Northern Europe's medieval economy   14
Pilgrimage routes   29
Bruges   44
Paris in 1300   61
The battlefield   130

Introduction

When Count Robert of Artois leaned forward in his saddle to survey the flat field before him, no doubt he smiled to himself at what he saw. Thousands of foot soldiers drawn from the towns of Flanders had gathered to challenge his force of some of the most distinguished knights of four powerful European states. He thought he knew a good deal about infantry, for large numbers of peasant foot soldiers accompanied most, if not all, medieval armies. Such troops seldom had clear-cut functions, and if opposed by horsemen, they dispersed with haste. Poorly trained and ill disciplined, they followed in the wake of mounted knights. Their weapons were little more than the tools of their farms and workshops, and their protective apparel consisted only of heavy leather garments and whatever armor they could glean from the battlefield. Under the feudal system, such irregulars served their masters out of obligation and had little or no personal desire to defeat their lord's enemies. Not surprisingly, the peasant infantry auxiliaries of the Middle Ages seldom played important roles in battle. Yet, as Robert could well see, on that summer day in 1302 near the Flemish town of Kortrijk (or in his French, Courtrai), an army composed almost totally of commoners on foot faced the flower of French chivalry. Little did the Count understand the strong sense of independence and civic pride which had developed in Flanders throughout the

1

Introduction

four hundred years leading up to the beginning of the fourteenth century.

Seven centuries ago, hundreds of golden spurs were nailed to the wall of a Flemish church, marking the end of 900 years of knightly supremacy. The year 2002 marks the 700th anniversary of this little known but fascinating and highly complex encounter, in which noble arrogance was pitted against common ingenuity. Much is both known and mythologized about this battle, given that its two sides, Flemish and French, remain in conflict in modern day Belgium. However, in a world which often focuses only on "great powers," few outside of the Low Countries are aware of the significance of Kortrijk. Despite mention by Dante and Longfellow, no major works on the battle have appeared in languages other than Dutch and French. The commemoration of this often overlooked battle is a national holiday in Flanders, but its significance reaches much further. Along with the Battle of Stirling Bridge, made famous in the film *Braveheart*, the Battle of the Golden Spurs at Kortrijk was a historical milestone in which an inferior force of common foot soldiers defeated knights on horseback. What follows is the story of a time, a land and a battle that have helped shape the world ever since.

1

Metropolis in the North

Early in history, the flat, open, and seemingly ordinary plains of Flanders saw many unique developments. Intended as a buffer state against the Vikings, the County of Flanders was created in 864 following one of the many divisions of what had been Charlemagne's Empire. Situated in the heart of Europe and claimed by the French crown, the county lay between the Holy Roman Empire and the North Sea, making it the crossroads of important trade routes. Vassals of the French king, the counts of Flanders were blessed with the most valuable fief north of the Alps and at the same time cursed with one of the most difficult to govern.

Despite the apocalyptic predictions of the era, after the year 1000, Flanders began to urbanize and prosper to an extent unsurpassed anywhere in Europe outside of the city-states of central and northern Italy. Unlike the early medieval period following the fall of Rome, the period after the turn of the millennium was more stable. Some towns grew out of or around earlier settlements or fortifications. Others were "planted" by kings and lords for military or commercial purposes. Most important among the urban centers, though not most populous, was Bruges (Brugge in the local Flemish). By the mid–1300s, the city's population stood between 35,000 and 45,000, twice that of the modern inner city. Northern Europe's biggest harbor, Bruges was possibly even

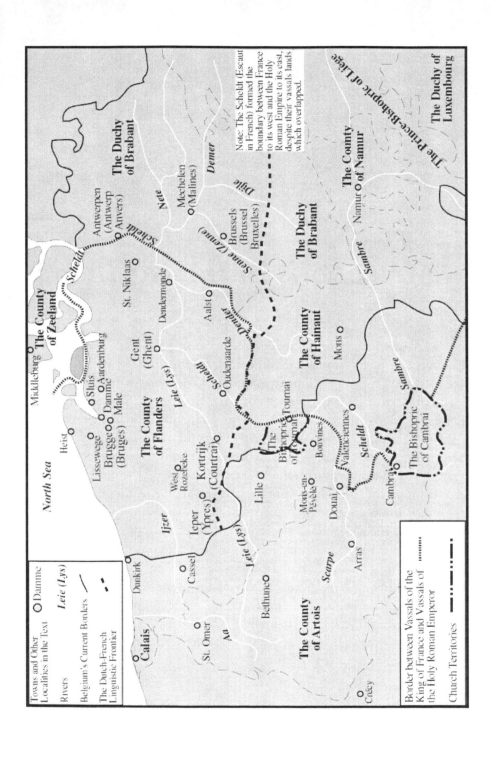

Towns and Other
Localities in the Text   O Damme

Rivers   *Leie (Lys)*

Belgium's Current Borders

The Dutch-French
Linguistic Frontier

Border between Vassals of the
King of France and Vassals of
the Holy Roman Emperor

Church Territories

Note: The Scheldt (Escaut
in French) formed the
boundary between France
to its west and the Holy
Roman Empire to its east,
despite their vassals lands
which overlapped.

North Sea

The County
of Zeeland

Mickleburg

The Duchy
of Brabant

Antwerpen
(Antwerp
Anvers)

Scheldt

Nete

Mechelen
(Malines)

Demer

Dijle

The Duchy
of Brabant

The County
of Namur

Namur O

Sambre

The Prince-Bishopric of Liège

The Duchy
of Luxembourg

Brussels
(Brussel
Bruxelles)

Senne (Zenne)

St. Niklaas

Dendermonde

Aalst O

Dender

The County
of Hainaut

Mons O

Gent
(Ghent)

Leie (Lys)

Scheldt

Oudenaarde O

Tournai

The
Bishopric
of Tournai

Heist

Lissewege

Brugge
(Bruges)

Sluis
Aardenburg
Damme
Male

The County
of Flanders

West-
Rozebeke

Kortrijk
(Courtrai)

Boûvines

Valenciennes

Sambre

The Bishopric of Cambrai

Cambrai O

Scheldt

Ijzer

Ieper
(Ypres)

Lille O

Mons-en-
Pévèle

Douai O

Dunkirk

Leie (Lys)

Cassel

Béthune O

The County
of Artois

Scarpe

Arras O

Calais

St. Omer

Aa

Crécy

more populous a century earlier, while Ghent saw its population increase to 60,000. In Northern Europe, only Paris was larger, with a population just exceeding 65,000. Ypres, Lille and Douai were other great Flemish cities exceeding 10,000 inhabitants. The surrounding countryside was dotted with market towns, monasteries and castles. At the same time Florence had about 100,000 inhabitants, while Londoners numbered only 30,000 to 40,000. Cologne, the largest German city, also had around 30,000 inhabitants.[1]

Unlike Florence with its public baths, sewers, and garbage collection, most towns were not pleasant places to live. Streets were noisy and dirty with garbage and sewage. Plumbing and refrigeration were primitive or nonexistent. Butchers slaughtered animals in the street. Rough carts squeaked and horses' hooves clopped on the cobblestones. Vendors called out their wares. Church bells marked the passage of hours and lives. Houses protruded over streets, cutting off light and hindering air movement. Despite the conditions, towns prospered and grew into cities. Opportunities seemed as abundant as the stars.

Bruges began as a Gallo-Roman settlement on the Reie River some 2000 years ago, although the area had been inhabited as far back as Neolithic times. Its inhabitants farmed and traded with England and the rest of Gaul. Around A.D. 270 the Franks settled on the Flemish coastal plain. When Saint Eligius came to the area to spread Christianity around 650, Bruges was already the most important fortification along the coast. About a hundred years later trade with Scandinavia boomed and the city's name developed from either *Rogia* (the Latin name for the Reie) or the Old Norse *Bryggja*, meaning "landing stage."

The name "Bruges" has appeared on documents and coins since the mid-ninth century. Around that time it had a strong citadel, which halted Norse plundering. Towns were often defined by their fortifications, or "burg" in Flemish and German and elsewhere as "burgh," "bourg," or "borough." Hence, the suburbs were called faubourgs (meaning "beyond the walls"). In the early fourteenth century the

Opposite: *Map of medieval Flanders.*

Grafenburg, the original castle of the counts of Flanders built by Baldwin Bras de Fer (Iron Arm), still stood. Both the fortifications and the large public square that followed would be known simply as the Burg. However, the Burg of today is dramatically different from that of 1302. Only scant remnants of the city's first wall, the count's castle, and its oldest church, St. Donatian's, can be found.[2]

Bruges has a long tradition as a port. The oldest settlement and early medieval port were accessible from the North Sea. However, the coastline of Flanders has been radically transformed by nature and man over the past millennium. The natural link between Bruges and the North Sea silted up around 1050. But the great Dunkerque Floods in 1134 profoundly altered the Flemish coast again. A deep estuary reaching from the North Sea, the Zwin, came to within a mile of Bruges, as far as present day Damme, where the Reie River connected the North Sea to the city center. Hence Bruges remained linked directly to the sea throughout the high Middle Ages.

Often called "The Venice of the North" because of its many *reien*, or canals, Bruges is in fact a city of waterways surrounded by land, whereas Venice is a city of canalized islands surrounded by the sea. In medieval times, the city's waterways had to be constantly dredged, adapted, or enlarged to allow ships to reach the city. Inside the city the Reie, which originally flowed through the city from the Minnewater to Dampoort, was transformed into a network of canals, enabling traders to bring their goods to large halls at the Markt, or marketplace, near the Burg. The precise origins of these canals and the extent to which they are natural or man-made remain unclear. The Reie entered the city at the Minnewater, mistakenly translated by nineteenth century romantics as the "Lake of Love" and a popular spot for honeymooners today. A more recent explanation is that "Minnewater" originally meant "water where a sprite lives." If this is true, the Minnewater does not date from the twelfth or thirteenth centuries, but was a much older natural waterway. This broad fortified waterway stretching north from the southern edge of the city was one of Bruges's harbors in medieval times. It is also believed that the canals in the southern part of the city follow the original course of the river Reie. Dijver,

Lange Rei, and Spiegelrei probably also follow a natural watercourse. The other canals of Bruges are more likely man-made.

After passing Damme, ships entered Bruges where the Dampoort complex is now situated. On the way to the city center the sailors followed the canals along the Langerei and Potterierei, where the shipyards were located, then the Spiegelrei and Spinolarei, near the Poortersloge. Lining the waterways were guildhalls and market- places. Various docks and quays provided unloading areas. A huge bird-like wooden crane unloaded boats in the city center. Operated by a human-powered treadmill, this peculiar structure was a technological marvel, which attracted the interest of onlookers and even appears in paintings down through the ages. Used from the thirteenth to the eighteenth century, it gave today's Kraanplein (Crane Square) its name.[3] The Groene Rei and Dijver were the quays of the two busiest canals in inner Bruges. The Pelikaan, or Pelican House, a hospital and almshouse for the poor, was built on the former. However, the merchants of Bruges were eventually compelled by siltation to use a number of more distant harbors, such as Damme and Sluis.

Like other Flemish towns, Bruges produced woolen and linen textiles. Not surprisingly, most clothing was made of these local products. Woven from both local and English wool, Flemish cloth was exported throughout Europe. Interestingly, England, the focal point of the Industrial Revolution in modern times, had a medieval economy based on exporting raw wool and importing finished goods. These trading conditions were little better than those fostered by nineteenth century European colonialism in Africa. Raw wool had been exported from England to Flanders since the time of the Romans. Charlemagne established the first fulling mill, which was built by Count Baldwin III of Flanders at Kortrijk on the river Leie (Lys), which was chalk-free and good for retting flax. The Counts of Flanders allowed Bruges to have an annual trade fair beginning in 957 and guaranteed privileges to those involved in commerce. Traders, moneychangers, and other merchants were allowed to deal outside the gates of the Burg. Noted in thirteenth century Spanish and Italian sources, weaving was practiced as a trade by many in Flanders well before 1200.[4]

The Great Crane of Bruges (© Stedelijke Musea Brugge)

1. Metropolis in the North

Made of flax and lighter than wool, linen was used for undergarments and summer clothing. Although flax had been cultivated for its fibers since 3000 B.C., linen was difficult to manufacture.[5] Available but expensive, cotton came to Europe with the Muslim conquest of Spain and Sicily and was not yet common north of the Alps.[6] Also originating in the East, silk and velvet were even more expensive and were used only by the nobility.

The most important contribution of the medieval town to civilization was to reintroduce the civic spirit of classical times. Neither towns nor their merchants fit readily into the patterns of feudal society. Unlike either peasants or nobles, townspeople were a new and different breed and learned the effectiveness of acting together. Expanding trade had required the abolition of feudal and manorial obligations in the towns. Without the direct protection of feudal lords, townsfolk had no way of securing themselves or their property. Guilds offered merchants and later craftsmen privileges of protection and support at a price, similar to that provided by lords to their vassals. A large measure of independence was given to both guilds and town councils. These freedoms coupled with the prospects of wealth reurbanized a Europe that had not seen true cities since the fall of Rome. Under the noses of the great lords, a powerful middle class emerged that would first bolster their masters and later lead to their demise.

Urban inhabitants were divided into two groups: burghers and commoners. Less than a tenth of the population, the burghers, or patricians, were commoners with old roots and old money. The Poorters, Bruges's commercial elite, formed a self-governing body that communicated directly with the Counts and were allowed to own property. They met in the Poortersloge, a special hall with a tall watchtower located at the head of the river, where goods would first enter the city. Later, concerts, banquets, and other festivities were organized by the elite in the Poortersloge. Throughout Flanders, such elites came to own most, if not all, of the land inside city walls. Most made their fortunes trading in cloth. These rich merchants proved important to lords in need of money. Taxes and fees for justice were levied on town residents. Tolls were collected for stalls in markets and for passage along roads and across bridges. In return for increased exactions and to attract settlers, lords conferred "freedoms" on towns by charter. Often merchant guilds founded towns by obtaining these charters. Communes, or corporate urban associations, were formed, and their members took oaths to support each other in struggles to win privileges from their lords. By negotiation and sometimes violence, townsmen gradually won recognition by acting collectively. Throughout the 1200s, French kings made extensive grants to existing cities and founded new towns. Peasants were drawn to urban areas until town governments began restricting immigration by denying citizenship rights to newcomers.

Merchant guilds were the first urban organizations to appear and constituted the nucleus of Bruges' civic life. At first, these guilds were composed of all artisans and merchants within a given town. Their main objectives were to protect their goods and develop monopolies. As early as the 900s, merchants combined for the mutual protection of their horses, wagons, and goods when traveling. In Bruges, they banded together in the London Hansa, an organization of merchants trading with England. Eventually, raw wool imports, finished cloth exports, and all stages of production were controlled by the patrician classes. Merchant guilds were separate and distinct from civic governments, but since the functions, purposes, and memberships of guilds and town governments overlapped, it was not always easy to tell them apart. Many well-to-do guildsmen were prominent in local government, and small hereditary commercial oligarchies dominated towns by their interlocking memberships in urban bodies. Copying the lifestyle of the nobility, the rich lived in great stone mansions, wore expensive clothing, and led local militias. They made sure that only members of specific families were chosen for official duties. All members of the town councils, or aldermen, came from this class. The councils guaranteed public order, carried out punishments, and watched over the city's interests. They could intervene in disputes between guilds and establish overall standards, such as weights and measures. By the 1100s Bruges had become self-governing, with an elected council and magistrates who collected customs taxes and supervised public works projects, such as canals and markets. Mayors were chosen from within the councils, to run administrations on a day-to-day basis, assisted by aldermen who implemented decisions and dispensed justice.[7]

These officials drew their powers from charters, which detailed the privileges or liberties granted to towns by nobles. Typical charter privileges included increased personal freedoms and rights to collect taxes and tolls on behalf of lords to hold courts to convey real estate, and to maintain militias. Many were very specific in their provisions. A good example of this is the charter Count Philip of Alsace granted to Bruges in 1190. Here are some excerpts:

> C.18. If the bailiffs, with the assent of the court of the Count, decree a toll on bread and wine and other merchandise for the improvement of the town, half the money which comes from the toll shall go to the Count, and the other half to the castellan and the town.
> C.19. If a merchant or other foreigner should come before the bailiffs for justice, and if those about whom the complaint is made are present or are able to come within three days, or at least within eight days, the bailiffs shall do full justice to him according to the law of the town.
> C.20. No one is allowed to put stalls in the market place of the Count; but if he does so and is convicted on the word of the bailiffs, he shall give sixty solidi to the Count.[8]

One charter, England's Magna Carta, went beyond defining local political relationships and listed rights to be offered to a king's entire realm. Although forced on King John in 1215 and ignored by other monarchs for centuries, the Magna Carta marked the beginnings of modern constitutions. Using the Salic law of the early Franks, influenced by both the Justinian Code and their own interests, the count's court and other royal courts could overturn the decisions of urban bodies. However, the nobility needed to think twice about upsetting the cities. The civic pride characteristic of first the elite and later of the general populace was considerable.

Although seriously impaired by instability, trade had never wholly died out even during the chaotic second half of Christendom's first millennium. Regional trade continued in wine, wood, fish, cheese and grain. Jews, Moors and Vikings all had trading traditions. Later, Venice,

Genoa, Pisa, and other Italian mercantile cities boomed. Increased agricultural surpluses and populations encouraged long-distance trade and economic growth. Except in Flanders, recovery was slower in the North.[9] Cloth manufacturing techniques remained unchanged for many centuries. Wool was processed by spinning, weaving, fulling, and even painting. The fleece needed to be washed and combed. Next, yarn was spun with a spindle. It took many hand spinners to supply a single weaver. But, contrary to the common view of medieval times as dark ages of poverty, disease, famine and instability, the thirteenth and fourteenth centuries saw much innovation. The invention of the spinning wheel in the mid-thirteenth century and the later addition of a foot treadle to power it speeded the manufacturing process.[10] Toothed warpers, square frames for preparing bundles of threads, were also used together with vertical two-beam looms. Initially, weaving was done on difficult vertical looms. By the twelfth century, horizontal looms that allowed the weaver to sit while he worked had spread westward with traders from China.[11] A trade by itself, fulling increased the weight of cloth by washing, shrinking, and matting, beating, or pressing.

A revolution also occurred in the way in which business was conducted. The existence of a cash economy and respect for contracts encouraged new economic activity in Flanders. Temporary joint companies became common structures for spreading the risks of long distance trade. Several merchants would lease ships to spread out both their cargoes and their risks. Courier services between the major commercial centers of Northern Europe and Italy ensured that letters arrived safely and in time. Account ledgers listing debits and credits kept track of transactions. Later the letter of exchange was developed as a document for transferring money. Several Italian banking houses, particularly from Florence and Lucca, lent huge sums to merchants and nobles, thereby financing both trade and war in the North. The Medicis of Florence and the Fuggers of Augsburg, Europe's most important banking families, opened branches in Bruges and the Brabantine port of Antwerp, respectively. They were joined by native bankers who enabled merchants to open accounts, transfer large sums, and change money. Flanders became an international marketplace, accepting most currencies from neighboring countries. This "paper" economy was unknown in most of Europe.[12]

At its height, dozens of cities were members of the Hanseatic League, a powerful trade alliance of cities that extended from northern Holland through Germany, Poland, Sweden and Finland to the Baltic States. From the Baltic, furs, hemp, flax, honey, beeswax, timber, and pitch entered the world market. Merchants from Bremen, Hamburg, Lübeck, and Stettin established trading ports further east at Riga, Reval, and distant Novgorod in Russia. Their commerce linked Britain and Flanders in the west to the Silk Road in the east. The Hanse had four important offices outside of its own territory, including one in Bruges. The burgher merchant class of Bruges served as brokers and landlords for Hanse merchants trading with Southern Europeans, especially Italians, Spaniards, and Portuguese. Along with the Crusades, trade gave the growing class of townsmen a wider view of the world.

In contrast to our modern age, the medieval marketplace was a clearly defined physical location. Merchants usually traveled with their goods. Commerce was based on a three-tiered system of grand fairs, regional fairs, and local markets. International trade took place at regular meetings, usually lasting several days or weeks. Grand fairs were usually held annually. Organized in large towns, these events encouraged long-distance trade. Particularly important to the Low Countries were the grand fairs in the French county of Champagne. The counts of Champagne and other enterprising lords sought to attract commerce. During the late 1100s a highly organized cycle of six fairs emerged, two each in Provins and Troyes, and one each in Bar-sur-Aube and Lagny-sur-Marne. Northern and Southern Europe were brought together. Genoese and Venetians traded with Flemings and Germans. At first the fairs were held on fairgrounds outside of town walls where long rows of tents were erected. Later, fortifications were extended around them. Built in 1250, the walls of Troyes enclosed its commercial areas. Each fair lasted six weeks with two-week intervals between them. A week was spent setting up stalls, and ten-day cloth sale, an eleven-day leather sale, and a nineteen-day general goods sale

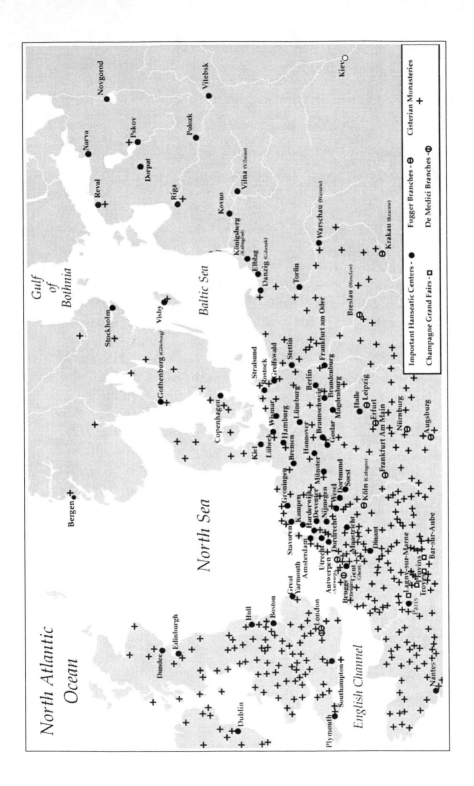

followed. A few concluding days were devoted to settling accounts. Traveling merchants attending the fairs often journeyed considerable distances, employing couriers to ride ahead and announce the variety and quantity of goods en route.[13] They would typically visit a number of local markets on their way to the next regional fair.

During the 1200s a trader's journey was largely determined by the pattern of the fairs he frequented. Regional fairs in large towns were organized in a sequence, allowing the merchants to attend all the fairs in their region. Markets, organized on a weekly basis to cater to the needs of local communities, complemented these fairs. The geographical spacing of these markets was largely determined by the distance a person could travel in a day (about seven miles).[14] Virtually every village had a market in some form. Small traders made their own goods and sold them themselves, either from storefronts on their own homes, from moveable carts, or by hawking them in the streets. These craftspeople were eligible to join guilds, which rural cottage workers could not. Early marketplaces had moveable and later fixed stalls.

Usually limited to one year's stay in a town or less, foreign merchants could not set up shop permanently. They had to sell to local guildsmen, who would then resell to their fellow citizens. In some cases foreigners were allowed to sell directly, but they had to pay a very heavy tax for the privilege.[15] Everywhere economic relationships were carefully spelled out and regulated, as witnessed by the details of grants.

Grant of Privileges to the Flemings at Cologne, 1197

Be it known to all that the merchants of Cologne and Flanders have agreed that, if any Fleming be prepared to depart by land or water, if any one seek a debt from him, and have witnesses, he should prove it by the law of Cologne, and should not delay him further: but if he have no witnesses he, who is accused, without aggression and without delay will purge himself on his own oath that he is byvanc and will be free. No one from their land can be provoked to fight a duel, or to go to the judgment commonly called ordeal except by chance he commit homicide, or wound any one, or be taken by reason of false

Opposite: *Northern Europe's medieval economy.*

money, or except he break the peace. Nothing shall be taken from them for the debt of another except he promise of his own will to repay, or except there be pledges.

Done in the year of the Incarnation of the Lord 1197.
Given at Cologne on the 25th of March.[16]

The grand fairs in Champagne and many local fairs in Flanders declined with the arrival of Atlantic shipping and the rise of Bruges and other towns as permanent trade centers in the thirteenth century. Around 1200, an important annual market was held in Bruges. From it would emerge year-round commerce with distant lands. However, the sequential fair system did not disappear until late in the Middle Ages. Groups of local markets sometimes banded together to form permanent trading centers. Commercial buildings replaced older markets. One such structure, the Cloth Hall of Bruges, was begun in 1280. Most of its famous belfry was not yet finished in 1302. Its counterpart in Ypres was completed in 1304.

Once the Genoese perfected the Atlantic route from the Mediterranean in the 1270s, the fortunes of Bruges rose rapidly. By the end of the thirteenth century, it became northwestern Europe's most important center of culture and international trade. A vast range of goods from amber and fish to spices and furs was traded as predominantly overland transport was supplemented by expanding sea-lanes. Canals opened up inland towns such as Ypres, Bruges, and Lille to the sea.

Centuries-old Roman roads and a few convenient waterways formed the backbone of Europe's transport system. With increased traffic, many needed to be repaired over and over again. Flanders was one of a handful of places which saw new roads built in medieval times. These were made of cobbles and broken stone on beds of sand. Bridge building also boomed. Wagons and carts met most long-distance transport needs throughout the high Middle Ages. Four-wheeled wagons with fixed forecarriages became common. Their wheels were strengthened by small iron plates, which were nailed on (iron wheel hoops were not invented until the 1500s). Smaller carts were pulled by breast harnesses. Wagons and carts could carry goods 12 to 22 miles a day cheaply. Noblemen, prelates, and their often lengthy retinues traveled in the safety of convoys and rarely did better than 28 miles a day. Pack animals carried short distance freight faster. Speeds of 35 and 37 miles a day were not uncommon. Messengers made even better time, carrying letters and parcels at amazing speeds for the day. One could leave Bruges in the morning and cross the Holy Roman Empire's border into Brabant by dusk.[17]

Around this same time, it was found that Flanders' salt meadows supported sheep producing extraordinarily fine wool, a resource that was then woven into textiles that were traded all over the known world. Sheep-raising replaced cultivation in much of Flanders. Artois and Picardy came to produce the surplus foodstuffs to meet the needs of the Flemish population, and the Frisians traded in Norway and Denmark for smoked and pickled herring, which was highly-prized throughout the region. However, the capacity of the Flemish woolen industry outstripped local fleece-production, and other sources of wool had to be found. Meanwhile, sheep-raising intensified in the Fens of eastern England. The Florentine banking house of Bardi compiled a list of wool-producing monasteries in England, which showed the value of wool graded by its quality.[18] Typically, values ran twice that paid to growers. Foreign merchants were given special privileges, causing much discontent among the English. However, English wool remained almost exclusively an export item, as successive monarchs were unable to stimulate a local textile industry. Bruges was particularly well situated to profit from this trade.

Towns along the Scheldt and Maas (Meuse), such as Tournai, Kortrijk, Ghent, Namur, and Liège, developed extensive textile industries and traded with grain and wine-producing areas upstream for local consumption and export. The greatest wine-producing region was the nearby Moselle valley and the narrower reaches of the Rhine, where vineyards date back to Roman times. Along the Rhine, dense populations grew with the expansion of trade with Italy over the Alps, the Danube above Lake Constance and the Rhone via the Moselle. The local economy diversified, with the growth of metalworking in Strasbourg and glass production in Cologne. Like Flanders, the Rhineland depended on grain and other commodities from elsewhere, particularly the Neckar, Main, Ruhr, and other valleys to the east.

By the eleventh century, a process of specialization unfolded in many areas of northwestern Europe.[19] With the development of new land and sea trade routes, an interdependent economy developed. At the center of this network, Flanders developed the first truly specialized economy in any modern sense.[20] Such economic integration meant that imports could mitigate local scarcities. But this web of dependence could also easily spread the misfortune of one area to another.

More humble commoners made up the vast majority of urban populations. Their lives were dominated by carefully delineated and highly disciplined craft guilds, created to preserve their members' privileges from encroachment by the merchants. Like merchant guilds, craft guilds maintained monopolies. The closed shop is not a modern invention. Members met, determined the demand for their trade, and then allowed as many masters to set up shop as the situation supported. Soon no one could do business without belonging to the appropriate guild. In many ways craft guilds resembled labor unions, while merchant guilds bore similarities to chambers of commerce.

As crafts began to develop and grow, the merchant guilds often split into increasing numbers of craft guilds, which the wealthy merchants who dominated town government often saw as threats.[21] According to Knox, in Augsburg there were seventeen guilds in 1350, thirty-eight by 1450, and over sixty by 1550.[22] A similar situation had developed earlier in Italy, where Florence boasted seventy-three guilds. Never numbering more than fifty-two, Bruges's guilds maintained monopolies by charter over their particular crafts. In the textile industry, different guilds performed different steps in the manufacturing process: spinning, weaving, fulling and dying. Hence each craft and occupation had its own guild, which fixed prices and arranged trade. Ranging from the lowly trades of tanning and tallow-making to the highest callings in education and the arts, virtually all economic activity was controlled by guilds. The mainstays of Flanders' lucrative wool trade, weavers were the largest single group, probably about half of all guildsmen. Fullers and dyers were also numerous. But all were under the thumbs of the burgher merchants, who depended on their cheap labor. Those who managed to accumulate a bit of wealth by hard work were still not considered citizens and had no major part in city government. Striking was forbidden and punished by banning or even death.

A wage economy grew. But fleshing out their story beyond official records, charters, contracts and work regulations is often difficult.

> The earners of wages in the Middle Ages are historically elusive subjects because of the long time before they developed, or were permitted to have, lawful organizations devoted to self-help. Hence employees mostly appear as items in records (guild statues, apprenticeship and work contracts, court cases) generated by people who hired them, and so the great mass of evidence concerns things done to workers rather than by them.[23]

In the second half of the 1200s, craftsmen and other members of what could be described as Bruges' middle class were permitted to join the Hansa. This broadened representation within city government and broke the monopoly of the merchants. A new type of small trader developed. Some artisans became merchants in their own right, employing small numbers of specialized skilled workers. Bruges, and to a lesser degree Ghent, differed from other Flemish towns in the size of their middle classes. This difference was heightened by the fact that towns like Kortrijk, Ypres, and Douai were purely weaving centers, while Bruges became an international trading hub involved in a more diverse range of activities. Craft guilds demanded shares in civic leadership and began to supplant the older merchant guilds, which disappeared except in towns too small for special craft organizations. However, the elites they had created continued to have substantial power. While much less restrictive than serfdom and much more specialized than previous economic orders, this system did not encourage individual freedom.

Admission to guilds was restricted and required long years of rigorous apprenticeship and lifelong submission to inspection to ensure adherence to standards. Virtually everyone was employed by age four-teen or fifteen. Work was strictly guided by guild rules. "Generations of intelligent people across Europe applied themselves to elaborating upon or changing whatever original rules guided the masters in the ear-liest years of the guild's existence."[24] To join a guild, one had to go through training stages as an apprentice and journeyman before becoming a master.

A master's house was a residence, dormitory, workshop, ware-house, and retail store rolled into one. Typically, workshops and a retail outlet opening onto a street were located on the ground floor of the master's home. The second story was the master's living quarters, while the third story housed journeymen and the attic apprentices. Apprentices were usually teenagers who lived with masters and their families after they or their parents paid fees to be taken on. There were many restrictions on apprentices. They were virtually adopted by mas-ters and received bed, board, and training but no pay. Apprentices were subject to masters and were not allowed to marry. This rudi-mentary training varied from two to seven years depending on the craft. They then became journeymen.

Journeymen were day workers entitled to earn wages. They were named journeymen, because many moved from master to master and some from town to town to perfect their skills. Using their own tools and materials, they were required to produce a masterpiece that would satisfy the guild as to their proficiency. Once a masterpiece was com-pleted, a guild could vote to accept the journeyman as a master. How-ever, personal considerations, guild politics, or the state of the economy could delay or deny acceptance.

Guilds regulated working hours for journeymen and masters. Workers relied on the sound of the local church bell to signal the day's end. Apprentices worked as long as daylight permitted. Prohibited at first, work at night was eventually allowed. However, few wanted the additional hours. Most Flemish artisans worked sixteen- to seventeen-hour days in the summer and about eleven-hour days in the winter. Depending on the season, midday meal breaks ranged from two to three and a half hours.

1. Metropolis in the North

Women were eligible to join guilds, though seldom independently. One exception was the handful of exclusively female guilds connected with the silk industry. Women who joined other guilds usually joined by default, by assisting fathers or husbands in their trades. A wife who joined a guild with her husband would be an independent guild member after her husband's death. Knowledge of a trade that could be practiced at home was of value in marriage. Women sometimes practiced more than one trade at a time, such as brewing and weaving. This undoubtedly helped their families, but may have contributed to their exclusion from guilds as independent specialized workers. Women's contributions to the medieval economy are reflected in English surnames. Names with suffixes -ster or -xter denote a trade practiced by a woman. Hence a Brewster was a female brewer, a Baxter a baker, a Spinster a spinner, and a Webster a weaver. Girls could be apprenticed to men or women, but they were usually under the direction of a male master's wife. While male apprentices could not marry, some female apprentices' contracts included clauses allowing them to marry with the payment of a forfeit to their masters.[25]

The guilds aimed to use urban markets peacefully and profitably for themselves alone. In protecting its members, guilds also protected consumers by demanding uniform quality. All prices were regulated, and price-cutting and the sale of foreign artisans' work were strictly forbidden. To regulate competition, guilds forbade most advertising. No member was ever allowed to corner the market by purchasing a large supply of a commodity. Most guaranteed every member the right to participate in any purchase made by any other member. It was considered unfair for any one member to derive advantage from a particular bargain. The use of improved methods of production, such as water power, was frowned upon unless all shared in its benefits. No one could employ his workers longer than another, nor pay higher wages. All members were required to charge the same price for the same item. No master could try to take another's customers or entice his workmen away. This kind of close supervision of the economy would later be branded as guild socialism or primitive communism. After 1250, guilds had to face slowed economic expansion. The reaction

21

of many was to restrict admission to master's status, cut wages and charity, extend the years of apprenticeship, lower working conditions and quality, and take work away from smaller guilds.

Despite the restrictiveness of life under the guilds, few left the system. The benefits were too great, not the least of which was the higher social status that went with membership. Guilds engaged in a vast range of economic, fraternal and civic activities. They provided their members with trade contacts, credit, housing, the only lay education available, and even dowries for poor girls and arranged marriages for members without heirs. Pooling capital, they set quality standards, production quotas, wages and prices. They maintained training standards, inspected working conditions, and examined candidates for journeyman and master. Represented on town councils, they served in town militias, local courts, and fire watches, maintained sections of city walls, and took turns at guard duty. Paying taxes collectively, they contributed the bulk of their city's treasury and bailed fellow-guildsmen from jail. Guilds were essential in the construction of churches, chapels and cathedrals. Their roles are illustrated in the stained glass windows they donated. Honoring their own patron saints, guildsmen were the mainstays of local festivals. They maintained charitable institutions, such as hospitals, cemeteries, burial funds, and almshouses and charities for paupers, widows, orphans, the aged, and the sick.

The mass discipline and loyalty fostered by guilds gave Flemish society a level of cohesion not existing elsewhere in the conspiratorial atmosphere of feudal Europe. In many ways the guild system resembled the organization of a modern army, particularly in its reliance on specialists drawn from the populace at large. The self-sufficiency of this system promoted esprit de corps and with it a kind of xenophobic pride which often clashed with the more urbane demeanor of the elite. This would make the conflict to come different from any other. From these craft guilds emerged two of the major figures in the conflict ahead: master weaver Pieter de Conink and butcher Jan Breidel.

Medieval Bruges had a very active religious life. The growth of the city in the thirteenth century is apparent from the development of its ecclesiastical institutions. In contrast to our modern era, the church was important for more than worship in this Age of Faith. The church had an effective executive authority, the pope and his curia, and a trained and organized network of personnel. It was wealthier than any state in Europe. Holding about a quarter of Europe's land and much other wealth in the form of endowments, it collected about 14 percent of the continent's gross production as tithes, "first fruits" taxes, fees for the delivery of sacraments, and special levies. A sophisticated system using canon law and professional lawyers, ecclesiastical courts handled a wide range of cases. Penance, excommunication, interdict and inquisition were wielded as sanctions. Directly under the Pope, Templars, Hospitallers, Teutonic knights, and other military orders were formidable forces. Holding a monopoly on sacraments, the church enjoyed great popular support as the only path to salvation in an era when the masses were genuinely concerned with spirituality. It was medieval society's most important source of education, counseling, health care, news, welfare, trade and marriage contacts, and the expression of grievances. It was most people's only experience with art, music and drama. The old, the sick and the abandoned depended on the church as well as the guilds. Through oblation, a process of formally giving children to the church, parents could assure better lives for their children than available to most commoners. Unlike the abandonment of later ages, oblation was history's most compassionate way of dealing with unwanted or unsupportable children.

Within the original fortifications, Bruges' oldest church, St. Donatian's, was built in Carolingian style around 900 but destroyed during the French Revolution in 1799. An impressive structure of Romanesque arches with numerous chapels, St. Donatian's served the city first as the count's church, then a chapter church and finally the city's cathedral. In 1127 Bruges was scandalized when Count Charles the Good was murdered while at prayer in St. Donatian's.

Churches were altered to accommodate the city's growing population, with the exception of St. Donatian's, which had already been rebuilt after a major fire in 1184. Beyond the Burg, the area around the present day Markt and Steenstraat grew fastest until around 1100.[26]

Dating from the ninth century, two other old churches, the Church of Our Lady and St. Saviour's, were on the edge of this district. The status of cathedral was later conferred on St. Saviour's, an imposing Gothic brick building with foundations laid in the tenth century. Burned down several times, its chapels were not completed until the 1500s and its 325-foot tower was not completed until the 1800s. Originating from *cathedra*, the Latin word for chair, a cathedral is the chair, or headquarters, of a bishop. Then and now, Europeans define a city as a place having a cathedral. But surprisingly, Bruges's cathedral was neither the oldest nor the most impressive of its churches.

Bruges most spectacular church is the Church of Our Lady, or in Flemish, Onze Lieve Vrouwkerk. Remodeled in Romanesque style in the twelfth century and rebuilt in Gothic style in the thirteenth, its most remarkable feature is its 400-foot brick spire, the tallest in the Low Countries. Although not finished until about 1350, this church undoubtedly already made an impression in 1302. Nearby, a few traces in the lowest part of its present tower are all that remain of the Romanesque Holy Saviour's, Bruges's oldest surviving church.

In 1149 Dietrich Thierry of Alsace is said to have returned from the Second Crusade with a crystal vile containing a drop of Christ's blood. This relic was housed in the plain, mystery-evoking Romanesque Chapel of St. Basil, built in the same year by Count Robert II of Flanders to house the relics of St. Basil he had brought from Palestine. In the 1400s an upper Gothic chapel known as the Basilica of the Holy Blood would be constructed on top of St. Basil's. Encouraged by the annual Procession of the Holy Blood each May since at least the late 1200s, a cult of pilgrims developed around these relics.[27]

Bruges' parish structure was adjusted in the mid–1200s. Incredibly, all but one of the town's thirteenth-century parish churches have survived.[28] Only the earliest, St. Walburga's, which began as the count's chapel and became a parish church in 1239, has disappeared. The parish of Sint-Jacobs (St. James) was founded in 1240 out of the existing parish of Holy Saviour's. Old St. James's Chapel, near the Ezelpoort in the city's original fortifications, became a new parish church. As a result the gate was also known as Sint-Jacobspoort. It was transformed into

The Church of Our Lady, or Onze Lieve Vrouwkerk, in Bruges.

an early Gothic cruciform church with a block tower before being altered again two centuries later to its present building with three aisles. The parish of St. Giles was founded around 1241, from Our Lady's. Its parish church was an early–Gothic building that was also fundamentally altered in the late Middle Ages. This three-aisled hall church has only a few remnants of the original cross-shaped building. Its solid tower, like that of St. James, gives it a rather squat appearance similar to the early–Gothic churches of the polders. The countryside around Bruges also saw rapid ecclesiastical development. Six and a half miles south of Bruges, Zedelgem was dominated by St. Laurence Church, noted for its exquisite baptismal font, dating from the turn of the eleventh and twelfth centuries.

Another reflection of civic pride was the establishment of forty-six almshouses, several hospitals, and numerous other religious institutions.[29] Charity was clearly a concern. St. John's Hospital, dating from the twelfth century, was given its Romanesque tower and the first of its three wards in the early 1200s. Together with the western façade of Our Lady's, it dominates Maristraat at the Maria Bridge to this day. Its north ward was added at the end of the thirteenth century and a south ward in 1310. The hospital brothers were given accommodations near the north ward in a monastery also dating from the early fourteenth century. With an estate of over four hectares, the hospital was a secular institution. Reference to the governors who ran St. John's on behalf of the city occurs as early as 1270. Earlier the bishop of Tournai attempted to establish his authority over the hospital in 1236. However, the city's aldermen managed to retain control until the end of the fifteenth century. One of their more interesting rulings was that the estates of deceased patients and members of staff should be inherited by the hospital.

Beguinages, or *begijnhofen* in Flemish, were closed communities of women, started in the late 1100s. They flourished in the thirteenth and fourteenth centuries in the Netherlands, France, and Germany and are still found in some Flemish towns.[30] They began as Catholic lay associations of female workers, who first met to discuss economic and religious matters but later decided to devote their lives ministering to the poor, sick, and old. These communities became subjected to strict church discipline and were housed in closed complexes with chapels or churches. Some were later made into parishes and finally into beguinages. They were "towns within towns," in which pious women lived either as groups in large houses or alone in small cells. The women did not take lifelong vows but promised to obey the rules of the community. A beguinage was headed by a *Groojuffrouw* or *Grande Dame*, a Mother Superior nominated by the bishop. The sisters lived in convents at first and did communal work, such as lace making and sewing. After six years they were allowed to move into little cottages containing two or four apartments. Two or three times a day they congregated for mass. They wore greyish-brown habits while at work and donned black Flemish hooded cloaks, known as *failles* or *falies*, when they went out. The beguines were allowed out alone by day but required to return to the beguinage in the evening. Despite the beguinage's restrictive life, few felt obliged to leave. The male equivalents of beguines were beghards, who looked also after the sick.[31]

The Wijngaard beguinage, or Beguine of the Vine, was established near the Minnewater in 1244, when the bishop of Tournai granted it independent parish status. The next year, Countess Margaret of Constantinople had a chapel moved from the Burg to the beguinage, giving the community its own church. The institution was removed from the city's authority in 1299, when King Philip IV of France placed it under the direct control of the sovereign, hence its title Prinselijk Begijnhof (Prince's Beguinage). The area of this beguinage has remained constant to the present; however, many buildings have been added over the centuries.[32]

Before the ninth century, the coastal plain north of Bruges was a salty marsh, criss-crossed with creeks. When this area dried up, its first inhabitants came from the north. Frisians and Saxons settled in the polder village of Lissewege, a Celtic name meaning "house of Liso."[33] A bit more than six miles from Bruges, it is mentioned for the first time in 961 in an act of Count Arnulf. Small though the community was, it attracted large numbers of pilgrims for two reasons. According to a local legend, fishermen from nearby Heist discovered a Madonna in a creek. After taking the statue home, they found it miraculously back in Lissewege the next day. This was interpreted as a signal that Mary favored Lissewege and soon pilgrims flocked to the village.

More importantly, Lissewege was the northernmost marshaling point for pilgrims on the way to Santiago de Compostella. Pilgrimages were an important part of medieval religious life. After the Holy Land and Rome, the shrine of St. James the Apostle at Santiago de Compostella in northwestern Spain was the third most important pilgrimage site in Christendom. Pilgrims, particularly those who were commoners, were undoubtedly awe-struck at this first stage of their journey. A village of 300 inhabitants, Lissewege built a parish church of cathedral proportions. The monumental early Gothic Church of Our Lady, built from 1225 to 1275, is a typical example of Scheldt-Gothic brick and limestone construction in the coastal area. From its 162 foot west tower, one can see Bruges and a vast stretch of polders and coastline. In the flat surrounding countryside the tower can be seen for many miles. In the church, various representations associated with the pilgrims' way of Saint James can still be found. The interior of the church was later decorated in baroque style. Sint Jacob house in front of the church and nearby Spaniehof were two of a number of guesthouses for pilgrims.

The Lissewege canal runs through the old village center. By deepening a natural watercourse in 1220 the village was connected with Bruges. During the Middle Ages it was used mostly for draining the polders, but also for trade. Up to 1940 coal and other goods were brought from Bruges in small narrow boats. Centuries earlier, similar boats brought limestone from Tournai to build the church and nearby abbey. Today, looking at this waterway, lined with flowers, little whitewashed houses and artists, it is difficult to imagine how so narrow a canal could be economically feasible.

Important though it was, Lissewege was over shadowed by the great Abbey of Ter Doest, a mile south of the village. By 1300, Christian monasticism already had a long history. Lissewege had seen a good bit of it. Throughout much of the medieval era, monasteries were practically the only repositories of scholarship and learning. The monks

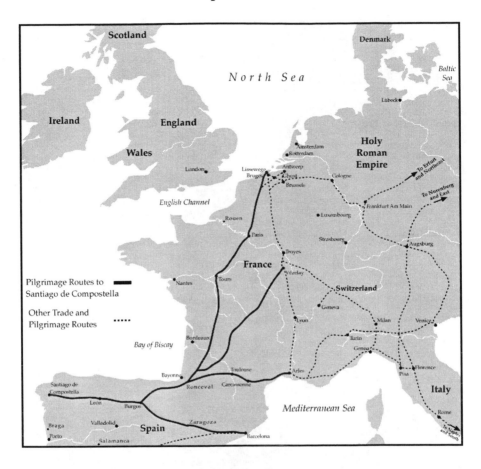

Map of Pilgrimage Routes.

were by far the best educated, often the only educated, members of society. Both the eremitical monasticism of hermits and the coeno-bitic monasticism of religious communities had their origins in late Roman Egypt. By the fifth century monasticism had spread to Ireland. Irish monks spread Christianity to Cornwall, Wales, Scotland, Northumbria and beyond. Often built on isolated islands, Celtic monasteries promoted lifestyles of solitary contemplation. But it was Saint Benedict of Nursia, founder of the Benedictine Order, who for-malized monasticism with *The Rule of the Master* in about A.D. 529

The Church of Our Lady or Onze Lieve Vrouwkerk in Lissewege.

1. Metropolis in the North

St. Benedict's vision was of a community, sworn to poverty, chastity, and obedience, working in prayer and isolation from the outside world. The marshes of Lissewege were ideal. The village's first monastic foundation dates from 1106. Lambert, Lord of Lissewege, gave a domain with a chapel called Thosan, later Ter Doest, to French Benedictines.

In the tenth and eleventh centuries a reform movement grew from Cluny, a great monastery in eastern France. Various abuses, such as the selling of church offices, or simony, and licentiousness and debauchery in the papal court, were condemned. Married clergy or Nicolaites were particularly blamed for infecting the Church with worldliness. Celibacy and strict discipline were advocated as solutions to the clergy's weakened spiritual life. Reformers founded several new religious orders, including the Carthusians.

However, the most important of these were the Cistercians established in Citeaux by Robert of Molesme and influenced by St. Bernard of Clairvaux. Evermardus, bishop of Tournai, transferred Ter Doest's modest priory to the Cistercians. In 1177 it was affiliated with Ter Duinen abbey at Koksijde. John of Bruges, second abbot of Ter Doest, was from Bruges' patrician Gruuthuse family and a relative of Robert of Bruges, abbot at Ter Duinen, a contemporary and companion of St. Bernard. Despite St. Bernard's intentional choice of poor land for his monasteries, the hard-working, enterprising Cistercians, who consumed only that which they produced, came to dominate much of Europe's economy. What many later described as the economic self-sufficiency of the church went far beyond subsistence. Meanwhile in Rome, increased attention was given to canon law and the formal establishment of the papal court, or curia, particularly after 1059 when cardinals were empowered to elect popes. Reforms introduced by Pope Gregory VII emphasized the "freedom of the church." This meant freedom from the political control of monarchs, particularly the lay investiture of bishops. Conflict on this issue led to the excommunication of Holy Roman Emperor Henry IV and his dramatic pleading in the snows in front of the pope's residence at Canossa in January 1077. The power of popes and monasteries was at a high point. Known for wine in France, wool in England, mining in Germany and a host of other

31

products elsewhere, the Cistercians became a major economic enterprise. Numerous gifts, particularly from Philip of Alsace, turned Ter Doest into a rich estate of some 10,000 acres. By the first half of the 1200s the abbey, situated near the sea and on the economically vital Cologne-Bruges axis, reached a high level of prosperity.

Another important source of revenue for monasteries was pilgrims. Monasteries and convents were safe havens for pilgrims, as well as other travelers and the less-fortunate members of society. Religious relics also attracted pilgrims to monasteries. The tombs of particularly saintly persons became magnets for pilgrims, who could generally be induced to buy an insignia, which proved they had visited a particular shrine. Ter Doest proved to be well situated in this respect.

Monastic life was generally one of hard physical work, scholarship and prayer. Monks were forbidden from owning property and in most cases from leaving their monastery. Emulating earlier Roman clothing, they wore long woolen habits: the Benedictines in black with linen coifs to warm their heads and the Cistercians in white or undyed wool. Their day was regulated by regular worship services in the abbey church. These routines of worship or offices involved singing, chanting and reciting prayers. The first office, matins, began at 2 a.m. and seven more followed at roughly three hour intervals, culminating in vespers in the evening and compline before retiring at night. Between offices, monks occupied themselves with copying religious texts and all the work associated with maintaining their self-sustaining community. These tasks were often carried out in silence.

Monasteries began as simple communities of barrack-like cells clustered around a chapel for devotions and a refectory for meals. Most had a centrally located calefactory, or warming room. Nearby a scriptorium was used by monks studying and laboriously copying sacred manuscripts. The first monastic buildings were built of wood, then gradually rebuilt in stone. The first priority for rebuilding in stone was the chancel of the church. The Cisterians introduced Gothic style at Ter Doest and Ter Duinen. Later, as monasteries become important economically, barns, guesthouses and other outbuildings were added. Ter Doest abbey's gigantic early Gothic tithe barn is the only building

The thirteenth century tithe barn is all that remains of the original abbey of Ter Doest.

remaining from the original thirteenth century monastery. Fighting during the Reformation destroyed all but the barn and the church, which was demolished in 1586. After churches and castles, tithe barns were the largest buildings of medieval times. Usually located in monasteries, they stored the tithe, the tenth of produce given to the church. Dating from 1230, the barn at Ter Doest is 66 feet high, 197 feet long, 82 feet broad, and supported by huge oak beams. The façade is decorated with Gothic blindniches and buttresses. Few tithe barns exist today, perhaps due to their prosaic function; however, they were vitally important in an era when a monied economy was not yet fully embraced.[34]

Monastic organization grew in complexity. Monasteries were led by abbots, often landless nobles who used the church as a means of social advancement. Next in importance were priors, who ran monasteries in the abbot's absence. There could also be sub-priors. Cellarers served as financial and production managers, while almoners dispensed charity. Novice masters would educate those about to take vows. Others included specialists in building, farming, education and medicine. Choir monks, often of noble birth, devoted their lives to worship, led by precentors or cantors. The Cisterians encouraged the presence of lay brothers, monks of common origins who did most of the work in monastery kitchens, workshops, fields and even mines, so that the fully-ordained monks could concentrate on prayer and learning. One of the major figures in the coming battle, Willem van Saeftingen was a lay brother at Ter Doest.

In reaction to the heresies rife in the 1100s, the Spaniard Domingo de Guzman (St. Dominic) and the Italian Francesco di Bernardone (St. Francis of Assisi) founded new holy orders. These orders, along with the later Augustinians, were known as the mendicants or poor friars and emphasized preaching. Mendicant orders founded monasteries throughout Flanders. Bruges had six monasteries and two convents and more friars and nuns than more populous Ghent. Apparently, Bruges the trading city provided more opportunities than Ghent the manufacturing center. Franciscans, Dominicans, Augustinians, Carmelites, Brothers of the Sack and Magpie Brothers, as well as Franciscan and Dominican nuns, all had foundations in or immediately outside the city. The mendicant orders responded more quickly to the needs of Bruges's growing urban population than the established clergy. However, all that remains of these today are a few traces of the medieval Dominican abbey incorporated into a modern apartment building. While the monasteries and convents of the mendicant orders left little mark on the cityscape, their influence cannot be overstated. The cosmopolitan nature of the mendicants meant that they had a great deal of contact with foreign merchants. As the 1300s progressed, groups of foreign traders set up chapels in the mendicants' churches. English merchants used the Carmelites' refectory as their meeting place after 1334. The German Hansa traders kept the little chest containing their standard weights in the Franciscans' dormitory from 1347. One of its keys was kept with the Carmelites. Manuscripts and miniatures inspired by Franciscan and Dominican doctrine appeared in Bruges around 1250, and were the city's first works of art that had more than regional importance.[35]

1. Metropolis in the North

Four miles northeast of Bruges was the outer harbor of Damme, which boasted as many as 20,000 inhabitants of its own. The Zwin reached to Damme, which received a charter from the Count of Flanders, Philip of Alsace, in 1180. Due to siltation, by the twelfth century most cargo bound for Bruges was unloaded at Damme or even more distant Sluis. The port was a forward naval base for the French in their perennial wars with England. In 1213, seventeen hundred ships under the command of French King Philip Augustus gathered to cross the Channel. On May 31, 1213, they were surrounded by an English fleet under the command of William of Salisbury and Renaud of Boulogne. The town and some 400 ships were destroyed by fire. "The French know little of naval methods," was the French king's sad conclusion.[36] However, the town rebounded quickly and became Europe's most important market for Scandinavian herring. Damme held monopolies on the storage, sale and resale of pitch from Norway and Germany, wood ash from Sweden, wine, and herring. Frisians and Danes sold horses and oxen here. The 147-foot tower of Damme's Church of Our Lady, already under construction by the beginning of the 1300s, was visible for many miles. The town also boasted Sint-Janhospitaal, an almshouse for the elderly founded by Margaret of Constantinople in 1249. Damme's Town Hall with its Cloth Hall also dates from the thirteenth century.

Like any other time in history, including our own, life varied enormously. Some lived on the edges of both their means and society's conventions. Some were burdened by the stress of shifting traditions. Others demanded constant change. Scandals, murders and changes in the price of bread made news. The arrival of pilgrims at their long-sought destinations and the completion of a church, whether a great cathedral or a humble parish chapel, were causes for rejoicing. While the health of most was seldom good, no major epidemics had occurred in hundreds of years. Mundane lives in workshops and fields were livened with gossip. Lives were short and work was grueling. Yet in Flanders, and particularly Bruges, an era of good feeling and high emotion was all that had been known for some time.

Despite its prosperity, thirteenth-century Bruges, like other towns

The size and beauty of Damme's Town Hall shows the medieval importance of Damme, which has dwindled to a small village today.

in Flanders, also had many poor people, who lived in frugality at best and hardship more often. The era's clothes were quite plain. Most wore woolen clothing with linen undergarments. The wool was sometimes combined with goats' hair to make chamlet. Most men wore hooded tunics, while women wore gowns with sleeveless tunics and wimples to cover their hair. Sheepskins, woolen hats and mittens were worn for protection from the winter cold. Leather boots were soled with wood to keep the feet dry. While underwear was regularly washed, outer clothes were almost never laundered. Luckily the smell of wood smoke permeated most people's clothing, acting as a deodorant. Only the clothing of aristocrats and wealthy merchants changed with fashions. The apparel of most was dictated by their trades.[37]

Just about everywhere in medieval western Europe, houses comprised dirt or stonework ground floors, wooden beams and frameworks of wooden posts, known in French as colombage (half-timbering). Dwellings were pegged together rather than nailed. From sill beams, framing a house's floor, walls were supported by wall posts, studs and tension braces and tied together with crossframes and tie beams. Windows and doors were added. Ceiling rafters were supported by arch braces or central king's, or crown, posts and connected by a crown plate, a beam extending the length of the house (usually the longest piece of wood in the construction). Spaces between the beams and studs of the walls were packed with small stones and covered with plaster. Wattle (woven sticks) and daub (mud fill) were also common, while brick was reserved for the rich. Stone was used by all if in abundance, but again only the wealthy could afford cut stone. Most cities had a white-washed appearance, which has long-since disappeared. After 1200 differences between houses of different classes increased dramatically.[38]

Most city dwellings were simple one- to three-story structures, built first of wood, later brick. They were cold, damp, and dark. It was sometimes warmer and always lighter outside than inside. The mansions of the burghers were primarily made of stone, and their floors were paved with stone or tile. Meanwhile, straw covered the dirt floors of the commoners. Many roofs around the city were thatched. Later, wooden, slate and tile shingles were more common. The number of fireplaces, chimneys and windows signified poverty or prosperity. Many poor homes had one of each and no more. Windows were small openings with wooden shutters that shut out bad weather and allowed those inside to see out, but kept outsiders from looking in. Windows with lattice frames covered with fabric soaked in resin and tallow, allowed light in, kept drafts out, and could be removed in good weather. Only the wealthy and the church could afford window glass.

Problems of waste disposal and pollution soon arose. Too many people wanted to live within the town walls. Their waste ran in open ditches, canals and rivers. Traffic crowded the narrow streets. Collisions were noted as a problem. The town was filled with smoke from cooking and heating. Fire hazards were numerous. Open lamps and candles were the norm. City authorities banned thatched roofs in certain districts shortly before 1232 to reduce the danger. Two centuries later, in 1417, following several devastating blazes on the edge of the city, a scheme was set up whereby subsidies were granted to householders who replaced their thatched roofs with tiles.[39] Cleaned weekly at the expense of the city, the streets were widened and the city council paid for demolitions. This is one of the first instances of the use of eminent domain. Wooden houses remained common, and were not prohibited until the seventeenth century. Two such buildings have survived in Bruges to the present.[40]

The furnishings of most houses were sparse. A rough table, some benches or stools, maybe beds and a chest or two were typical. Looms, spinning wheels or workbenches, which generated a household's income, were also evident. Animals were never far away. Even the mansions of the rich were quite bare of furniture until the Renaissance. However, the wealthy could afford tapestries to hold out the damp so common to the Low Countries. One common feature of all dwellings was pottery.[41]

Essential to medieval life and within reach of even poor households, pottery came in many shapes and sizes, but was always functional. Both locally produced and imported from neighboring countries, it was used not only for storage, but also for cooking and serving. Pots and pans were designed to be placed on hot ashes. Most medieval jars and jugs did not have smooth undersides made on a wheel, like modern pottery. Glazing, a costly process involving a second firing, served a functional waterproofing purpose and was used sparingly, usually on the inside only.

Cheap earthenware made of local clays was bought by all social classes and found in every medieval kitchen. Red and gray variants, made from brown clay and sometimes glazed with lead, were standard in many parts of Brabant and Flanders. If glazed, these pots were usually white, yellow or green. Highly prized Andenne earthenware, made of fine white clay from the Maas (Meuse) valley, was white or pale yellow with a transparent glaze inside and out. Produced as early as 1075, it was sold throughout northern Europe. The proportion of locally produced earthenware decreased in the 1300s. Meanwhile, imported earthenware included luxury goods, such as high quality blue-gray pottery from Elmpt and Brüggen in the Holy Roman Empire.

Made from clays found in the Rhine valley and the Westerwald, stoneware became popular in the 1200s and occupied an important place in all households during the high Middle Ages. Fired at high temperatures that almost melted the clay, it was extremely hard and completely waterproof. Clear salt and purple or brownish iron glazes were used later. Such luxury products as stoneware jugs, mugs and bowls were used mainly for serving and were rarely found in the kitchen.

Pots, iron kettles, open fires and lots of smoke characterized medieval kitchens. A stone hearth in the center of the room was used not only for cooking, but also as the house's main source of heat. People of all stations cut their meat into cubes with daggers and ate with fingers. Wooden spoons were sometimes available. The fork had been invented, but was viewed with suspicion as a newfangled Italian gadget.[42]

Bread was the mainstay of the medieval diet. However, baking required ovens, only found in the largest homes. Communal ovens in rural areas and bakers in the towns provided most people's daily staple. Bread varied greatly in terms of texture and color. Additives including peas, beans and even acorns were ground into wheat, barley, oat and rye flour, resulting in all shades of yellow, brown and black.

Trenchers, slices cut from loaves of wholemeal bread, were used to hold food, salt, and even candles. The word "trencher" is derived from the French verb *trenchier* or *trancher*, meaning "to slice." Wholemeal loaves were left to harden for three or four days, then four-by-six inch plates were cut from them for each meal. One's status dictated how many trenchers were given. Clean trenchers with cheese and delicacies were expected at the end of a meal. In wealthy households, used trenchers, covered in sauces and morsels of food, were tossed to the dogs or given to the poor as alms. For commoners, trenchers were most of their meal. Sometimes two people shared a trencher and drinking cup. Dipping the stale slice in wine made it more palatable. In the 1500s trenchers of wood, earthenware or metal gradually replaced those of bread.[43]

Fish was eaten on Fridays and numerous other days. Chicken, beef, pork and a variety of game were consumed sparingly and almost never in large portions. Sausages were more common than meat in other forms. Mentioned in Homer and Aristophanes, they have a very long history. Variations in contents and regional origins have been great. Stuffed in animal intestines, sausages were mixtures of veal, pork, ham or other ground meats boiled with native herbs such as sage, parsley, fennel, onion, marjoram, caraway, mace, and coriander. More expensive varieties included nutmeg, cinnamon, cloves and other imported spices. Sausages and other meats were dried or smoked to aid preservation and enhance flavor. Smoked sausages were more common in the cold climates of the north than the dry sausages or salamis of the warmer Mediterranean south. By the tenth century, butcher's guilds created their own proprietary recipes which led to the development of sausages still known today by place names, such as Bologna, Salami, Mettwurst and many others.[44]

Even more common were broths and potages, or stews. Added to these potages, cabbages, leeks, and onions became known collectively as pot-herbs. Among the culinary delights of the medieval Flemish kitchen was nettle potage, a stew made of onions, bay leaves, parsnips, leeks, garlic, lard, water, salt, milk, butter, a couple handfuls of young nettle leaves and a bit of beef.[45]

1. Metropolis in the North

Tomatoes, potatoes, maize, tea, chocolate and coffee were unknown and fewer varieties of peppers and beans were available. Turnips, peas, and sorrel were common in Flanders. Apples and cherries were consumed in large amounts when in season. Sauces were thickened with breadcrumbs or ground almonds rather than flour. Eggs were used sparingly, while honey was the most common sweetener. Rightly considered suspect, water was seldom drunk. Wine was available. However, beer was most common among all classes and ages. These were not heady alcoholic drinks but weak concoctions with little effect on sobriety. In addition to beer, Flanders was and is also known for mustard. Salt was often the only seasoning at the table. Herbs were used in the kitchen, often to mask the true taste of questionable meat. Imported spices were too expensive for most.[46]

Feasting and fasting were integral parts of medieval societies. Most of the calendar was dominated by one or the other. Accompanied by rich sauces and greater than usual amounts of meat, feasts celebrated weddings, betrothals, births, and holy days. Fasting was typical prior to religious feasts and was practiced in various forms, which included the exclusion of certain foods, the allowance of only one daily meal and the addition of unpalatable items to other foods. Both fasting and feasting were of equal importance during the Middle Ages. Those who ignored either were frowned upon. Fasting on feast days was considered as much a sin as feasting during a fast.[47]

Not surprisingly, as the towns grew, demand for agricultural produce skyrocketed. The use of water and later wind power increased production. By the end of the eleventh century, thousands of flour and oil mills dotted the countryside of Western Europe. The large portions of manpower previously needed to move grindstones were put to other uses. Such structures were built of timber and sometimes stone. Wind power was used in Castille from the tenth century and spread northwards during the twelfth. The Low Countries began to acquire their distinctive windmills. By 1302, Ypres alone was surrounded by 120 windmills.[48] Requiring regular maintenance and iron parts, mills represented a level of investment that only the rich could afford. To recover their investments, lords imposed heavy taxes on peasants bringing

41

them grain. Many peasants were tempted to continue to use their old grindstones. As a result, lords confiscated handmills, obliging tenants to use manor mills. Lords and peasant farmers alike started cutting down the County's forests at alarming rates for firewood and in order to extend cultivation. Farming methods improved, leading to higher yields and less wasted land. Many in rural areas were relatively well off and some even became modestly rich.

Meanwhile urban life became progressively more crowded and more expensive. Until the third quarter of the 1200s, Bruges proper, the area governed by the city council, was largely limited to the territory within the city's fortifications. One exception was the Braamberg district, south of Groene Rei, which was added to the town before 1246. By the 1200s Bruges had its first rudimentary water supply. Lead pipes carried water from the city reservoir at Saint Bavo's (now the Sint-Andries district) to public wells. Steady economic growth caused Bruges to burst its seams. The city's original fortifications, erected in 1127, were no longer truly its boundaries. Available land outside the walls was rapidly divided into building plots, primarily for the small, one-room dwellings of laborers. Inside the old walls, spacious townhouses were built for the wealthy. Bruges's oldest surviving stone frontages date from around 1300.[49]

The city's earliest fortifications (from Speelmansrei, Augustijnenrei, Gouden Handrei and Verwersdijk to Groene Reij) are probably combinations of human and natural watercourses. Just after 1275, the city boundaries were adjusted to take into account both the changed circumstances and possible future growth. Officers of the count arbitrarily placed ten boundary posts around the city. They deliberately ignored existing roads, waterways and other landmarks. New walls were built in 1297, surrounding an area that was to remain unchanged until 1795. They still mark the boundaries of the inner city and are clearly visible in the modern cityscape. This second set of defenses enclosed an oval area measuring 1,064 acres, with a circumference of four and a quarter miles. Old moats were then used as canals and quays facilitating the transport of goods. Bruges's city walls and stone gates were not added until the second half of the fourteenth century. Of the nine gates the five most important were the Ezelpoort to the northwest, Gentpoort to the southeast, Smedenpoort to the southwest, Kruispoort to the east, and Dampoort to the outer harbor of Damme in the north.[50]

Civic pride was reflected in architecture. Bruges established a pattern of public investment in infrastructure and monumental civic structures later followed by Antwerp and Amsterdam. However, few of the city's surviving civic buildings date from the thirteenth century. The belfry and market hall on the Markt are the largest complex of buildings of that era. The first wooden market hall was built no later than the early 1200s. The stone hall and the earliest belfry probably date from around 1240. The market hall was, of course, used for commercial purposes, while the city aldermen used to meet in a chamber in the belfry. The municipal council, treasury and archives containing Bruges privileges were all based here, as were the city's bells. The belfry thus served as a clear symbol of municipal autonomy. The city also financed the construction of the Waterhalle, a great hall for storing and selling wool. It spanned the river, so that the bundles could be unloaded without being exposed to the elements.

The counts, meanwhile, resided less frequently at the Burg and more often at their huge moated castle at Male, three miles east of Bruges, while the Gravensteen, or Castle of the Counts, was their principal residence in Ghent. By 1302, even more building was going on in the city. Construction work on churches, public buildings, fortifications, markets and houses provided a steady income for generations of masons, quarriers, carpenters and smiths and involved hundreds of carts, wagons and boats to transport building materials into the city. Throughout Flanders, the landscape was transformed with belfries, castles, churches and cathedrals.

The differences between rich and poor were great and growing. Meanwhile expectations climbed. Social tensions sometimes led to unrest, such as the Moerllemaye troubles of October 1280. In the summer of 1280, Count Guy of Dampierre granted generous privileges to Aardenburg, which led some foreign merchants leave Bruges. That same year Bruges's belfry was seriously damaged by a fire, which destroyed the city's archives, including the charter setting out its

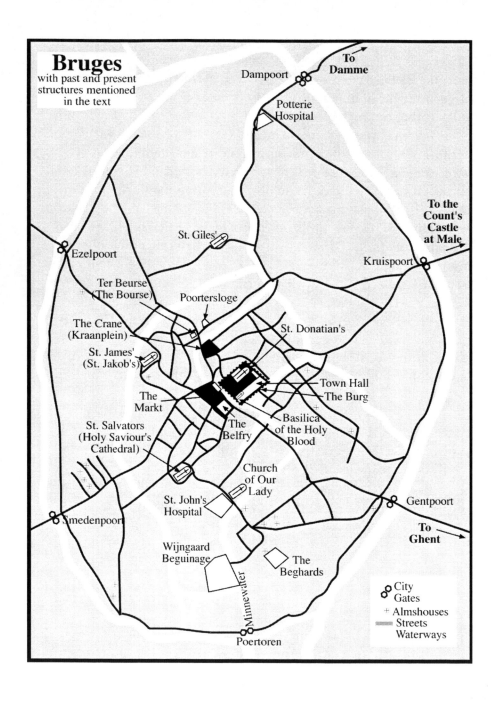

Map of Bruges.

44

privileges. The mayor and aldermen moved to the Burg, where they occupied the Ghiselhuus on the site of the later Town Hall, begun in 1283 and finished some eighty years later. The Count showed little inclination to renew the charter and decided instead to consolidate his authority over the city. Angered by these attempts to undo their power, a group of prominent burghers pitted themselves against the Count and mounted a coup within the city council, supported by the commoners. Around the beginning of October, members of the previous city government fled or were imprisoned, and their houses were plundered and burned. A list of grievances was presented to Robert of Béthune, the Count's son. However, within a year, the rebellion was crushed and a heavy price was exacted from the town. A new charter issued on May 25, 1281, consolidated the power of the Count and curtailed that of the council. A second revolt that summer was crushed even more ruthlessly. The fourteenth century dawned with even greater tension.

2

The Overlords

The counts of Flanders were officially subordinates of the French monarch. But as subordinates, they proved to be greater thorns in the king's side than many of his enemies. Scarcely recognizing Paris's authority, they built huge castles to defend their realm. When the policies of their French masters didn't suit them, they schemed with whomever they could. Siding occasionally with the English whose wool was Flanders' chief import, the counts offset the French kings' unceasing desire to bring them under more centralized control. Other times they looked eastwards to their neighbor, the duke of Brabant, a similarly independent-minded vassal of the Holy Roman Emperor. Although Brabant was not as economically developed as Flanders, Brabantine knights had an impressive record of success and their presence helped to keep the French at bay. Meanwhile, town councils no longer accepted the interference of counts in their affairs. In several conflicts, they turned directly to the French king, the Flemish counts' liege lord. They realized too late that what they thought to be independence, turned out to be direct royal rule. With the cities the king thought he had an ideal weapon to get rid of the counts and annex Flanders to his royal domains. Eventually, many commoners came to see the counts as allies against the burghers who ran the cities. Because of this dangerous, complex game of playing enemies against each other, Flanders edged towards the precipice of a crisis. A cutthroat world of competitive arrogance had emerged.

But first, an examination of Flanders' wider European context and its overlords, the French kings, is essential to fully comprehend what lay ahead. The history of France began with Julius Caesar's invasion of Celtic Gaul. Rapidly assimilating Roman culture, language and law, Gaul covered all of present day France and Belgium, the northern quarter of Italy and parts of Germany. After 395, Germanic peoples who had long inhabited the area east of the Rhine came under pressure from the Huns further east and began to migrate westwards. Burgundians, Vandals, Visigoths and others passed through history. In 451, Aëtius's defeat of Attila on the Catalaunian Fields ended the threat of the Huns. But by then Gaul's prosperity had disappeared.

The arrival in Europe of the stirrup, an Asian invention, revolutionized warfare. Stirrups welded horses and riders into powerful fighting units, enabling riders to use the force of their galloping animals to strike enemies. The degree to which this was significant has been the subject of many disputes.[1] The supremacy of cavalry began with the Visigoths' victory over the Romans at Adrianople in 378. Rulers recognized the potential of heavily armed cavalry equipped with stirrups, and began to gather large numbers of retainers. But horses and armor were terribly expensive. It also took considerable time to train effective cavalry. The sword and horse became the hallmarks of the knight.

The most important of the Germanic migrants were the Franks, indeed they were the only Germanic group to establish a lasting political presence anywhere. United by Clovis, they overran Gaul. Adopting Catholic Christianity, Clovis was recognized by the pope. The Salic law of the Franks was fused to the remnants of the civilization of Roman Gaul. Based in Tournai, Clovis established the Merovingian dynasty, named after his grandfather, Merovech. Over a period of two centuries, Merovingian power weakened while the mayors of the palace acquired more and more power. A long line of puppet rulers followed, and the dynasty was only nominally enthroned.

In the absence of governmental activity apart from that concerning the military, the Church played a major role in the political structures, which followed Rome's fall. The papacy centered in Rome based its organization on that of the fallen empire, complete with dioceses, vicars and a pontiff (all based on features of Roman government). The Church sought to moderate the excesses of the warrior class by implementing a code of chivalry, but morals were often shed for other considerations.

The Carolingian dynasty (from Carolus, Latin for Charles) began with one of the Merovingian's mayors of the palace, Charles Martel, who defeated the Moors at Tours in 732 and halted the Muslim advance into Europe. In 751 one of his successors, Pepin the Short, took the title as well as the power of king. After consolidating his position by granting lands to the pope, Pepin died in 768 and was succeeded by his son, Charlemagne (Charles the Great). Standing 6 feet 4 inches in height, a foot taller than the average man of his time, Charlemagne personally led his men in victories over Lombards, Saxons, Avars and Danes and became the overlord of Western Europe. Until his empire grew larger than his reach, he frequently traveled throughout his domain on horseback, impressing his subjects with his greatness in physique and authority. His official policy was "Renovatio Romani Imperi," the restoration of the Roman Empire. On Christmas Day 800 he was crowned emperor by the pope. Thus the Holy Roman Empire was established to embody the medieval ideal of world domination by pope and emperor working together. Church and State were separated to a large degree, though in theory the pope ruled all.

At the center of Charlemagne's system was a royal household, a palace court and a chancery. Within the royal household was a chamberlain, who supervised other subordinates within the circle immediately around the emperor. The Palace, or Palatine, Court was headed by a count, while the chancery was administered by a chancellor, an educated cleric who also served as court chaplain. An elite of counts monopolized the high offices of the Carolingian Empire. They dispensed justice, waged wars, and collected taxes. For most people, they were the government. At first countships were not hereditary, but they tended to remain within the same family. In the eighth and early ninth centuries, regional concentrations of power depended on family connections and political influence at court. The powers of counts were curtailed by mandatory attendance at a triennial assembly and by the assignment to church leaders of bailiffs, or secular retainers, by the emperor. To consolidate his power, Charlemagne regularly sent royal messengers or *missi dominici*, to inspect the activities of the counts, although there was little chance of a corrupt count being removed from office. Special military governors, or margraves, administered border areas, or margravates.

Based in Aachen, the Empire fostered a short-lived renaissance of building and literacy. However, the Frankish custom of partible inheritance divided the empire among Charlemagne's sons Charles, Pepin and Louis. Three decades of quarreling weakened the power and prestige of kings who were able to do little to stem a growing tide of violence. Finally, the 843 Treaty of Verdun divided Western Europe into three realms, roughly France, Germany and Italy.

For the next century and a half, Europe's history is a story of constant instability. France was harried by Moors in the south and invaded by Vikings in the north. Aachen fell into Viking hands and in 886 Paris witnessed a terrible siege. Kings could do little to halt the invaders, and the common people sought local protection from the counts, who they came to consider their rightful rulers. Great aristocratic families governed virtually independent territories in which distant and weak kings could not interfere. Civil and military powers were assumed by landowners. Some of these new lords were imperial officials, which the kings could no longer control. Others emerged independently as local rulers. By the 900s, dukes of Aquitaine, counts of Toulouse, counts of Flanders and other local lords had become powerful enough that they began to absorb the lesser lords and territories around them. Political power became private property, which could be loaned, given away or passed on to heirs. The distinction between private rights and public authority disappeared.

First Charles the Fat, then Count Odo, an elected king, and later Charles the Simple tried to buy off the Norse. By the 912 Treaty of Saint-Clair-sur-Epte, the mouth of the River Seine and Normandy (land of the Northmen) was ceded to Danish Viking leader Rollo, who established himself firmly at Rouen, converted to Christianity and agreed to pay homage to the king. These Normans, as they became known, were to play important roles in Europe's history for centuries to come. Meanwhile, the Carolingians became as weak as the Merovingians. Hugh, Count of Paris, overshadowed the king. Although he could have easily declared himself king, he maintained the charade of the Carolingians for one more generation. His son, Hugh Capet, founded the Capetian dynasty in May 987 when Louis V, the last of the direct Carolingian line, died.

Hence a complex series of events devolved power from monarchs to the nobility in what later became known as feudalism. The adjective "feudal" is often used disparagingly to describe something unjust, antiquated and barbaric. Modern sensibilities have promoted a view that the feudal order was little more than gang rule dominated by conflicts over "turf," financed by taxes that were little more than protection money. It is similarly commonplace to think of medieval feudalism as a system that allowed a small group of lazy military leaders to exploit the producing peasant class, the tillers of the soil. This is neither an accurate nor a very useful approach. Societies ranging from ancient Greece to the antebellum American South to some twentieth-century Latin American countries have been characterized by sharp divisions between exploiters and exploited. To call all such societies feudal strips the term of significant meaning and distorts any understanding of medieval feudalism. The fact remains that when and where feudalism developed it served the needs of society very well. Isolation was dangerous, and it was common for humble individuals to seek protection from some powerful lord or cleric. Most were happy to exchange the distant, ineffectual imperial government for familiar, effective local lords. Sometimes freeholders seeking noble protection gave up the rights to their property. Such were the feelings of insecurity. The system was well suited to conditions caused by ineffective central government, a moneyless economy, inadequate communications and constant threats of armed attack.[2]

Although the term feudalism was only first used in the 1600s, the aristocratic political order which characterized Western Europe from about 900 to 1500 was based on authority as a private heritable possession divided among a large number of lords. It was a form of personal rule in which land rights were exchanged for military obligations at a time when central authority had failed to perform its functions. In practice, feudalism meant that political power was not centered on kings but on lower lords, who administered their own estates, dispensed their own justice, minted their own coinage, levied tolls and taxes, and demanded military service from a subordinate warrior class. Lords could often field greater armies than kings. In theory the king was the chief feudal lord, second only to the pope in authority. In reality individual lords were supreme in their territories and many kings were little more than figureheads.

Feudalism actually existed at two levels: lords, such as counts, who ruled territories and armed retainers who became knights. Until the eleventh century, political power was concentrated in a small group of counts. A wide and deep gap in social standing and political function separated counts from knights. Because knights were not involved in government, and only men who exercised political power were considered noble, knights were not originally part of the noble class. The old count-knight distinctions were blurred as the era continued. Eventually, the noble class extended to include knights, and a complex hierarchy of ranks emerged. Dukes were most important, followed by counts, viscounts, marquis and barons. In England the term "earl" replaced count and elsewhere other localized variations of title and rank were common. To avoid confusion, this book uses the general term "lord" for any noble above the lowest of knights. Those who were not noble were not even part of the feudal system, but rather were part of the noble-dominated economic relationship known as manorialism, frequently confused with feudalism.

As the value of retainers increased, rulers bound their knights by oaths of loyalty and ceremonies of homage. These bonding rituals included exchanges of gifts and vows by the liege lord and his kneeling vassal. The vassal became a member of the lord's family. The words used in these relationships have interesting origins, which shed light on feudalism's beginnings. "Homage" emerged from the French word for man, homme, because feudal contractants agreed to become the man, or servant, of their lord. Rooted in the Germanic word vieh, or "cow," an early German measure of wealth, the term "fief," later came to mean "something of value," by then usually land. "Vassal" was derived from the Celtic word for "boy."[3] Here is a ninth-century oath of fealty:

> Thus shall one take the oath of fidelity: By the Lord before whom this sanctuary (some religious place) is holy, I will to N. be trufaithful, and love all which he loves and shun all which he shuns, according to the laws of God and the order of the world. Nor will I ever with will or action, through word or deed, do anything which is unpleasing to him, on condition that he will hold to me as I shall deserve it, and that he will perform everything as it was in our agreement when I submitted myself to him and chose his will.[4]

Lords tried to ensure the support of their retainers with weapons, jewelry and usufructs or benefices of land as payment or reward. The great lords gave fiefs or estates to their vassals or armed subordinates. Hence land produced income to maintain knights and their families. Vassals were required to attend the lord's court, help administer justice, and contribute resources if needed. They had to answer summonses to battle, bringing an agreed-upon number of fighting men or paying scutage, a hefty fee in lieu of service. They were also required to feed and house the lord and his retinue when they traveled across their land. This last obligation could involve enormous feasting expenses in the form of thousands of chickens, rabbits, fish, eggs and loaves of bread, and hundreds of geese, hams, and casks of wine, beer and cider. Lords, on the other hand, were obliged to protect vassals and their families. Sometimes, this duty was specifically limited to three nights' hospitality, a commitment still difficult for many lesser vassals. A number of traditional services were often included such as aid in ransoming the lord if he was captured in battle and presents and money on occasions such as the wedding of the lord's eldest daughter and the knighting of his eldest son. If a daughter inherited, the lord arranged her marriage. If there were no heirs the lord could dispose of a fief as he chose.

The Golden Spurs of Kortrijk

Feudalism developed differently in different parts of Europe and also quite independently in Japan. In theory, kings could ennoble any of their subjects. All land was his property and its use could be revoked. Subjects could appeal cases through the system to the King's Court, though this happened infrequently. This system operated very informally at first. But time led to increased emphasis on ceremony, procedure and other formalities. Really the rituals of a simple contract, ceremonies of homage and fealty became formalized, romanticized, and overlaid with symbolism. They were powerful bonds that generated centuries of legends and tales based on the relationship between lord and vassal. Many of these rituals have persisted to the present in the traditional customs of courtship and marriage. The kneeling suitor, the showering of gifts, the exchange of rings, the formal procession and the lavish feasting of modern times are rooted in knightly ceremony.

Despite the celibate example set by the clergy, marriage had a valued status in medieval times. Most people married in their early twenties, typically within their same class. Lords seldom permitted their serfs to marry beyond their fiefs, since they would lose control of the offspring of such unions. However, "mixed" marriages, particularly between free peasants and serfs, did occur. More than 90 percent of Europe's population married in the 1200s. Despite the popular ballads of courtly love, marriages in all classes tended to be arranged. Annulments were rare, but possible, based on violation of Church laws relating to the partners' age, consent and consanguinity. Medieval households were surprisingly like those of the twentieth century, having nuclear families of two parents and an average of three children. The large farm family common in the 1800s was not typical of the 1300s. Frequent pregnancies were accompanied by high infant and maternal mortality. Childbearing was the greatest hazard of a woman's life and changed only gradually as diets improved and body fat increased. Medieval attitudes towards wives present many contradictions. Wife-beating was common. However, society assumed that a wife would control a purse, which she used for her own shopping, alms-giving and other expenses. As in ancient Rome, hen-pecked husbands were themes that appeared so often in popular culture that their existence must have been familiar to all. Viewed as individual souls separate from their parents, most children were not burdened with great expectations or seen as reflections of their parents. However, this view promoted neglect, often shaded with brutality.

Because feudal society was a military society, men held the dominant positions in it. However, the legal and social position of women was not as insignificant as might be expected. Charters recording gifts to the church indicate that women often held or inherited land, which obviously meant economic power. They frequently endowed monasteries, churches, and other religious establishments. Countess of Flanders Margaret of Constantinople is an excellent example of a medieval philanthropist. In southern France, Navarre and Catalonia, women inherited feudal property as early as the tenth century. Other evidence attests to women's varied status. For example, in parts of northern France, children were sometimes identified in legal documents by their mother's name rather than their father's, indicating that the mother's social position was higher than that of the father. In an 822 treatise on the organization of the royal household, Archbishop Hincmar of Rheims placed the queen directly above the treasurer. She was responsible for giving the knights their annual salaries and supervising manorial accounts. Thus, in the management of large households with many knights and complicated records to oversee, ladies of the manor had very important responsibilities. With such responsibility went power and influence.

The first Capetian kings were no more than great nobles who were given the royal title and nominal allegiance of other nobles. In reality, they only had power over their own personal holdings. Hugh Capet and his successors had great ambitions. But the might of the Normans was at least as strong. The Capetians revived old Carolingian claims to the Middle Kingdom and to sovereignty over the church. Henry I had been defeated by Normandy. Later Duke William of Normandy strengthened his realm further by successfully invading England. Despite their differences, various French, Flemish and Norman nobles cooperated in the First Crusade.

The Crusades were a major departure from the Christian ideals of the early Middle Ages, when canon law recognized no death penalty. But with Constantinople and the Holy Land threatened by Muslim armies, Pope Urban II issued his famous call for a crusade at Clermont on November 26, 1095. He later offered indulgences to those going to fight the Saracens. Indulgences offered forgiveness from the earthly consequences of one's sins. Many would interpret them as tickets to heaven. Four centuries later, abuses related to the sale of indulgences would spark the Lutheran Reformation. While the Crusades and increased trade opened the eyes of Europeans to the outside world, in many ways they sealed the fate of Europe's traditional society. New ideas brought new expectations. Europeans realized that much lay beyond their small continent. Another result of the violent turn in church policy was the belief that crusades within Christendom could deal with heresy in Europe. This was particularly important in France, where campaigns were initiated against first the Waldensians in the southeast and later the Cathars or Albigensians in the southwest. In both cases the power of French kings and their relationships with Rome were strengthened.

Under Louis (VI) the Fat, the Capetian monarchy grew stronger. Instead of quarrelling with the papacy like his predecessors, Louis VI forged an alliance with the church. He attacked Henry I of England in Normandy and tried to check the power of the counts of Blois, which was strengthened by the accession of Stephen of Blois to the crown of England. This was temporarily neutralized by the 1137 marriage of Louis VII to Eleanor of Aquitaine, the heiress to the vast Duchy of Aquitaine in the southwest. In 1152 Louis divorced Eleanor, who six weeks later married Henry of Anjou, King Henry II of England. Henry's power was the greatest danger the French monarchy had yet faced. With his marriage Henry II established an empire that extended from the Pyrenees to the Scottish border. In France he ruled in Normandy, Maine, Anjou, Touraine, Gascony, Aquitaine and Poitou; a realm greater than that of the French king. Flanders meanwhile was a fiefdom divided by the Scheldt into Crown Flanders (western areas under the French king) and Imperial Flanders (smaller eastern holdings of the Holy Roman Emperor). Roughly, the area of the present day

2. The Overlords

Belgian provinces of West and East Flanders, together with French Flanders, formed the historic County of Flanders. The Belgian territory known today as the Flemish Region is much bigger and includes the provinces of Brabant, Antwerp and Limburg, historically part of the Holy Roman Empire as the Duchy of Brabant.

By 1200, medieval society was a three-tiered hierarchy of those who prayed (the clergy), those who fought (the nobility) and those who worked (the commoners). The manorial system, which took root, provided wealth to the military class and, in theory, protection to the producing class. Most people were serfs, peasant farmers bound to their lord's land. Their conditions were little better than slavery. But while slavery would divide families, serfdom promoted a narrow view of the world that would not vanish with its abolition.

Descended from Roman villas, manors were the principal economic and social units of the early Middle Ages. A manor consisted of a manor house, often a castle, one or more villages, and up to several thousand acres of land divided into pasture, forest, and cultivated fields. The center of life in manors and castles was the great hall, a huge chamber built on the safety of the second story. Dimly lit due to the defensive need for massive walls with small windows, these halls were used to hold court, to entertain guests and for numerous other purposes. Typically, villages consisted of one- to five-dozen families living in rough dwellings along with the livestock. Built to last only about twenty years, the typical village's mud and wood-frame houses were not permanent structures. The only buildings to last from one generation to the next were the community's focal points: the castle, church and mill. Roads and footpaths were damp trenches. Furnishings were sparse: three-legged stools, a trestle table, beds on the floor softened with straw or leaves. The diet was mainly broths, porridge, cheese, black bread and vegetables.

The feudal lords exerted great economic control. Forests were the lord's possession. Lords were paid for the firewood and game taken from their woodlands and the animals put to pasture there. Used only for building and weapons, hardwoods were cut with special permission. Lords built ovens and mills as monopolies, which villagers had to patronize. This gave them opportunities to grant fiefs other than land, such as the income from a certain mill or fishing rights in a certain stream. Agriculture was typically based on an open field system with a three field rotation. Intercropping, or the cultivation of more than one crop in a field, was common. Fields were divided into narrow strips. A third was the lord's fields or *demesne* (from which the word "domestic" originates). Some was given to the church, and the remainder was for peasants and serfs. Land was distributed and sometimes rotated so that everyone had equal shares of good and bad. At least half a week was spent tending land belonging to the lord and church. Other duties included maintenance, clearing land, cutting firewood, and building roads and bridges.

Free peasants often had hard lives, but they did not work on Sundays or on the many saints' days. They could travel to nearby markets. The lot of serfs was harsher and more restrictive. Although not sold as slaves, serfs were bound to a manor and its land for life. They could not own property and needed the lord's permission to marry. They were not free to leave the land unless they chose to run away. If they ran to a town and stayed there for a year and a day, they were free. However, serfs did have rights. They could not be displaced if land changed hands. They were entitled to the lord's protection and could not be required to fight.[5]

Prior to the Middle Ages, horses were used for transport and warfare. After Rome, the chariot fell from use and the wagon remained a vehicle for the farmer and merchant. Horses were expensive to buy and keep, compared to oxen and donkeys, which were foragers. They required special feed, constant care, and good shelter. With the advent of iron horseshoes, the needs of horses went beyond what a single tiller of the soil could afford. Hence, lords often supplied farmers with horses for field use.[6]

Brought from Asia like the stirrup, the horse collar revolutionized the rural economy. Roman and early medieval beasts of burden were hitched to plows and wagons with harnessing that gradually choked the draft animal. This meant that animals had to be changed every few hours. With the horse collar, the burden was shifted to the animal's shoulders and a horse could plow all day without danger. For the first time in history, horses were used on a large scale in agriculture. Many fields which grew animal fodder could now be converted to food crops for humans. The density of Europe's rural population skyrocketed.[7]

Europe was far from urbanized, and only a tiny portion of the continent's population lived in towns. Those cities which existed were small by both classical and modern standards. Most were in Italy. However, with the end of Viking raids and the return of trade, a few cities north of the Alps were beginning to have an impact. To many landowning rural lords, places such as Paris and Bruges were suspiciously powerful concentrations of independent commoners beyond their reach. One word used to describe those who lived in the ville or town was "villeins." As cities gained reputations as centers promoting rebellion and vice, the modern term "villain" developed.

The forty-three-year rule of Philip II (Philip Augustus) marks the high point of Capetian power. Enthroned at the precocious age of fourteen, Philip consolidated royal power in the north and allied himself with the rebellious sons of Henry II, the future English kings Richard (I) the Lionhearted and John. In 1191 he took part in the Third Crusade with the former. The 1199 death of Richard cleared the way for the overthrow of Angevin power in France. Defeating the unpopular John at the Battle of Bouvines in 1214, Philip consolidated power in northern France. Engaging in a questionable crusade against the Cathars, he gained a presence in the south that would be strengthened by his son and grandson. In February 1182, he had all of Paris's Jews arrested and confiscated their gold, precious cloth and houses. This gave him the wealth necessary to make a mark on history. Administration and law were firmly established during his reign. Begun in 1163 and finished in 1330, the cathedral of Notre Dame de Paris symbolized this era of rapid expansion and intensive construction. Indeed the Paris of 1302 was largely the Paris Philip Augustus had resurrected after more than six centuries of post–Roman stagnation.[8]

The most famous of Philip's many building projects was Paris's first medieval wall.[9] This wall on the Left Bank began at the Tour de

Nesles opposite the Passerelle des Arts and swept southward, encompassing old Roman Lutetia. Near its southernmost point, it crossed what is now the boulevard Saint-Michel near the northeast end of the Luxembourg gardens. Continuing northeast, it finally ended at the Seine near the present boulevard Saint-Germain. On the Right Bank, the wall began on the quai des Célestins and ran northeast and then northwest. Its northernmost point was the Tour de Jean Sans Peur on the rue Etienne Marcel. Continuing southwest, it ended at the northern entrance of the Cour Carrée of the Louvre. To complete the city's defense, chains could be stretched across the Seine. The area enclosed by the wall was about 600 acres. To estimate the number of Paris's inhabitants is difficult. The population probably grew from 25,000 to 50,000 during Philip's reign and reached 65,000 by 1302. The city quickly expanded beyond its walls, particularly in the north, around the Louvre and beyond the Porte de Buci on the Left Bank.

Even though no danger had come up the river Seine for three centuries, Norman invasions were still feared by the Parisians at the beginning of Philip Augustus's reign. The king had a fortress built where the city's defenses were weakest. The unused land at the western end of the wall by the river was called the Louvre, a name whose origins remain unclear. There he built a fortified castle with a huge square keep, surrounded by a wall, covering an area a quarter the size of the present Cour Carrée. It was about 96 feet high, with cone-shaped roofs. Its walls were almost 13 feet thick at the bottom. Spiral staircases led to rooms inside the walls. There were no underground prison cells. The surrounding wall, particularly thick on its western (Norman) side, was 231 feet from north to south and 210 feet from east to west. Two crenellated towers graced each corner. Living quarters completed the construction. The main entrance was from the south, though there was a smaller gate on its eastern side. The walls were surrounded by an 18-foot-deep moat, filled with water flowing downhill from Belleville and the Prés St Gervais. Philip Augustus would keep his treasure, archives and arsenal in the Louvre, but never lived there.

Paris also became known for its scholars. Northern Italy, then Europe's population center, had its greatest concentration of universities.

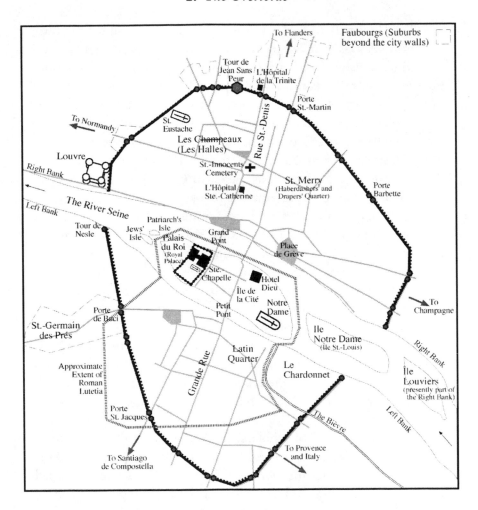

Paris in 1300.

Bologna, Padua, Vicenza, Piacenca, Arezzo, Pavia and Vercelli all date before 1300. Founded in 1173, Salerno was Europe's first medical school. Elsewhere, Oxford (1167) and Cambridge (1229) were founded in England, and Salamanca (1243) and Valladolid (1250) in Spain. Louvain, the great university of the Low Countries, would not be founded until 1425. In southern France, Montpellier, founded in 1289, was the center of learning.

The Golden Spurs of Kortrijk

The University of Paris, or the Sorbonne, as it would be known for centuries, was founded in July 1200, based on privileges granted by Philip Augustus. Its head was the pope himself, and students were under the control of ecclesiastical faculty. This was unlike the model of the University of Bologna, founded in 1088, where secular faculty were under the control of the students. By 1210 the chronicler royal noted that Paris rivaled Athens and Egypt as a place of scholarship and attracted students from around the world.[10] The university district on the Left Bank became known as the Latin Quarter, so common was the scholar's language there until the 1800s.

In 1206, one of the first colleges founded in Paris was Constantinople College, or "Greek College," at Place Maubert, near some of the present-day *premières écoles*. Founded for Greek students, it fell into decay and was bought in 1362 by Guillaume de la Marche, who created a new college in 1402. Standing students listened to masters who lectured on physics and Aristotelian philosophy from raised pedestals. Later the students moved to colleges on Saint-Geneviève hill. Place Maubert was taken over by gallows and torture chambers. In 1213 the various faculties instituted procedures for masters to acquire a license to teach. By 1215 the university was described as a *universitatis magistrorum et scolarium* where medicine, theology, and canon and civil law were taught. This reflected the fact that *universitas* meant a corporation or guild of scholars. In 1219, Masters of Arts were so numerous that they began to organize national groupings. In 1221 the university was granted its own seal. The name *Sorbonne* developed from the name of the University's faculty of theology, founded by Robert de Sorbon in 1257. Among the university's scholars were many of Europe's best, including Peter Abelard, Duns Scotus and St. Thomas Aquinas.

The reputation of the Sorbonne grew rapidly, resulting in a housing shortage. Many seeking education came to Paris. Typically, rents had to be paid a whole year in advance. The first guest houses are said to have operated from this time. In 1215 the pope regulated rents, set by two of the university's masters, in order to stop abuses. Landlords not complying with these fixed rents were banned from letting for five years. This was not aimed at safeguarding the students' welfare, as some generous landlords, having pity on poor students, undercut the fixed rates and were penalized.[11]

As today, Parisians were great consumers of food. Herds of cattle and sheep were driven from Maine and Perche and sometimes even from as far as Limousin and Marche. There were two markets: one in the Pourceaux square at the junction of rue de la Ferronerie and rue des Déchargeurs (Unloaders), the second on Place aux Veaux, close to the Grande Boucherie. Grain arrived on the River Seine and was unloaded at the Place de Grève (currently Town Hall square). The mills on the Grand Pont ground it to flour. The Grève market became too small. In 1135, Louis VI moved it to Les Champeaux. At first it was in the open air. Later under Philip Augustus, two large market halls were built with secure doors, which allowed traders to leave their merchandise there safely overnight. In 1181 the King had "la foire St-Lazare" moved to Les Champeaux. This was the origin of Les Halles quarter, or the market district. Attracting mainly traders in small wares, greengrocers and grain merchants, the market was situated between the church of Saint-Laurent and the Léproserie Saint Lazare and was further enlarged in 1182, following the confiscation of Jewish property. Traffic dramatically increased in the district previously known only for its cemetery.

Probably dating from the tenth or eleventh century, the Saint-Innocents cemetery was the largest in Paris for 800 years. Sharing the Champeaux district with later markets, it was an open space, where people came for a walk, children played, and laundry was hung to dry. Guillaume le Breton in his *Philippide* describes it as "open to pigs and full of refuse, [where] prostitutes exercised their trade."[12] In 1187 Philip Augustus ordered the cemetery to be enclosed by a wall to separate it from the market. He also ordered it closed at night. Thus both the district and market were cleaned up. Philip also supervised the establishment of the Lendit market in 1215 in the then open countryside on the Saint-Denis road. On market days, Lendit traders were banned from trading at Les Halles. In 1222 a pork market was established in the square in front of Notre Dame one day a week.

The Golden Spurs of Kortrijk

Like Flanders, Paris also had its guilds. The Livre de la Taille of 1292 lists all trades and the number of craftsmen in each.[13] All paid dues in order to have special rights. Dating from at least 1146, the butchers appear to be the oldest guild. In 1182 Philip Augustus reinforced their privileges and granted them the right to buy and sell cattle without having to pay a special fee. By the mid-thirteenth century, their guild was a close-knit brotherhood, in which membership passed only from father to son. Water carriers (boatmen) were known as far back as 1121. A charter granting them control of river traffic and a monopoly on transportation on the Seine within the city was confirmed in 1170. In 1220 the King assigned to them the surveyance of weights and measures, and the collection of the salt tax. Drapers (sheet makers) and furriers were prominent after 1183, when Philip Augustus gave them houses he had confiscated from the expelled Jews. Glove-makers were registered in 1208, but were only allowed to make leather gloves, since the right to produce cloth gloves had been given to the hatters. Mentioned as early as 1268, the jewelers' guild required a decade of training for membership and played an important part in the city's economic evolution. Grocer-pharmacists and wine merchants were also important among Parisian traders. In 1182, Philip Augustus bestowed upon the nuns of Saussaie a half tithe of the wine brought to the royal cellars in Paris. Later, in 1192, he regulated the Paris wine trade. Consequently only wine merchants living in Paris had the right to unload wine in the city. Banned from unloading their cargoes in Paris, other merchants were only allowed to sell wine from their boats or to buy it in Paris and sell it outside the city limits. The need for wood workers was limited to carpenters.

The River Seine cleaned Paris's crowded center. But without the flushing effect of a canal system like Bruges's, the French capital faced serious sanitation problems, despite serious floods which washed through the city in 1119, 1196 and 1206. Up to the 1100s, public baths had been plentiful. However, the presence of naked men and women together brought the Church's disapproval. Public bathhouses became rare until the 1800s. In the 1200s, Paris was transformed from feudal estates to a municipality dominated by the church and state. Philip

Augustus ordered the paving of the roads with cobblestones. This cut down on the muck and its offensive stench, which still remained considerable, but also created the need to get rid of garbage and sewage, which could no longer be assimilated into the ground. As the city grew taller and more densely packed, sunlight no longer penetrated to street level to light the way and dry the muck.[14]

Philip also established the royal gallows north of the city at Montfaucon, which also served as the city's dump. Thousands were hanged there and left to rot on a huge two-tiered scaffold. Their remains would then be dumped with the household waste, excrement and rubble. Along with the denial of Christian burial to criminals, the smell emanating down through the city served as a deterrent to crime. This practice continued well into the 1700s. Early nineteenth century hygienist Alexandre Parent-Duchâtelet referred to Montfaucon as the "Epicenter of Stench."[15] Others noted that the wealth of Paris could be measured by its stench. However, medieval society was not ignorant of environmental concerns, and urban bodies frequently imposed restrictions on building, trade, mining and waste disposal with those concerns in mind. Evidence of this is found in the development of Paris, Flanders and the city-states of Italy.[16]

The accumulation of refuse in the streets reached a point that in 1348 Philip VI passed an ordinance requiring residents to sweep in front of their doors and to transport garbage to dumps or risk fines and imprisonment. In desperation, he made the nobility set an example. But they just dumped their waste on public property away from their own doors. He established the first sanitation corps to clean the streets. Even with ordinances issued every few decades up to 1780, garbage, water and sewerage continued to make some streets completely inaccessible. It was not until 1370 that Hughes Aubriot created the first covered sewer in Montmartre. Called the Fosse de St. Opportune, it dumped into the Seine right by the Louvre, offending Louis XII and later leading Francis I to move his mother to the Tuilleries to escape the smell. Both before and after this development, other sewers were simply gullies running down the middle of streets. They smelled odious and overflowed regularly. Some enterprising souls made livings by charging fees to cross particularly notorious streets on boards.[17]

The Seine was used by industries placing themselves along its banks to benefit from particular chemicals dumped upstream. Tanners and dyers were often on opposite sides to avoid contaminating each other's wares. Skinners, furriers and glovemakers located themselves downstream from dyers to benefit from dumped alum. Urine and feces were used in papermaking, dying, and making saltpeter, a replacement for the scarcer alum.

Long periods of war from the fourteenth to seventeenth century limited the physical expansion of Paris. Constant influxes of peasants spurred population increases. But the number of deaths almost always outpaced the number of births. Water was available from only a few fountains and wells and the addition of new water supplies barely kept up with demand. Paris's chronic lack of potable water caused outbreaks of water-borne diseases well into the 1700s.

A few hospitals can trace their origins back to this period. Unquestionably the most important is the Hôtel-Dieu. Many legends offer differing origins for the Hôtel-Dieu, which has had a great influence on Paris throughout history. Most likely Saint Landry, the 28th bishop of Paris, was responsible for founding the hospital rather than druids or Emperor Julian II as suggested by others. Saint Landry is known as a benefactor, who gave his income and even sold precious objects from his cathedral for the relief of sick poor people. Sometime around 600 or 651, he is said to have established l'hôpital de Saint-Christophe near the cathedral for the needy. Still operating some fourteen centuries after St. Landry, this hospital is the same one later known by the name of Hôtel-Dieu (Domus Dei), a name used first in an official document by Louis VII in 1157. Up to the middle of the thirteenth century three names are used for this institution: hôpital Saint-Christophe, hôpital de Notre-Dame, and Hôtel-Dieu.

L'hôpital de la Trinité, a shelter for travelers and pilgrims founded during the reign of Philip Augustus, was at the corner of rue Saint-Denis and rue Grenata. La Trinité was serviced by religious orders from 1210. To avoid the risk of overcrowding, a fixed maximum number of patients could not be exceeded. L'hôpital Sainte-Catherine, situated on rue Saint-Denis on the southern corner of rue des Lombards, was founded in 1184. Run by friars, its original name was l'Hôpital des Pauvres de Sainte-Opportune. A papal bull of Pope Honorius III dated January 17, 1222, placed this hospital under the protection of la Maison-Dieu-Sainte-Catherine. The friars were joined by sisters in an association lasting from the fourteenth century through the sixteenth century. Dating back to 1184, Paris's first "unemployment center" was located in Sainte-Catherine's Hospital. It was a hostel for women, mainly widows and young girls who couldn't afford a place to stay when they came to Paris in search of work. Other similar centers later existed, maintained by commenderesses, or female wardens. These hospitals inspired public confidence and, as D. Louis Mackay noted, "assured that alms would be used for the poor and not to maintain a group of idlers."

After giving his wealth to Paris's poor and to those knights who accompanied him to the Holy Land, Philip Augustus died after months of illness at age fifty-seven. Interest in securing the south of France ran high. As predicted by his father, Philip's son and heir Louis VIII contracted a fever in the malarial south and died only three years after his coronation. His brief reign continued his father's work. His son, Louis IX, later canonized as Saint Louis, was only twelve years of age when his father died. His mother, Blanche of Castile, ruled as regent and successfully suppressed a revolt of some of the nobles. Known also as a great, though unsuccessful, crusader, Louis IX oversaw the development of the parlement de Paris and the subjugation of the feudal nobles by depriving them of their rights to private war. During his reign the University of Paris was expanded. Sainte-Chapelle, the tiny but magnificent Gothic royal chapel was built in 1248 to house the Crown of Thorns, which Louis had bought from the emperor of Constantinople nine years earlier. Philip (III) the Bold succeeded Louis IX. Anjou, Toulouse, Auvergne, Provence and Champagne came under royal control. However, in Sicily French rule ended with a massacre, known as the Sicilian Vespers of 1282, an event strangely similar to one that would happen later in Bruges.

The Golden Spurs of Kortrijk

Philip IV became king of France in 1285, at the age of seventeen. Born in Fontainebleau to Philip the Bold and Isabelle of Aragon in 1268, he married Joan of Navarre a year before his accession to the throne. Beyond the influence of Salic law, Navarre permitted female succession and Philip's marriage led to his being named king of Navarre. Joan would bear Philip four children: a daughter Isabella, future queen of England, and three sons, all of whom would become kings of France (Louis X, Philip V and Charles IV).

Ruling until 1314, Philip was cunning, unscrupulous and ambitious. Called "Philippe le bel," this king's name always appears as "Philip the Fair" in English. The name refers to his tall, blue-eyed and blond appearance, certainly not to his sense of justice. A man of few words, he felt that minor details were beneath the dignity of a ruler. Cold, secretive and vengeful, he wanted to weld France into a powerful empire.[18] For this he needed land and wealth. In 1286 he recognized the claim of Edward I of England to Gascony and Aquitaine, but using quarrels between the sailors of the English Cinque Ports and Normandy as a pretext, Philip claimed Gascony and Aquitaine. Edward then built an alliance against Philip, who in turn allied himself with the Scots, beginning the Franco-Scottish "Auld Alliance," which lasted until 1560. The conflict between France and England was temporarily suspended with the 1298 Treaty of Boulogne-sur-mer. Count Guy of Flanders, Philip's godfather, was one of many vassals that stood in the way of the King's limitless ambitions. Annexing wealthy Flanders to his royal domains became a high priority. Guy was vilified by Philip. One painting of the era depicted the count of Flanders as one of the horsemen of the Apocalypse.[19] In the meantime, a new Cathar revolt needed to be suppressed in 1300, and an even more serious crisis with Rome loomed.

Geography and history had combined to create a bewildering diversity of political systems in Europe, ranging from Venetian oligarchy to Swiss democracy to French monarchy. While Western Europe grew stronger and more populous, the Ottoman Turks weakened the Byzantine Empire, and the great Arab caliphs succumbed to Mongol Conquest. The Church's ideal of a centralized and disciplined Christendom was challenged as political stability and economic growth encouraged new and competing poles of loyalty. Kings, dukes and even lesser nobles upheld the supremacy of secular political interests and sought to eliminate the "foreign" authority of popes. This was true not only in the strong unified monarchies of France and England but also within the less cohesive collections of states in what would become Germany, Italy and Spain.

The legacy which Philip Augustus and St. Louis passed on to Philip IV was impressive. In addition to "building" medieval Paris, Philip Augustus doubled the area under the direct control of the French king. Philip the Fair would see it doubled again. France comprised more than 20 million people, a population not regained until the 1700s. Strong precedents were set for centralized control. Corruption was minimized. More importantly, Philip Augustus and Louis IX gained the adulation of the French masses with their pious, crusading zeal. Despite his fondest dreams, no exploits in the Holy Land would be attributed to Philip IV. However, the reputation of his ancestors served him well. Known for his piety, he embarked on pilgrimages and prayed daily for his dead parents and saintly grandfather, around whom he created a cult.

Philip surrounded himself with unscrupulous subordinates who were more than willing to do the king's bidding. The most important of these was the lawyer Pierre Flotte, a commoner who became Chancellor and was knighted by Philip. Chronicles characterize Flotte as wily and scheming. Chief among Flotte's protégés was Guillaume de Nogaret. Born in the middle of the thirteenth century at St. Félix-en-Lauragais, de Nogaret was one of the chief counselors of Philip the Fair. Allegedly descended from an Albigensian family, he studied law, gaining a doctorate and a professorship. In 1294 he was appointed royal judge of the seneschal's court of Beaucaire. By 1299 Philip the Fair conferred the title of knight on him as he had done with Flotte. Influenced by his study of Roman law, de Nogaret espoused the doctrine of the absolute supremacy of rulers and had no scruples when royal power was in question.[20]

Philip the Fair's relations with Rome deteriorated alarmingly. One of the great dangers to his position was the authority of the Church. French bishops were powerful men, commanding large tracts of land

Philip the Fair with the relics of St. Louis, as shown in a manuscript illumination in the Grands Chroniques de France *(© Bibliothèque Nationale de France).*

and vast quantities of money, all technically outside of royal authority. Determining who controlled the French Church (also called the Gallican Church) was a pressing matter for the king, who faced frequent wars with the English King Edward I. In particular issues related to the Church's wealth interested Philip. Louis IX had already asserted absolute royal control over the Church in France at the Council of Lyon in 1247. However, what St. Louis was able to accomplish and what Philip the Fair would be allowed were two different matters.

2. The Overlords

The Colonna and Orsini families of Rome had one or another of their members elected pope for decades. In 1297, to break a deadlock, a pious monk related to neither family was elected as Celestine V. He proved to be a very weak leader. Meanwhile a highly qualified Italian lawyer, Benedetto Caetani stepped into this power vacuum. Born in the village of Anagni near Rome in 1235, he had made a career in the Roman Curia, participating in numerous missions to various countries before being made a cardinal in 1281. After playing a role in persuading Celestine to stand down after less than a year in office, he outmaneuvered both the Colonna and Orsini and was elected pope as Boniface VIII at a conclave in Naples on Christmas Eve 1294. A stubborn Philip was soon in a stand-off with the equally stubborn Boniface VIII.

The new pope's authoritarian demeanor helped to consolidate his personal and family position in Rome and defeat his enemies, especially the Colonna family. To assert his authority, he intervened unsuccessfully in numerous disputes including those between Genoa and Venice, France and England, and the Guelphs and Ghibellines in Italy. 1300 was a Jubilee Year in the Roman Church's calendar. On Sunday April 10, all Europe paid homage to the institution, which had emerged as the arbiter of European affairs. But Boniface's failures made him very unpopular. Like his adversary, Boniface was stubborn, ambitious, intelligent, vain and unscrupulous. Notorious for his temper and his hatred of the French, he believed that anyone who opposed him opposed God. His plan to restore the papacy's absolute spiritual and temporal power took on a fervor equaled only by Philip's own empire-building obsessions. Meanwhile, Philip called on the services of the vengeful Colonnas. In 1300 he dispatched de Nogaret to Rome to justify his alliance with Albert of Austria, usurper of the throne of the Holy Roman Empire. De Nogaret and the Pope clashed badly, setting the tone for future contacts between the two and guiding the former's influence on his king. Boniface angered the French king by forbidding the clergy to pay taxes, after Philip had attempted to make levies used to fund the Crusades permanent. In a direct challenge, the pope emphasized the dominance of church over state in *Bull Unam Sanctam*. The

French king publicly burned his copy of the bull. The Pope in turn offered the throne of France to the Austrian monarch. A master of careful timing, Philip awaited the right moment to deal with his adversaries.

3

The Deadly Politics of Medieval Flanders

Nobody ruled Flanders for long against the will of the cities. Accompanied by the grandeur of fortified walls, cathedrals, belfries and town halls, the cities of Flanders led the medieval world through a profound political transformation. The region's seemingly limitless prosperity increased the townsmen's appetite for greater control over their affairs. The existence of the French threat enabled the rising Flemish middle classes to gain more and more privileges from the counts. This was a slow process, which took centuries. As the counts maneuvered to gain freedom from the French kings, the townsmen slowly undermined the counts and French alike. The power of the Flemish cities was felt quite early. In 1127 a count died without issue and his successor chosen by the king was rejected by the cities. The townsmen forced the selection of Dietrich (Theirry) of Alsace, who, of course, remained indebted to his nominators.

The counts of Flanders were not only liege lords of French kings, but also territorial lords who could call up all men to serve in their army. Every community could be forced to provide troops. Most were common citizens without any military training. Local lords and councils were required to arm their men, but commoners frequently carried only basic pole arms or even the tools of their trade. The quality of these poorly armed and often unarmored troops left much to be desired. Along the coast, hired or press-ganged merchant vessels and civilian fishermen provided the count with a navy of sorts. No strict separation existed between soldiers and sailors.

After 1100 a new but unnoticed military power appeared throughout Europe. Wealthy and powerful towns insisted on providing in their own defense. Town councils soon discovered that militias were not only useful for guarding city walls against hostile raiders but also were perfect instruments for securing urban interests and undoing political competitors. With many charters, city folk won rights to bear certain weapons, such as crossbows, pikes and maces. These arms, all of which required specialized skills, were to become deciding factors in many future battles.

Nowhere was this more the case than in Flanders, where booms in wealth and population enabled militias not only to defend their own walls but also to carry their influence into the hinterland beyond city gates. By 1302, Flemish militias already had a long history. Foot soldiers from the cities helped knights on the battlefield and defended fortresses very early in Flanders. The Flemish communal armies were first explicitly mentioned in 1127 but existed well before that. Brotherhoods of citizens, called *communio*, at Ghent and St. Omer were recognized by the counts.

The militia of Ghent was particularly noteworthy. Unlike peasant levies, the Gentenaars were specialists. Pikes and heavy hand weapons were their *forte*, and they were sought far and wide as siege engineers and sappers.

> The soldiers were well armed and had at their disposal a baggage train and siege equipment: they were battle-seasoned and enjoyed the reputation for being specialists in besieging fortresses... The men of Ghent had ladders, which took ten men to carry them, and a sort of tower equipped with ladders, which were intended for besieging and storming strongholds. They also had iron hammers, and implements for boring through walls, and siege engines to shatter them. Their baggage was carried on waggons, of which they brought thirty to Bruges to besiege the murderers of Count Charles the Good. They also

74

had a corps of experienced workmen who could set up or take down the siege engines, and rebuild the wooden towers to make a battering ram.[1]

The use of townsmen and peasants in the Crusades and in the various wars of the medieval era sharpened such skills. Leaving as an undisciplined mob of servants and camp followers, they returned with military skills and a knowledge of the world beyond their looms and fields. By the thirteenth century the militias in all Flemish cities were organized by guild, with each having its own uniforms, banners and leaders. The role of earlier militias in Philip Augustus's army has sometimes been exaggerated. The towns were required to come to the king's help if needed. But kings were not inclined to resort to a mass mobilization, and were satisfied to receive from the cities small contingents recruited and equipped by them or money to hire mercenaries.[2] The count of Flanders had the right to commandeer town militias, but could not deploy them beyond his territory without their council's permission. Feudal Europe's knightly warriors should have been disturbed by such developments. But it was never doubted that armies of commoners would always be inferior to mounted knights on an open battlefield.

All men living within city walls could be called up to serve in town militias when needed. Town councils maintained arsenals and registers of all able-bodied males. But most owned their own weapons, which were kept at home. Militias were composed of a variety of soldiers. Most soldiers were heavy infantry or archers, who typically fought in close order. Typically crossbowmen outnumbered their shield-bearers two to one. One out of every nine militiamen was a sergeant, and in 1303 a militia contingent of 1346 men contained one physician.[3] They were subdivided into *vouden*, or folds. A *voud* numbered about 600 men, both burghers and craftsmen. Forming a communal yeomanry, the burghers provided a number of men in proportion to their districts' populations. Those with assets of more than 300 Flemish pounds were required to own a horse, weapons and armor. However, no cavalry appears in Bruges's accounts for 1302.

Using trumpeters to communicate their orders, a militia's commanders were the members of its town council.[4]

The craft guilds provided set numbers of infantrymen according to the size of their membership. The weavers traditionally were most numerous and therefore supplied the strongest contingents. Town councils called up numbers of folds according to the demands of the campaign. During the early fourteenth century, Bruges was able to assemble a dozen folds, or a force of some 7000 men.

Each fold had several *coningstavelryen*, or constabularies, each with about 20 *serjeants* (sergeants), six horses and two wagons. Such a unit was commanded by a *coningstavel*, or constable. Town councils paid for horses and wagons, but serjeants hardly received a penny. Archers were armed almost exclusively with crossbows. In 1302, Bruges had 16 archer constabularies, each having about 20 archers, 10 servants and 2 supply wagons, totaling 320 crossbows supported by 160 servants carrying pavises, or large shields, behind which they could safely span their bows. Archers formed the communal army's elite, and members of the exclusive Saint George's Guild of Archers were paid wages of four shillings a day, an amount similar to a squire's pay.

A militiaman wore braies, or loose fitting linen underpants. Also known as drawers, they covered the legs from the waist down. Worn in either long or short versions by men of all classes, they were pulled over hose and held to the waist by a string. A coif of mail was placed over a linen shirt. Then a cotte, or outer shirt, was covered by a surcotte, a tunic-like outer garment smaller than a knight's to facilitate movement on foot. These were held with a belt. A pointed cowl or hood, sometimes attached to a cape or worn separately, and simple cloth or leather shoes or clogs completed the militiaman's attire.[5]

The arms of militiamen were quite specialized and varied.[6] The sword-like falchion was designed to have the greatest possible cleaving power to cut through armor. Unlike the swords of knights, which could be used to both cut and thrust, the falchion was for cutting only. Its single edged blade widened towards its point. Cheaper to produce than swords, it was common in town militias.

The pike was a much-favored weapon of medieval foot soldiers.

Two to four yards long, it was shorter than the similarly tipped lance, but had a thicker shaft. A pike could be used in two ways. In attacks it served to keep an enemy at a safe distance. As a defensive weapon, its butt could be planted in the ground to take the shock of a cavalry charge.

The crossbow, introduced in the eleventh century, proved useful during sieges. At first it was no more than a simple wooden bow mounted on a frame, which allowed the bow to be spanned. By the late thirteenth century, it had evolved into a portable weapon with a short, stiff, composite bow of layers of wood, horn and sinew, mounted on a wooden stock with a trigger mechanism. Later many of the crossbow's parts would be made of steel. The bowstring was made of linen or hemp. The carreau, or crossbow bolt, a short, thick arrow with a small, sharp iron tip proved to be far more aerodynamic than an ordinary arrow. Such a crossbow was spanned by placing a foot in a stirrup on the bow's front and pulling and fixing the bowstring to the trigger mechanism with a hook, kept on the shooter's belt. Winches and other spanning devices associated with crossbows date from much later. In combat, crossbowmen were often aided by servants with pavises.[7]

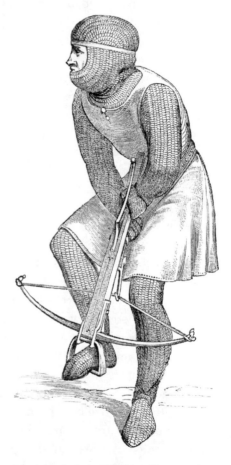

Clad in chain mail a crossbowman reloads his weapon (© Bettman/ CORBIS).

However, the weapon that captured the imagination of Flanders in 1302 was far simpler and easier to make than any of the above: the goedendag. Literally, *goedendag* means "good day." However, this term (also *godendac*) appears only in French sources and its origins remain unknown. The Flemings themselves called it a "pinned staff." During the 1800s some misconceptions spread about the goedendag, which were perpetuated by many historians, writers and teachers. The famous French architect Eugene Viollet-le-Duc thought it was some sort of stretched halberd. Others speculated that it was a plowshare on a pole or an iron ball with pins suspended on a chain from a short wooden stick.[8]

In reality the goedendag was a sturdy wooden staff, four to five feet long and slightly thicker at the top, on which an iron pin was fixed with an iron ring and pitch. Evidence for this view is found on the Courtrai Chest at Oxford University's New College and from the now lost frescos of the Leugemeete in Ghent. Additional archaeological finds have yielded its metal parts. The goedendag is a simple, cheap, effective weapon, much used in Flanders during the late thirteenth and early fourteenth century. The staff's handle could be used as a club to unhorse a knight and the spike served to punch holes through armor.

The equipment of Flemish foot soldiers, while a pittance by knightly standards, was a considerable expense for a commoner. Mail tunics cost between £10 and £20 depending on length. A buckler cost £1 and a goedendag cost 10 shillings. Body armor, gauntlets, armored hose, and possibly a doublet would be added to this. Rich burghers from Ypres were reported to have equipment totaling at least £100. Thirty to 35 pounds was more the norm.[9]

An important role in all of the era's political maneuvers was played by Flanders' most populous city, Ghent. Like Bruges, Ghent dates back to Roman times. It began on a small island at the confluence of the rivers Scheldt, Lieve and Leie (Lys). In the 600s a missionary, St. Amandus, founded two abbeys in the area. The threat of Norse invasion led Count Baldwin Iron Arm to build the city's first fortifications around the year 867. A town rapidly grew around Baldwin's castle, which became the seat of his domain. The 1100s saw the development of the cloth trade, the designation of Ghent as a city and the enlargement of its castle. Its population may have surpassed Paris's in this era.

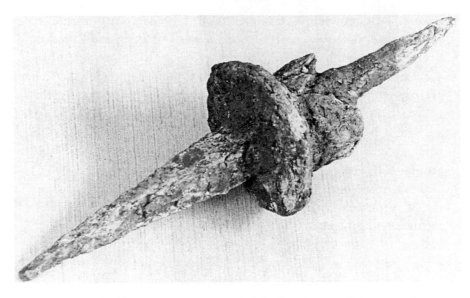

A goedendag point (© Stedelijke Musea Kortrijk).

After Philip of Alsace's death the Gentenaars gained a very advantageous charter from his widow, limiting their military service and gaining the right to fortify the city. The French chronicler William the Breton wrote with much exaggeration that the city was able to provide up to 20,000 soldiers at its own expense. In 1211, the city refused to receive Ferdinand of Portugal as the new count. Two years later it was the only Flemish city able to offer resistance to Philip Augustus, who with Duke Henry I of Brabant placed the city under siege. After his defeat at Bouvines, Holy Roman Emperor Otto was advised to continue the struggle with the militia of Ghent.[10]

By the beginning of the fourteenth century, Ghent was also in the midst of much construction. The city's cathedral, Sint-Jans, was a majestic building of brick and granite with a Romanesque crypt. Years later it would be renamed Sint-Baaf's (the Flemish name for the local Saint Bavon). In 1300 work on the cathedral was continuing, and in centuries to come it would host some of the finest art of the Van Eycks, Pourbus, and Rubens. Facing the doors of the cathedral, Ghent's Belfry was begun about 1300 and finished 38 years later. The Belfry was the city's watchtower and alarm bell. In its basement was a huge iron chest where the city's charter of privileges was kept. Sint-Niklaas Church rose next to the belfry. It too was a work in progress, but this Scheldt Gothic structure already dominated the Korenmarkt (corn or grain market). Along a nearby canal the city's most important guild-halls were established. However, Ghent's famous Graslei and Koren-lei hardly had its present stately appearance. The only surviving commercial building of the era is the Spijker, a grain storehouse built around 1200.

Ghent was a city surrounded by abbeys. Sint-Pieter's Abbey on the city's southeast side was probably founded in the seventh century. Further east, Sint-Baaf's Abbey was founded in 630 by St. Amandus and destroyed by the Norse in the 900s. West of the city on the other side of the Leie, the Cistercian abbey of Bijloke became one of the rich-est in Flanders. Though not as well endowed as Bruges, Ghent also had its share of charity houses: a number of almshouses and hospitals

Ghent's medieval economy was centered on its guildhalls on the Graslei.

and first one, later three, beguinages. Joan of Constantinople and her sister Maria founded Ghent's Small Beguinage of Our Lady of Hoyen in 1234. However it would not acquire its present look until the beginning of the 1700s.

On flat, higher ground, the Vrijdagmarkt, or Friday Market, was the center of political life in medieval Ghent. It was here that the counts of Flanders swore public oaths to observe the city's freedoms. Also here the guilds regularly fought each other like cats and dogs. Indeed, Ghent's reputation as a city of turbulence stems largely from what went on in the Vrijdagmarkt.

But Flanders was not unique in having demanding townspeople. A twelfth-century abbot described a revolt against the bishop and nobles of Laon in 1115. During the bishop's absence, the townsmen were offered the opportunity to form a commune by paying the bishop's customary dues. On his return, the prelate was not amused, and friction quickly developed between him and the newly created citizenry. On Good Friday a mob of citizens entered the bishop's palace armed to the teeth. Some nobles rallied to the bishop's side; others fled in disguise. The bishop himself hid in a wine cask but was eventually discovered and killed. His body was found minus his ring finger.[11] The masses had spoken, but seldom were they sufficiently organized or deliberate to have a lasting effect.

Retribution by nobles against rebellious commoners was usually severe, although church and state did not always agree. In 1210 a mob in Chartres, incited by officials of the Countess of Blois-Chartres, assaulted the house of the dean of the cathedral. After a lengthy battle, the citizens were only able to storm and plunder the forecourt of the dean's house before retreating. The cathedral's canons were outraged, and a lengthy process of punishment followed. The inhabitants of the city and its surroundings were excommunicated as blasphemers. Priests were ordered to ascend their pulpits daily only to repeat the sentence of anathema. Holy relics were removed from public view and church bells were silent. Public wrath increased with riots and fires. King Philip Augustus eventually intervened and appointed three knights to conduct an inquiry. On All Saints Day 1210, the King ruled that the countess and the city's provost make amends to the dean. A fine of £3000 was levied on the city. The count of Boulogne was to oversee the enforcement of the king's decree. Those malefactors against whom the dean had made specific and detailed complaints were paraded naked through the streets and lashed with switches in front of the cathedral's altar on the next feast day.[12] These punishments were far less than the local ecclesiastical officials had hoped for.

Despite the increasing boldness of commoners, the counts of Flanders could not be regarded as spent forces. The Crusades, all of which had Flemish contingents, increased their prestige. Count Robert II of Flanders was a leader of the First Crusade. From 1204 until 1261 the counts and countesses carried weight as the "Latin Emperors of Constantinople." One of Western Europe's strongest moated fortresses, the intimidating Castle of the Counts, or in Flemish, Gravensteen, was completed by 1200. Modeled on a Crusaders' fortress in Syria, this castle was built on the orders of Philip of Alsace amid the canals near the guildhalls in the city center "in order to subdue the excessive pride of the people of Ghent."[13] Along with their two castles in Bruges, this was where counts of Flanders resided and held court. Complete with encircling moat, battlements, turrets and walls six feet thick, it was intended to be a message to the burghers as well as to the French and other potential invaders.

Seven miles east of the city, Laarne Castle formed part of the city's outer defenses. This pentagonal moated fortress was begun in the eleventh century and reached the prime of its military utility in the 1300s. But the counts were not content to just rule behind walls. Their power was felt throughout Flanders in the form of intrigue, torture, midnight arrests and assassinations. They moved in a world where military power had been monopolized by their class since the fall of Rome, but such power was available in even greater quantities to the king of France.

In the nine centuries following the victory of Visigoth cavalry over Roman infantry at Adrianople in 378, the knighthood was bolstered by a potent combination of technology and mythology. In early medieval times, it was the duty of every free man owning land to serve

The Gravensteen (Castle of the Counts) in Ghent.

in the army on reaching age of fifteen, later raised to twenty. But an army composed of only landowners irregularly equipped would have been insufficient. A royal call to arms, or hériban, was sent to all dukes and counts, who as liege lords assembled the men of the fiefs they governed and led them to an appointed rendezvous. Defaulters were punished by fines. Permanent service was not required and regular armies were nonexistent. As soon as the campaign for which they were levied was over, troops were disbanded. Armies usually broke up with the approach of winter. Periods of service rarely lasted as long as six months, three months being the average. Even thus limited, it was a heavy burden for many lesser vassals. Early medieval soldiers received no pay or allowances for clothes or weapons. Their only hope of gain lay in plunder.

Sixth century Merovingian armies were composed of almost all infantry. Some wore helmets and body-armor, but many used only animal skins for protection. They carried shields and fought with swords or axes. By the seventh century the proportion of horsemen increased. Still, campaigns were little more than plundering raids, unable to conduct sustained attacks on fortified places. There were no lines of communication or supply. The raiders lived on the invaded land and left it only when they had exhausted its resources. Battle was a series of single combats; the idea of maneuver was unknown.

The eighth and ninth centuries saw much improvement in armor. Over the two centuries which followed, true feudal armies developed. Cavalry grew to be their main element; infantry was still more numerous but subordinate. Missile weapons, long out of use, returned with improvements. Thus, when William the Conqueror's army embarked for England, it included a strong force of archers, a fair number with steel crossbows. In the twelfth century, a revival of military science, engineering, fortification and siege warfare took place under Philip Augustus and Richard the Lionhearted. However, during this period little changed in the conduct and discipline of operations. There was also little difference in weaponry and armor between the armies of Philip Augustus and Louis IX. Proven successful in battle after battle, chain mail, conical helmets, swords, lances, and oblong shields were the norm for knights. Mainly leather-clad infantry were armed with pikes, maces and bows.

To obtain troops, the Capetians appealed both to their own vassals in royal domains directly under their control and to their feudal lords and their vassals. But they could only expect limited support from both of these sources. Feudalism had replaced unconditional military support with intermittent obligations fixed at an average of forty days a year. Such short service rendered the formation of stable military forces impossible. Hence armies of the period were increasingly composed of professional mercenaries, which included both knights, of more or less noble descent, and crossbowmen, archers and other common foot soldiers.[14]

Armored knights were well honed, efficient weapons. Their advanced training and esprit de corps gave them seemingly insurmountable advantages in battle. Usually the sons of knights entrusted to other knights, squires were engaged in court duties as well as training.[15]

Learning to withstand fatigue and endure the elements and depriva-
tion, they were taught from childhood to handle horses and weapons,
and when finally knighted, they could draw on this long and intensive
training. Medieval nobles were also convinced that they were chosen
to be above the common man. This meant that they would unhesi-
tatingly ride into a line of common infantry. These attitudes were
amplified by the macho ethic of knightly honor, which encouraged
these warriors to be aggressive and unyielding, against all odds if necessary.

The Church endeavored with some success to limit the warrior
class. It exercised a great influence in easing the lot of prisoners and
local inhabitants by banning the enslavement of captives and speak-
ing out against looting.[16] Less successfully, the popes also forbade the
hiring of mercenaries.[17] Forced upon the knights by the Church, the
code of chivalry placed limits on military behavior on one hand, but
created a heroic ideal which encouraged knightly arrogance on the
other. Popular culture reflected these values in numerous ballads and
tales, The Song of Roland being the best known.

> The ideology of knightly conventions and customs was indeed pene-
> trated by Christian doctrine and this led to a more humane type of
> warfare. But this was also tempered by the scarcity of nobles, who
> were fighting against members of their own class, by the efficient pro-
> tection given by their armor, and the understandable self-interest,
> which encouraged the taking of prisoners. No one wanted to fight to
> the death because it would only make the enemy more anxious to
> fight.[18]

Chivalry and its associated sporting events gave rise to a complex
body of customs and behavior. Knights spent a great deal of their time
training. They were professional soldiers always prepared for war. Militias frequently trained, but were by no means comparable to knights
in terms of preparation for battle.

Historically, sports have often prepared individuals both physi-
cally and emotionally for battle. In medieval Europe, the tournament
became the most popular form of noble recreation and could include
jousts (individual contests) or melees (group competitions). The events

of a tournament kept knights in condition for their role in warfare. The church opposed tournaments, but the nobles saw them as training grounds and sources of income as well as pastimes. Undaunted by the criticism of the clergy, tournaments increased in popularity.[19] They lasted well after the heavily armored knight became obsolete and remained a sport in which noble valor and grandeur continued.

The *pas d'armes*, or "passage of arms," was one form of tournament. Traditionally, a proclamation was sent to different countries announcing that a knight would take on challengers at a certain time and place. The hosts were called tenants or holders and the challengers venants or comers. The tenants hung two shields, symbolizing war and peace respectively, from a tree. When a venant approached, he would touch the peace shield if he wished to joust with a blunt courtesy lance or the war shield to indicate a pointed lance. Once a challenge was accepted, the venant was inspected by a heraldic expert to ascertain if he was of honorable standing. If the venant chose, he could fight on horseback or on foot with a sword or an axe. Once a challenge was made, a venant was treated with hospitality based on, in the terms of the day, *ce que vouldrez*, meaning "whatever you like." Horses usually had tents for stalls, where grooms pampered the mounts. Horses in a joust "ambled" (paced) to give knights smooth rides and better aims with their lances. The pas d'armes was a grand pageant for both man and horse.[20]

Fighting to the death was not common. No one wished to decimate their military capabilities or finances, unless some sort of vendetta was underway. In one form of the joust, horses were blindfolded to keep them from shying. They wore huge cushions stuffed with straw to protect their chest and shoulders and their riders' knees and legs. Nevertheless, much drama unfolded at such events, as evident in this passage:

> Quickly he returned to where he had left his horse. He strapped on his helmet and prepared himself at once. He mounted his horse quickly. The other did not neglect to prepare himself likewise. Each of them took his shield and drew it close to his body. The lord of the park and the guest urged on their horses. Truly they both showed

fierce anger. They spurred the horses on and charged at each other with all their strength. The oaken shafts were lowered and aimed at the four nails over the handgrip. Their aim was good and they both hit the mark. The spears passed through the shields and went in as far as the hand. The strong shafts remained whole, however forcefully they had been driven. They pulled out their lances again with manly eagerness and rode away from each other, the two like-minded men, both intending to joust again. The horses were again spurred roughly and firmly, and driven together a second time. Here began a love affair for a great prize. They needed no bed to make love. The goal of their love was such that whoever lay down would be rewarded with death. They kissed one another on the breast with their lances through the shields with such passion that the oaken shafts splintered right down to the hand so that the chips flew like dust.[21]

Along with tournaments and wars fought in service to their lords, knights also gained experience in private wars, frowned upon by church and king alike. Particularly in the eleventh century, small conflicts over land and vendettas for revenge proliferated, often between family members. Increased royal power led to a drop in the number of private wars. Indeed, tournaments originated from distractions from private wars.[22] Though not the spectacle of a tournament, hunting stag from a horse was a more common noble sport, especially in France. In a more varied natural environment, this too honed a knight's skills, as did daily training, sword exercises and target practice.

Dressing a knight was a painstaking process, best accomplished with a few servants.[23] Over the top of a linen shirt and braies, or underpants, went a long quilted garment known as a gambeson. Quilted leggings, or *cuisses*, covered the lower legs and stockings. Shoes were better but not different in design from those of commoners. A hauberk was then slipped over the gambeson. Unquestionably heavy and difficult to wear, this was a knee-length shirt of mail, small interlaced iron rings, each connected to four others. Other pieces of mail were then added and connected to the hauberk with staples known as vervelles. These included a coif covering the head and shoulders and gloves of mail, which were sometimes built into the hauberk. Mail stockings or chausses covered the cuisses. The knight then donned a coat of plates, plate armor riveted onto a leather jacket encasing the torso. The lower legs and shins were protected with greaves. Other pieces of plate armor typically were added: brassarts for the upper arms, couters for the elbows, and poleyns for the knees.

Covering all was the surcotte, a linen poncho-like outer garment. Forerunners of epaulets, ailettes, or decorative rectangular shoulder pads, were usually added. Bearing the knight's colors the surcotte and ailettes were typically the only dyed parts of the knight's apparel. Gauntlets protected the hands and spurs were strapped around the ankles. Finally, only a helmet was needed to fully protect a knight. Helmets in 1300 were varied. Old ones tended to be conical and the latest cylindrical. As they were heavy and restrictive, many regularly wore no helmet and depended on the protection of their coifs. Accompanied by a shield, a misericorde (dagger) for dispatching fallen foes, a yard-long sword and a sheath often decorated with gold, enamel and jewels, a knight was armed cap-à-pied (literally "head to foot").

Knights were distinguished by their possession of a horse and sword. The words for knight in continental European languages, *rid-der* in Dutch, *chevalier* in French, and *ritter* in German, are particularly descriptive the their significance as horsemen. In the Middle Ages, horses were specially bred to meet the requirements of warfare.[24] Medieval breeders believed that horses fell into two broad categories: cold blooded and warm blooded. However, there is little biological difference and certainly no blood distinction between them. Cold-blooded horses were typical of northern Europe and the Asiatic steppes. Warm-blooded horses were smaller mounts used by the Moors, who bred Middle Eastern Arabian and Barb horses with indigenous Spanish stock. While the added weight of the European-descended mount provided extra power, the Arabian horse was better for quick maneuvers and endurance.

Weighing twice as much as a conventional riding horse, the destrier or great war-horse was once thought to have been bred to support an armored knight's weight. But a typical suit of armor weighed no more than 70 pounds. Therefore, a mount only needed to carry some 250 to 300 pounds. The real reason this large horse was useful was because of the greater force its weight gave to the impact of a knight's lance. Stirrups were essential to keep the knight on the mount and use the horse's momentum to add power to a thrust with his lance or sword. Striking a conventionally mounted opponent was usually devastating. Riding a destrier required firmness. Bits used on them had long shanks and high ports to provide greater leverage to curb the animal. Reins were covered with metal to prevent them from being cut by an opponent's sword. War saddles with raised backs, or cantels, gave knights even greater leverage and stability when charging. Destriers were sometimes shod with sharp protruding nails to dispatch trampled enemies in their path. Despite being a potent, high-strung weapon, the destrier is most closely related to the docile workhorse of today.

A destrier would not have been a comfortable mount for duty beyond the battlefield. Instead, a knight rode a palfrey, a short-legged, long-bodied horse with a gentle ambling gait. The palfrey's smooth ride made it a suitable mount for the wounded, aged or others who had difficulty riding a taller mount.

The need for speedy messengers between courts and armies gave rise to the courser, the race horse's ancestor. They were strong, lean horses, which probably had "hot" Arabian or Barb blood. A principal European source of coursers was the kingdom of Naples, where horses acquired from Africa were bred with European stock. The result was an extremely fast horse popular throughout the continent.

The innovations in equipment associated with the knight's horse were complex. As a type of horse, the destrier had been in existence for some time, but increased use led to new designs in equipment. The bard, or horse armor, used in 1300 typically included a chanfron covering the horse's face and a peytral protecting its chest. The horse and its armor were usually covered with a caparison or comparison, a large ornamental cloth prominently decorated with heraldic arms for identification.

Spurs in medieval times came in two general varieties. Prick spurs were simple spikes strapped around the ankle. Similar to those used today, rowel spurs had multi-spiked wheels strapped or screwed to the heel.[25] Ornate spurs were bestowed on young warriors in colorful ceremonies commemorating their entry into chivalry. Spurs were made of different materials to indicate the owner's rank: a knight's spurs were made of gold, a squire's of silver, and a man-at-arm's of iron or brass.

The sword is the Middle Ages' most evocative weapon. A late thirteenth century knight's sword was about a yard long. Its tapered blade was double edged. A ridge or fuller ran about three-quarters of the length of the blade to add stiffness. Its cross-guard was straight or slightly curved towards the blade. Its hilt, typically with a heavy, round pommel, allowed it to be wielded with one hand. The pommel acted both as a counter-weight for the blade and as a club in cramped quarters where the sword could not be used as intended. However, the sword was not the knight's most important weapon in battle. Only when his lance was lost or became too difficult to use, would a knight draw his sword.

During the late thirteenth century a knight charged with an oak or ash lance, three to five yards long, couched under his arm. Unlike the pikes of common foot soldiers and throwing spears, which were very seldom used in the late thirteenth century, a knight's lance enabled him to thrust while on horseback. Its tip was small and sharply tapered to pierce mail and plates of armor. The lance's shaft was not tapered. An ordinary knight often attached a small triangular pennon to his lance, bearing his colors. A bannerlord, commanding a banner of about twelve to twenty-four knights and squires, had a rectangular flag, also known as a banner.

Tactics did not come natural to knightly armies, whose emphasis on honor, fame, courage and individual combat was not conducive to order.[26] Cavalry was usually deployed in densely packed formations. Horses often touched each other, forming small fronts with enormous punching abilities. Banners would form squares six to eight horses across, two to three rows deep. Three or four banners formed a battle of sixty to eighty horses. The battle was the era's standard tactical unit. These numbers varied considerably as units were based on noble holdings and relationships. As had been the case for 900 years, there were no universal tactical rules. However, strict discipline was important. Commanders wanted their warriors to be in total control of their weapons and horses and insisted on a tight battle. If cavalry charges were to be successful, they could not afford loose formations. Tightly packed battle orders were the best guarantees for successful break-throughs, and disciplined mobility could swiftly outmaneuver the flanks of opposing forces. In general medieval defensive strategy was based on avoiding rather than offering battle. Fortresses were nearly always strong enough to withstand attack.[27]

Knighthood was extremely expensive. The best destriers cost £300 and all the horses of a single knight could cost as much as £1,200. Added to this were the costs of chain mail, helmets, swords, lances, armor for the chest, shoulder, knees and elbows, banners, tents, kitchen utensils, food, and beasts of burden to carry it all. A full set of armor was an estimated £1000. In comparison, a craftsman would have made only a few pounds per year. The ability to buy horses, armor and supplies, maintain retinues of auxiliaries, and regularly engage in tournaments and warfare was something few could afford. In 1302 Zeger of Ghent and his son were accompanied by 22 squires. Nine knights from Zeeland were accompanied by 111 squires. Income from fiefs needed to be high to afford such power.[28] Many noblemen experienced considerable difficulties in meeting these requirements. By the thirteenth century the number of knights had dwindled due to this expense. Therefore, by the end of the thirteenth century feudal armies had large proportions of mercenary squires, who did not feel up to the duties and expenses of knighthood. Medieval chronicles make a distinction between knights and armored cavalry, who were almost certainly squires who hoped to be dubbed knights before a battle but wished to avoid the expense until then. By the 1200s armored cavalry typically outnumbered knights two to one.[29]

More specialized foot soldiers were also available for hire. Most fought with crossbows or pikes. Like knights, these soldiers of fortune were also better trained than militiamen. However, it should be noted that thirteenth century foot soldiers, whether militiamen or mercenaries, had more opportunity to train than ever before. Particularly, in the last ten years of the 1200s, there were endless campaigns in which to practice.[30] In the late thirteenth and early fourteenth centuries, many mercenaries were recruited from the Rhineland and Meuse districts. In 1297, 1300, and again in 1302 hundreds of these were employed in the armies of the counts of Flanders. Chroniclers report that while these mercenaries fought bravely, they were very greedy. Louis van Velthem noted that they loved wine, good food and money.[31]

Like most of their counterparts in feudal Europe, the counts of Flanders were in constant need of money. Military prowess was expensive. Hence they were forced to either tolerate many of their wealthier subjects' demands or kill the geese that laid their golden eggs. They chose the former. Thus the counts allowed their towns to be ruled by groups of wealthy merchants and landowning burghers. In Ghent this took the form of a thirty-nine-member council of aldermen led by a mayor, similar to the bodies ruling Bruges, Ypres, Lille, Douai, and Kortrijk. This council always appears in Roman numerals as "the XXXIX." By co-opting their most powerful subjects, the counts tried to ensure their own security. However, the burghers generally sided with the French king to counter the intimidating presence of their lords. Over the years this urban elite became more and more detached from the craft guilds and peasantry, from which many of them had risen centuries before. Eventually, their oppression and corruption rivaled that of the haughtiest aristocrats. Unfortunately for all leaders concerned, wealth and power were distributed too widely for such a tiny elite to maintain order. The commoners would eventually look to the counts to defend them from the burghers. This was illustrated by the fact that the Flemish leadership and ranks at Kortrijk would both be composed largely of skilled craftsmen and workers, as opposed to members of either the princely class or the mercantile elite.

Town governments found it increasingly difficult to maintain control. This situation was complicated by an Anglo-Flemish dispute in 1270. In 1230 and again in 1270 Countess Margaret of Flanders had expelled English, Welsh, Irish and Gascon merchants and seized their goods in payment of alleged pension arrears owed her by Henry III.

Trade declined and hostility to the urban burghers grew. Edward I (as prince) had all Flemish merchandise seized and embargoed all wool exports to Flanders. The Treaty of Montreuil between Edward and Margaret's son Guy Dampierre settled this dispute in 1274.

Ghent had the weakest craft guilds of any major Flemish city. But even there, craftsmen had militias and treasuries. In 1275, in response to complaints from commoners, Countess Margaret tried to replace the XXXIX of Ghent with an annual magistracy of thirty members. The XXXIX appealed to its overlord, the parlement of Paris, that Margaret's actions violated Ferrand's constitution of 1228. In 1280 the parlement restored the XXXIX on condition that they submit to external financial control. That same year an anti–XXXIX faction of burghers asked the count to abolish hereditary tenure of aldermen. They asked for representation in the city government from the craft guilds, their allies against the entrenched elite. They wanted the freedom to import wool without joining the Hansa and sought the restoration the privileges of the counts' bailiffs, which had been restricted by the XXXIX in 1279. These demands were rejected. Hence, unlike the situation in Bruges, Ghent's craft guilds gained no political rights before 1302.[32]

Bruges was less firmly a textile manufacturing center than Ghent and Ypres. Even the definition of a burgher there was problematic, as possession of town property did not change one's legal status as in Ghent. In Bruges the ruling elite included artisans and wholesalers as well as the very wealthy. The city depended on trade with England. Blaming the rupture in commerce in 1270–4 on the aged Countess Margaret of Constantinople, the city council refused to participate in peace negotiations.

Margaret abdicated on December 29, 1278, in favor of her son Guy of Dampierre, who had returned from the Crusades in 1274. Until his older brother Guillaume died in 1251, Guy was not destined to become count of Flanders. Thereafter he shared rule with his mother and was already in his fifties when he became count. During his reign, the towns reached the peak of their power and refused to accept any interference in their affairs. Almost immediately on accession, Guy faced with serious internal rebellions. The misfortunes of his last years detracted from his considerable achievements.[33]

The fastest growing Flemish city in the late 1200s, Ypres (Ieper in Flemish) was also the county's town most dominated by textile manufacturing. The situation there was more complicated than the obvious factional struggles of burghers in Bruges and Ghent. Much confusion in the textile industry, and in subsequent histories of it, developed over the status of the city's drapers, small operators who subcontracted work to individual cloth producers but were not members of the ruling oligarchy. Only after 1280 do Ypres sources speak of master weavers. In 1281 the Count distinguished "aldermen and merchants" from "drapers, weavers, fullers and shearers."[34]

Both the aldermen and count issued regulations in September 1280 that led to unrest. One was a wage scale regulating what drapers could pay fullers and what the latter could pay their journeymen. Drapers who paid more were fined and fullers who accepted more lost their livelihoods for a year. A second ordinance regulated the wages and work conditions of shearers. The fullers, weavers and shearers had professional organizations, with the three represented on a committee which met three times a year with the aldermen to judge violations.[35]

Another issue was the administration of Bruges's weight standards, a fief held by the Gistel and van der Woesijne families. Inequitable administration had led foreign, mainly German, merchants to ask the Countess to give them their own scales. Guy supported the Germans and made the aldermen responsible for punishing violations. When they refused, Guy gave the German Hanse weighing privileges at nearby Aardenburg on August 26, 1280.[36]

In late September the Count departed for Paris for five months, leaving his eldest son, Robert of Béthune, in charge. A good soldier who earned his spurs during the last Crusade, Robert did not differ much from his father politically. He too tried to secure his position before looking to the concerns of his people, whose Flemish language he probably didn't speak. Nevertheless, he came to be known as the Lion of Flanders.

From Paris on September 30, Guy issued a sweeping regulation favoring Ypres' drapers. Drapers were given the right to buy wool overseas, thereby breaking the London Hansa's monopoly. But those manufacturing cloth were forbidden from exercising another trade. However, if a draper married a woman from another craft, they both kept their trades. Municipal accounts were to be audited, but unlike elsewhere, drapers and other commoners made no effort to be present at these audits. Unlike earlier charters, which punished those who refused to accept the aldermen's judgments, decisions could now be appealed to the Count.

The troubles later called the Moerlemae began in Bruges on October 1, 1280.[37] This uprising was directed specifically against the count. Mobs aroused by aldermen took control of the city, imprisoning those of the count's supporters who did not flee. The commoners in turn asked Robert to review all laws and give them seats on the council and board of aldermen. The ringleaders of the rebellion were virtually all burghers, as were the count's supporters. This was an aristocratic power struggle. Excited by the mentality of mobs and possibly standing to gain a voice in government, the masses and some lower burghers supported the rebellion but did not lead it.

Ypres exploded six days later in the Cokerulle revolt. An attack was launched against the city from Poperinge, six miles west of the city. Virtually all of Poperinge's population consisted of textile artisans working for employers in Ypres. The insurrection was not so much a struggle within Ypres as a revolt of Poperinge against Ypres. Two rich but clearly disgruntled Yprois visiting Poperinge armed the local artisans and marched on Ypres. Their force was supplemented by aid from the town's unwalled suburbs. The rebels, all textile artisans except for one baker and a butcher, were unable to seize the city. Despite much noisy disorder, only two aldermen were killed. The count's authority was re-established by November 6.[38]

Order in Bruges was also restored quickly. By spring the count imposed on Bruges a large cash indemnity, rent and compensation for damage sustained by him and his supporters. The charter, which Philip of Alsace had granted Bruges, was lost when the belfry burned as the disturbances began. Guy replaced it with one limiting the city's autonomy.

Punishments were now "in the count's grace," and only the count could alter laws. To the commoners he granted a yearly audit and representation on urban bodies. Of the 328 residents of Bruges who were held as surety to keep the peace, only 158 were guildsmen, of which only 34 came from textile trades.[39]

Judgments in Ypres were moderate. Assemblies exceeding ten persons were forbidden. Claims for damage largely canceled each other out, but the Count confiscated a quarter of the drapers' property. Apprentice weavers were fined four shillings a month until 1283, since their real masters were the drapers. The earlier regulations were confirmed except for a clause giving the Count the right to modify Ypres' laws and customs at his pleasure. Most of the provisions of Ypres' charter were repeated in a new charter Guy granted to the town on April 1, 1281. Ypres' aldermen were back in the Count's grace by July 2, 1281. In contrast to his attitude towards Bruges, Guy did his best not to make things difficult for them. He honored his two-year-old promise to ask for no more money from Ypres for seven years. In 1294 guildsmen became aldermen in Ypres for the first time.[40]

Details of a second Bruges uprising in August 1281 are very sketchy. The Count imprisoned those doing surety and beheaded five of them. Their descendants later built the "Chapel of the Five Lords" at their burial place in Sint Andries' chapel. The families of the ringleaders left public life for years, with some returning by 1288 and others not until 1296.

Unrest spread beyond Flanders. Accused of having "hindered and disturbed" trade, the fullers were imprisoned at Tournai in mid–1279, and the weavers followed in 1281.[41] There were also disturbances at Douai, Saint-Omer and some smaller towns in September and October 1280. At the same time Damme's commoners alleged maladministration of taxes on bread, wine, beer, dye stuffs, rents and commercial transactions and complained of illegal courts and detentions. Accusing their aldermen of nepotism, they demanded an equal role in tax collection. Their complaints were ignored.[42]

Except for the introduction of annual auditing, all these troubles had minimal long-term consequences. Borrowing from the bankers of

Arras and the city council of Lille and raising levies on consumer goods, Bruges paid off its indemnity by 1287. Its rent was discontinued after 1296. In January 1297 Philip the Fair invalidated Guy's charter of 1281 and restored that of Philip of Alsace. To pacify the drapers and other guilds, the Count revised textile statutes after 1280. German traders returned to Bruges in 1282, and other foreigners followed. Weights and measures were entrusted to sworn officials and deposited in church institutions.[43]

The fines assessed in 1281 exposed the cities' alarming inability to meet the financial demands placed on them. Overpopulated, disorderly, and in the midst of an economic downturn, no Flemish city had healthy public finances between 1281 and 1302. Attempts to collect direct taxes were extremely unpopular and rarely tried by 1300. To meet less pressing expenses, cities sold annuity rents. Some wealthy town families moved to rural estates beyond city walls. Hence in 1286 Ghent became the first Flemish city to levy a tax on those leaving the city.[44] Other towns, such as Arras and Bruges, borrowed heavily from bankers, causing resentment among commoners, who demanded regular accounts, suspecting, with good reason, that magistrates were lining their pockets.

Most thirteenth century Flemish cities also received significant income from orphan money. When either parent died, a child's share of that parent's property was removed from the surviving parent's portion and deposited by guardians with city governments, which paid 10 percent interest. This system was similar to the dowry funds established by some Italian cities. In Ypres and Lille such money was kept in separate accounts, but in Bruges it went directly into the town treasury and was spent. In 1281 and 1282 orphan money accounted for almost 30 percent of the city's income, while almost 18.5 percent came from other receipts, mainly controversial taxes on food, beer, peat, wool and industrial raw materials. The remaining 52 percent of the budget was borrowed. The seriously indebted town's reputation for financial integrity was stretched to its breaking point. In 1301 Bruges defaulted on its orphan debt, which it was still repaying in 1408.[45] In 1288 Count Guy authorized new taxes and raised Ghent's rates to help put the city's finances on a firmer footing.[46] These levies would be major issues in the approaching conflict.

Wool continued to be the center of controversies. On Easter 1275, Edward's first parliament approved a new duty on wool, fells (sheepskins), hide and leather. This became the basis of a royal tax on all imports and exports. Between 1292 and 1294 both trade and rivalries increased. Seamen of Great Yarmouth and the Cinque Ports engaged in a private war with Flanders. English and Gascon sailors were expelled from Flanders as a consequence of the burning of Flemish ships, and England retaliated by seizing goods and ships belonging to Flemings in England. French interference brought naval engagements from the North Sea to the Portuguese coast. By 1296 Edward I was at war in Gascony with Philip the Fair, who annexed Aquitaine. In 1294 a new English tax, the "maltote" or "maltort," was levied on wool. Used to pay for the war, the maltote of 1297 was five times higher than the previous ones, which provoked a crisis in London.[47] Between 1299 and 1304, wool duties were assigned to the men of Bayonne in payment of money lent to Edward.

A wool staple was established in 1294 at Dordrecht, in Holland. Insuring control and minimizing fraud, a staple was an official location where all of a product had to be sent for foreign merchants to buy it. Centralizing control of exports to Holland and Brabant, it was moved to Mechelen in Brabant in 1303 and finally to Antwerp.

From the time of Guy's grandfather Baldwin IX, the nobles of Flanders had been divided into pro–English and pro–French parties. By 1290 this split had spread to the commoners in the towns. Opposing the Count's interference in their trade monopolies, Leliaart factions loyal to France fought Liebaarts, who sided with the counts and their often pro–English policies. *Leliaart* is derived from the golden fleur-de-lys (lilies) on the blue field of the French king's coat of arms and the Leliaarts' use of lilies as ornaments in their houses. *Liebaart*, a term of heraldic origin meaning lion or leopard, a zoological distinction not made in thirteenth-century Europe, was related to the Flemish counts' black lion on its golden field. The term *Klauwaart* has often been used in relation to this era. However, it is of mid-fourteenth century origin.[48]

3. The Deadly Politics of Medieval Flanders

The conflict between these parties was not that of aristocrat versus commoner. In the beginning the Count's only supporters came from portions of the Flemish nobility. As feudal lord, the Count tried to limit the power of the cities as much as possible. But commoners became Liebaarts when it became apparent that they shared the Count's goal of keeping Flanders free of French occupation. Although the Leliaarts were largely noble or burgher, the Liebaarts included prominent aristocratic opponents of the Leliaarts as well as artisans. Ghent property records confiscated in 1297 and 1298 show that the Leliaarts there were a very wealthy group of almost all burghers.[49]

But even Ghent's elite was not unified. Some prominent families were deeply divided. For example, Philip uten Hove furnished the Count with a complete inventory of his Leliaart brother Gilbert's property.[50] Within the XXXIX, complex political maneuvers did not always correspond to Leliaart-Liebaart affiliations. Some also changed sides. Jan uten Hove, Jan uten Dale, and Wasselin Haec were Liebaarts in 1297, Leliaarts by 1302.[51] Bruges's elite was more evenly divided between the parties. Townsmen whose wealth obliged them to do mounted military service for the town in 1292 and who lent the town money in 1297 were almost evenly divided, with the Liebaarts probably holding a slight advantage.[52]

Leliaart-Liebaart politics exacerbated personal hostilities and family factionalism in the towns, which were barely able to keep order within their walls. Surviving inquest records offer particularly good details of the Borluut and van Sinte Baafs feud in Ghent, a family conflict that would partially shape the coming battle and Ghent's role in it.[53]

After sustaining severe losses in the trade stoppage of the 1270s, Ghent's Borluut family was pushed to the margins of the ruling elite. In 1282 a broken engagement with a member of the equally patrician van Sinte Baafs family outraged family honor and led to murder. The families made peace, but in 1286, alderman Gerelm Borluut died and his colleagues violated custom by passing over his son in favor of Matthew van Sinte Baafs. Most of the van Sinte Baafs were not technically Gentenaars, as they had a fortress and numerous clients in St.

Baafs' village and abbey, across the Scheldt in Brabant. The Borluuts increasingly aligned themselves with the "popular" (pro-commoner) party within the elite.

In 1294 a nephew of now alderman Matthew van Sinte Baafs provoked Jan Borluut, son of the man bypassed for that office, into breaking the truce by attacking him. This bloodless violation led to an exceptionally high fine of £100, but at Matthew's request, the aldermen condemned Jan to an additional ten years' exile. The Borluuts then decided to murder the alderman and Jan led a band of armed youths under cover of darkness to St. Baafs' village, where they mistakenly killed Matthew's nephew, the village bailiff. Borluut declared that his revenge had been satisfied and returned to his fortress in Ghent.

Jan's father got his brother Fulk, the prior of the Franciscan abbey and confessor to Countess Margaret, to give his son sanctuary. An armed Borluut cohort prevented the bailiff from arresting Jan and processed to the abbey, where Jan stayed for several weeks. Uncle Fulk was most hospitable. He had a brother write love letters on Jan's behalf to his fiancée and even encouraged the abbey's librarian to translate into Flemish an erotic Latin poem that was used as a morality exercise for novitiates.[54]

When Jan finally went to Tournai in exile, Pieter de Visschere, brother of the abbot of St. Pieter's, called on the Borluuts' friends to kill another van Sinte Baafs to avenge the unjust exile. But he urged the perpetrator to do his work in St. Pieter's parish, so that the abbot could shield him with his immunity. Three weeks later, de Visschere's cronies ambushed and killed a servant of Eustace van den Kerchove, a nephew of the van Sinte Baafs. A lenient sentence from the abbot's court followed. But killing a servant was deemed insufficient revenge. When de Visschere learned that Jan Staes, nephew of the murdered bailiff of St. Bavo's, was going to France to buy wine, he alerted the exiled Jan, who ambushed him on the way.

With these actions beyond Ghent's jurisdiction, the still unsatisfied parties agreed to a three-month truce in October 1295. Meanwhile Eustace van den Kerchove, a van Sinte Baafs kinsman, plotted his enemies' demise. On January 7, 1296, Pieter de Visschere was killed in a riot that erupted at a funeral attended by virtually all of Ghent's burghers. When Jan Borluut got the news in Tournai, he came to Ghent in disguise and attended de Visschere's funeral under the abbot's protection. A few days later he knifed Eustace van den Kerchove's nephew in the back and killed another unsuspecting relative of Matthew van Sinte Baafs en route back to Tournai.

The Borluuts were the leaders of the Liebaart minority opposed to the XXXIX and had considerable support among the craftsmen. When the van Sinte Baafs, who were Leliaarts, left the city for France in 1297, the Borluut's power returned. They asked the aldermen to condemn the van Sinte Baafs for the truce violation, which had led to Pieter de Visschere's death. Two succeeding boards of aldermen failed to reach a judgment and the case was referred to the higher council of the "good towns," who ruled in favor of the Borluuts. But old scores would not be forgotten.

Thus kings and counts, merchants and artisans, and knights and militias jockeyed for power. Hostage-taking, banishment and political murder were commonplace. Blood feuds increased in size, scope and intensity. Such was the atmosphere of Flanders, a rich land where passions ran deep and little was sacred.

4

The Matins

The sparks which ignited the crisis, which in turn led to the confrontation at Kortrijk, occurred when Philip the Fair sought to bring Flanders and its riches under his direct control. Motivated by dreams of empire, Philip allied with whomever in Flanders would help maximize his power. Despite being the godchild of the independent minded Count of Flanders, Guy of Dampierre, the French king worked against the Count whenever possible, while Guy fought to preserve his fief's traditional privileges.

Guy of Dampierre had seen the annexation of his southern neighbor, the County of Hainault, by the French in 1280. The Avesnes of Hainault became Philip's main allies. Ill will between the rulers of Flanders and Hainault went back to Louis VIII, who forced Countess Margaret to marry William of Dampierre, thereby making her sons Baldwin and John from her previous marriage to Burchard of Avesnes illegitimate. Louis IX confirmed the Dampierres' hold on Flanders and awarded Hainault to their Avesnes half-brothers. Disputes between the two erupted immediately and continued for decades. The Holy Roman Emperor enfeoffed John of Avesnes, who had acquired Holland by a marriage alliance, with Imperial Flanders but lacked the means to enforce it. Imperial Flanders managed to stay clear of Philip's conflicts and would later refuse to help Crown Flanders pay fines owed to the

103

French. In turn, Guy allied himself with Edward I of England to offset the increasingly centralizing powers of the French monarch. Descended from a poor but noble family of Champagne, Guy was one of the most influential lords of his time. He was a ruler well matched to his subjects and his times. It was the high point of European minstrelsy and he was a lavish patron of music, literature and art. He built and strengthened numerous fortifications in his realm. Well tempered, courageous and capable, his downfall seems to have stemmed partly from the fact that he had 16 children he sought to marry off strategically. Guy's diplomatic emissaries were kept busy arranging far reaching marital alliances.

For centuries, intermarriage between the rulers of England, Normandy, Burgundy and Flanders had strengthened trade. Count Baldwin II of Flanders had married Alfred the Great's daughter Aelfrida. William the Conqueror's wife was Matilda, daughter of Baldwin V. Her sister Judith had married Saxon Earl Tostig Godwinson. Alice, daughter of Richard II of Normandy, married Count Renaud of Burgundy. Richard's sister Eleanor was the wife of Count Baldwin IV of Flanders.

Count Guy's oldest son, Robert of Béthune, married Blanche of Anjou, who died in 1269, then Yolande of Burgundy. Second son Guillaume, Lord of Dendermonde and Crèvecoeur, married Alix de Beaumont. Philippe, his fifth son, became Comte di Teano after his marriage to the Italian Countess of Chieti, Mahaut de Courtenay. His oldest daughter Margaret was the wife of Duke John I of Brabant, while her younger sister Beatrix wed Count Floris V of Holland. However, Guy of Dampierre later had difficulties with Floris over Zeeland, and after 1290 Floris allied with the French. His third daughter Marie married William of Gulik (Jülich) and then Simon II de Chateauvilain after William's death in 1278. These were the children of Guy's marriage to Matilda, heiress of Béthune, Dendermonde, Richebourg and Warneton, who died in 1264. Guy then married Isabella of Luxembourg, who in 1298 also preceded him to the grave. Isabella's sons included Margrave John of Namur, who married Marguerite de Clermont; Guy of Namur, who married Margaret of Lorraine; and Comte

Henri de Lodi, who eventually in 1309 married Margaret of Cleves. Guy's daughters by his second marriage included Margareta, married to Prince Alexander of Scotland, who died in 1283, and later Count Reinald of Geldren. Also Isabelle, who married Jean de Fiennes, chatelain de Bourbourg; Philippa, who Guy labored to pair with the English crown prince; and a second Beatrix, who married Hugues de Chatillon-sur-Marne, count of Blois and Dunois. Another daughter Jeanne was a nun at Flines.

After 1285 a series of untimely deaths disrupted Guy's ambitions. Margaret died in 1285. Guy's fourth son Jean, who became Bishop of Metz and Liège, died in 1290. His third son Baudouin as well as both the elder Beatrix and her husband Floris of Holland all died in 1296.

In order to strengthen his sons' influence and provide dowries for his daughters, Guy ran up vast debts, raised taxes and offered privileges for gold. Poet Jacob van Maerlant critically compared the commoners of Guy's Flanders to "sheep wandering among the ravening wolves who have become their shepherds now that pride and avarice have given to every man who possesses gold the right to speak in the council chamber of princes."[1] Combined with the elitist nature of Flemish urban democracy, Guy's debts placed the burgher class in a position of domination. His large family proved very costly.

Even so, such a situation was hardly uncommon and the wealth of Flanders could have supported him. However, Guy hoped to see the day when his county would be detached from France. To this end he tried in succession to affiance his daughters, particularly Philippa, to the heir to the English throne. These moves irritated the French king who encouraged Guy's rivals to question his claim to Flanders. Several important Flemish vassals, including the Lords of Oudenaarde and Gavre, as well as most of the higher clergy and the merchant class sided with Paris. Guy, who was worried by the growing independence of urban commoners, found himself continuing the policies of his mother, who often championed the cause of the artisans, particularly the weavers, in opposing the questionable practices of the elite. Margaret's attempts to break the power of Ghent's aldermen had resulted in the Gentenaar elite aligning themselves with the French king.

The Golden Spurs of Kortrijk

Not since Philip Augustus had the Flemings had to deal with such a determined and unscrupulous monarch. But Guy of Dampierre lacked the means, the energy and perhaps the will to play the diplomatic games at which both Philip IV and Edward I of England excelled. Philip hoped to weaken Edward, who held Gascony to the southwest of the French king's domain. Marriage alliances secured the collaboration of Duke John II of Brabant, whose own position had been strengthened by his father's annexation of the Duchy of Limburg following the Battle of Woeringen in 1288. Luxembourg also aligned itself with Paris.

Philip the Fair's major initiatives involved granting privileges to the burghers and commoners, though never at the same time. Eager though they were to secure city finances, the commoners protested Guy's taxes of 1288. Philip responded to public outcry by installing a French "guardian" in Ghent, allegedly to provide relief from a "despotic prince" (Guy), but actually to bring Flanders under royal administration. The XXXIX thus came to depend on the crown. Royal guardians were also installed in Bruges and Douai to supervise the count's administration. Appeals to the parlement of Paris, bypassing Flemish courts, were encouraged.[2] Guy protested against such interference but was ignored. The Count was forbidden to plead his case before a special court of his peers, comprising the twelve highest vassals of the French crown.

By the Treaty of Lier of August 31, 1294, Guy arranged the marriage of his daughter Philippa to the future Edward II of England. Using the pretext of an appeal from the XXXIX, Philip summoned the count before parlement and imprisoned him and two of his sons. Guy was released four months later, after he had renounced the treaty and agreed to send Philippa to France to be "educated." Contrary to the interests of the cities, Philip mandated the exclusive use of French coin in Flanders, ignoring the Count's own right to mint coin. The French regularly debased their coinage to pay the high costs of their diplomacy and warfare. Guy was ordered to artificially undervalue the English esterlin and forbid circulation of issue from the Holy Roman Empire. In 1295 the King demanded that all precious metals in Flemish possession be surrendered to him in return for compensation in French coin. Revalued against Flemish money, French coinage flooded the county.[3] Then on June 10, 1295, Philip cleverly gave Guy the duty of enforcing a trade embargo on England and the right to take the confiscated proceeds.[4]

By early 1296 Philip realized he was driving Flanders into an English alliance. His embargo on trade with England was coupled with a concession that Flemish cloth would be free of all foreign competition in France. He declared a two-year moratorium on debts owed to him by the Count and Flemish burghers. Reversing himself he limited the competence of his officials in Flanders and restricted Flemish appeals to parlement. Though confirming urban privileges, he effectively ruled Flanders directly. The Count dissipated his popularity further on January 6, 1296, by agreeing to the King's imposition of a 2 percent property tax with the Count getting half the proceeds. Except for Ghent, the cities escaped this tax by agreeing to pay lower "free will" contributions to the King, from which the Count got nothing.[5]

Guy's most serious blunder came in March 1296, when he accepted an invitation to rule Valenciennes, the chief town of Avesnes-ruled Hainault, and declared it annexed to Flanders. In June the five great cities of Flanders (Bruges, Ghent, Ypres, Lille and Douai) were again placed under royal guardians. Guy was summoned to Paris, while John of Avesnes invaded Flanders from Holland. Guy asked for trial by his peers to settle his grievances with the King, which had been guaranteed by the Treaty of Melun of 1226. Philip refused, going so far as to hold the trial in the presence of representatives of the Five Cities. Guy's fief of Flanders was declared confiscated, then restored for a fine. An exception was made of Ghent, then the chief bastion of French influence in Flanders, which the King continued to rule directly. Guy swore not to retaliate against Flemish townsmen who were royal allies and the King kept the right to put his own officers in any town to oversee the Count's conduct.[6]

Flemish relations with England had been turbulent since 1270. However, in 1290 Guy of Dampierre gave English merchants new privileges in Flanders. Just before he arrived in England to arrange a final peace in 1292, the English embargoed wool exports to Flanders, a ploy that was lifted as part of the settlement. Encouraged by continuous French provocation, Guy opened negotiations for a political alliance with the English in 1293. But in May 1294 Edward revoked safe conduct for Flemish merchants as subjects of the French king, hoping to force the Flemings into a firm alliance against Paris.[7] War raged between France and England after 1294. Moving closer to the English, on September 20, 1296, Guy refused a summons to parlement, again banished the XXXIX, and made overtures to the commoners.

On January 7, 1297, Count Guy openly allied himself with Edward I. This alliance also permitted the wool trade to resume. Two days later he declared himself absolved from all bonds holding him obedient to the French king. Guy accused the King of violating his duties to a loyal vassal in a long, moving letter without the official rhetoric that often accompanied such declarations. Philip conferred with Guy at Kortrijk, where he offered the Count trial by his peers. Working to undo royal influence, Guy abolished and exiled the XXXIX and replaced them with a new council, also of 39 members, mainly burgher enemies of the XXXIX. On April 8, 1297, he issued Ghent's Great Charter, the comprehensive criminal and civil code that would govern the city for the rest of the medieval era.[8] Posing as a champion of communal freedom, Philip responded with a lightning strike into Flanders on June 15, 1297.[9]

Most Flemish nobles sided with the Count at this early stage. But England provided little help, and Guy was unprepared for war and overextended financially. High status had high financial implications. The count's army is a good example of how knightly armies were raised and how costly they could be. When called up by Guy in 1297, each of his vassals was to bring a number of mounted men, which totaled about 1200. Some two thousand foot soldiers accompanied the force. Knights and squires received wages based on their status. Flanders had 43 bannerlords, each commanding units of about 20 nobles. Under Guy, these commanders were paid an amazing 20 Flemish shillings each per day. Knights were paid half that and squires a quarter, but only if they had a full set of mail. Each was required to bring enough baggage, food and tents for the campaign.[10]

On August 20, 1297, at Bulskamp near the town of Veurne, this hastily formed Flemish army was mauled by the French, who continued their advance. Eight days later Edward I landed at Sluis with a small expeditionary force to bolster Guy. He marched to Ghent where the count was residing. Bruges swore allegiance to Philip on September 18, 1297, after which the second set of city defenses was begun. That same month the French took Lille and Kortrijk. Despite their high wages, a majority of Flemish knights changed sides during this period. Financial difficulties drove many knights into the French camp, particularly during the rampant inflation of the 1290s. Military prowess went to the highest bidder. Philip promised lands, offices and privileges on the same terms as Guy. The French king lent money and redistributed property confiscated from those loyal to the Count. In 1299 John of Avesnes became count of Hainault, Holland and Zeeland, to which Flanders was forced to abandon all claims. By 1302 barely a hundred nobles would associate themselves with the Flemish cause.[11]

By October, with more than half of Flanders occupied by the French, a three-year armistice, the truce of Sint-Baafs-Vijve, was reached. Concluded on October 9, 1297, and extended to January 6, 1300, this treaty divided Flanders into royal and comital zones. During this period Philip bought off several of Guy's important supporters and made a secret treaty with Edward I, who gladly withdrew his forces from Flanders in March 1298 in order to use them on the Scots. Edward was also encouraged to withdraw after problems developed between his soldiers and the rambunctious citizens of Ghent. By reconciling with the French king in July, Edward abandoned Guy of Dampierre. Worn out by age, Guy was isolated. At the end of 1299, Guy once again transferred power to his oldest son Robert of Béthune. As soon as the truce expired on January 6, 1300, French forces under Charles of Valois invaded again and overran the County. In May 1300 the last of the count's strongholds, Ypres, fell and he had no choice but to capitulate. The French king absorbed Flanders into the royal domain. With the complete occupation of Flanders by royal forces, an independent Flemish army no longer existed. Guy, Robert and some fifty members of their family and court went to Paris to treat for peace. On arrival they were thrown into prison as felons.

Philip the Fair of France meets Edward I of England as shown in a manuscript illumination in the Grands Chroniques de France *(© Bibliothèque Nationale de France).*

With these hostages in his hands, Philip the Fair apparently thought that the County had been pacified. However, the king had overlooked the power of the guilds and the Flemings' stubborn independence. In 1297, the communal militias did not have a good relationship with the Count, to whom they sent a bare minimum of soldiers. Philip had no intention of keeping his promises of greater freedom, and tensions rose when Jacques de Châtillon de Saint Pol, the king's hand-picked governor of Flanders, began trampling on traditional privileges, hoping to eliminate domestic support for Count Guy. Brother of the Count of Saint-Pol and uncle to French Queen Joan of Navarre, de Châtillon was a typical French knight who felt nothing but contempt for commoners. Appointed as guardian of Flanders in June 1300, he understood neither the traditions of Flemish urban independence nor the fact that Bruges and Ghent were much richer and more powerful than any French town. His contempt for commoners produced widespread hatred, which ultimately undermined the integration of Flanders into France.

Beset by continual war, trade stoppages and then occupation, times were hard for the Flemish people. Tensions were also rising with the county's neighbors Hainault, Zeeland and Holland. Given these conditions, townsmen paid increasing attention to the organization of their defenses. With French occupation came deeply resented restrictions on the size of militias. Still, most townsmen owned their own arms, so militias were still able to call on a majority of local men. The burgher elite supported the French in these moves since it was in their interests to weaken the classes both above and below them. Gaining converts to their cause, the Liebaarts reminded their countrymen that they "had been all corrupted by the gold or the promises of the French king, who would never have dared to cross their frontiers if they had been true to their count."[12]

In late May and early June 1301, a year after Flanders' capitulation, Philip the Fair and his wife, Joan of Navarre, visited their newly acquired territories. The largest city north of Paris, Ghent greeted the French king with cheering crowds and fawning magistrates. A group of commoners asked the king to lift the city's unpopular taxes on consumer goods. Philip granted this, noting the magnificent feast held in his honor. This measure caused considerable trouble for the quietly alarmed Leliaart aldermen who had been exiled in 1297 and who now were reinstated. Public finances, particularly debt servicing, had come to depend on these levies, and the city's burghers profited greatly from farming out their collection.[13] Philip's Edict of Senlis of November 1, 1301, replaced the XXXIX with two boards of thirteen annually rotated aldermen, chosen by electors appointed by the monarch and city government. This structure, which reaffirmed burgher dominance, continued in Ghent for the rest of the medieval era.[14]

Spending much money and effort to receive the King in splendor, Bruges' burghers wanted to avoid impositions similar to those placed on Ghent. Hence commoners were forbidden from addressing serious questions to the King on penalty of death. Consequently, and much to the King's surprise, Bruges's commoners stood silently by the side of the road as the royal party passed. However, this was not the only uncomfortable moment during the visit.

Political tensions were heightened by the social haughtiness which seemed to be part of princely custom everywhere in Europe, but which in Flanders only hardened resentment against the envious French and their burgher puppets. One example of this behavior was related to the women's fashions of the era. The quantity and quality of a medieval woman's clothing reflected the status of its wearer.

The basic garment worn by everyone, the cote or tunic, was put on over the head. Its length varied from floor to ankle to knee and even shorter. Cotes could be very simple or elaborately decorated. Sleeves varied from wide at the top and tapered at the wrist, to a fitted sleeve with a wide, hanging cuff. Generally they were belted with a girdle. The cotehardie, a fitted tunic with large funnel sleeves and hooks and eyes down the front, would have been also popular during the early 1300s. Women's tunics were also called kirtles. The cyclas, an over-garment worn over the cote, developed from the tabard knights wore over armor to reduce the heat and glare of their armor. Loose garments pulled on over the head and tied at each side, tabards became the theater's oft-used costume for heralds and trumpeters in modern times.

Derived from the German word *bliald*, meaning cloth, the bliaut or bliaud was a garment also worn by both sexes from the eleventh century through the early fourteenth century. As a woman's gown, it touched the ground, fit closely around the torso, had long wide sleeves and was belted or worn with a girdle of contrasting fabric. Becoming longer and more decorative through the early Middle Ages, linen, woolen or, for the wealthy, silk girdles were worn around the hips, over tunics and bliauts. Often the upper half of the bliaut was laced to create a more fitting form, and it was usually decorated with embroidered borders on the neck and hem. For men, the bliaut's sleeves widened gradually from shoulder to wrist, the torso was looser, and there was a slit in the hem for ease of movement. Men wore bliauts at ankle, calf, or mid-thigh length under a coat of chain mail.

Lower class women had extremely limited wardrobes, mostly handed down through families, or cast-off from ladies of the manor. Their rough woolen shifts were sometimes made warmer by woolen mantles in cold weather. One of the most common forms of outerwear, mantles were single pieces of square or rounded cloth, fastened over one shoulder. Long mantles, often lined with fur, were favored by the nobility. Common women had little or no access to cotton or silk. The era's only undergarment consisted of a long, soft linen — or for the wealthy, cotton — shift, worn against the skin. Often the poor did not have the protection of such undergarments, which for the rich would be covered with long-sleeved gowns with wool or fur petticoats underneath during the winter months.

Sleeveless surcottes covered cotes and bliauts. In use for several centuries, surcottes were garments worn by both sexes over cotes. Their length and fullness varied and they could be worn with or without belts. In the early fourteenth century, women wore houppelandes, surcottes with rolled collars and either closed necks like the men or an open v-necks. Sideless surcottes with the wide, off-the-shoulder necklines and large arm-holes reaching the hips were fashionable between 1340 and 1460.

The average wardrobe of the period contained very few cotes or bliauts, but an assortment of surcottes of various materials. The rich and powerful had a wide choice of blue or oriental damasks, taffeta, silk and other more mundane fabrics. Some surcottes had detachable sleeves, making them seasonally adaptable. Noble women also wore capes, mantles, and shawls made of wool, fur, silk, or velvet. The hems and sleeves of their garments were often decorated with embroidered dagges, or dagging, in squared, curved, pointed or other fanciful shapes.

The Golden Spurs of Kortrijk

Women wore veils of various sizes and shapes to cover their hair, which hung in braids or was wrapped into buns at the back of the head. From the beginning of the twelfth century women's hair was covered as completely as possible. Often not cut in a lifetime, women usually let their hair grow very long. Smaller in the late medieval period than in earlier times, the couvrechef or coverchief was a veil made from a rectangle or half circle of linen, usually held in place by a circlet or fillet, or in the case of royalty a crown or cornet. Circlets, round decorative hair adornments worn by women, especially nobles, completely encircled the head and were often made of gold. Veils were often worn over wimples, linen or sometimes silk coverings for the neck, chin and sides of women's faces. Worn in a variety of ways, wimples were most often draped under the chin and fastened at the temples. Fur caps or high domed cloth or straw hats were sometimes worn by the wealthy over wimples and veils. Scorned by the Church, the cone-shaped hennin, typifying modern popular conceptions of a medieval damsel's headdress, was only worn by upper class women during a forty-year period in the mid-fifteenth century. Reality was much more mundane.

Often made of wool, hose were close-fitting leg and foot coverings usually ending just below the knee. The wealthy had linen undersocks. The women wore short, soft, leather shoes, which looked almost like modern socks. Sometimes fitted with carved wooden soles and leather laces, women's shoes were similar to those of the men, but without exaggerated toes. Heels were either small blocks of wood or layers of leather. Shoes were not only a luxury, but they were not really comfortable for walking. Wooden clogs were also popular in much of Western Europe.

Belts were symbols of fashion and money among the nobles. Upper class women's belts were leather studded with gold bosses. The poor would have either worn a piece of dull colored fabric around their waists or no belt at all. Often imported, jewelry common after the twelfth century included mantel fastenings, necklaces, bracelets, broaches and rings. Not merely decorative, it was often used as security against loans. Gems had little sparkle, as gem-cutting would not be invented until the fifteenth century. Diamonds were not common until late in the 1300s. By then laws were enacted to control who wore what jewelry. Gloves with separate fingers appeared for the first time in history. Other accessories included purses, fans and handkerchiefs.[15]

From the art of the period, we can see that dyes were widely used. Purple garments with gold embroidery were a favorite at the court of Justinian and most monarch since. Other favored colors were green, brown, black, white, blue, red, gray and plum. The dyes used on the clothing of commoners were made from lichen, onions, and alder plants.

Looking at a gathering, one could easily discern social status, particularly if observing women. The wealthy could afford more accessories and better garments, but even for them the variety of dyes and styles was limited. The Crusades had improved the supply of silk, gauze, sating, damask, velvet and jewelry from the East. Trade with the North added furs and amber to the era's apparel. Brighter colors, better materials, and longer surcotte lengths became signs of wealth. Men of the wealthy classes sported hose and jackets or tunics with surcottes. Their female counterparts wore flowing gowns and elaborate headwear. On festive occasions, such as the tour of the royal couple, the elite often sparkled with gold or silver threads sewn into silk garments. Being fashionable was an option open only to the wealthy and nobility.

During the French royal family's visit to Bruges, Queen Joan of Navarre, upon seeing the fine clothes of the city's women remarked indignantly, "I thought I alone was Queen, but here I see six hundred."[16] So richly were the Flemish townspeople dressed. The air of Flanders was too free for such attitudes to be tolerated for long. To add injury to the insult, the guilds of Bruges were billed for the expenses of the royal visit.

Philip was lulled into believing there would be no resistance to his annexation, by the pageantry and fawning Leliaart enthusiasm accompanying his triumphal tour. But the conflict between Leliaarts and Liebaarts was aggravated during and after the royal visit. Leliaart burghers were able to enrich themselves further during the French occupation. The commoners were exploited even more. Tax questions continued to trouble Ghent. Following a hard winter, 1302 was a year of famine. Rural areas supported the Count's sons, while the city government, supporting the French king, boycotted food supplies. With de Chatillon's permission, the Leliaart aldermen restored taxes on food on April 1, 1302. The next day the craft guilds declared a general strike, which resulted in an armed struggle in which mobs killed two aldermen and eleven other burghers, injured many others and trapped several hundred Leliaarts in the count's castle before the French could restore order.[17] To keep Ghent from joining in the growing unrest in Bruges and the countryside, Jacques de Châtillon agreed on May 11 to abolish indirect taxation, punished the magistrates who had reinstated it with his approval, and guarantee free commerce for all Gentenaars.

The French king had not abolished taxes in Bruges, as he had in Ghent. In June 1301, the Leliaart aldermen incarcerated the commoners' leaders, Pieter de Coninck, Jan Breidel and twenty-four others, who led the guilds in refuting the governor's invoice for the royal visit. A confusing rebellion ensued when a mob released the prisoners. De Châtillon successfully marched on Bruges and the Leliaarts chased the rebels out of town. De Châtillon insisted that the city's walls be destroyed. However, not realizing how many friends he had, de Châtillon became even more heavy handed with the townsmen and suspended Bruges' privileges. His policies and lack of understanding, combined with news of the treachery committed against Count Guy by Philip the Fair, rapidly changed the political atmosphere.

A fairly well-to-do local butcher about 38 years old, Jan Breidel captured the popular imagination. He helped lead a successful raid on the French garrison at Male on May 1, 1302. However, it was Pieter de Coninck, a simple, poor weaver from Bruges (and not the head of his guild as is often presumed), whose intelligence and oratorical talents motivated listeners to follow him in an unprecedented series of uprisings. Though short in stature, he was clearly the commoners' champion and a much more important figure than Breidel.[18]

Meanwhile, seeing the commoners' cause as the only hope of regaining their inheritance, John and Guy, the sons of Guy of Dampierre who remained at liberty, restored a skeletal administration in

116

Flanders and made their move. The Margrave of Namur, John signaled for a general uprising against French occupation. One of the Count's many grandsons, William of Gulik (or Jülich or Juliers), arrived a few days later with a number of German auxiliaries to assist his uncles. Son of Guy of Dampierre's third daughter Marie, his father was the count of Jülich (Gulik in Dutch). Because no noble title had been bestowed on him, William had become a cleric and later Provost of Maastricht and Liège. Many assumed he would probably be the next archbishop of Mainz. Despite his ordination, he enjoyed worldly pleasures and thought of himself as a soldier more than a priest. About 25 years old and by all accounts handsome, he was a natural leader, and his presence gave the entire undertaking a degree of legitimacy and professional leadership. As the closest in line of succession as count, he was accepted by the people in Flanders without hesitation as the count's official representative and eventually their commander-in-chief. Although they spoke hardly a word of Flemish, the few nobles joining the guildsmen were given a hardy welcome, while most of the Flemish aristocracy remained neutral and awaited the outcome. Recognizing de Coninck's importance, the count's sons sent him to Bruges, where he took over the town's council in December 1301 and became undisputed leader by March 1302, only to be ousted in early May.[19]

Jacques de Châtillon reacted to these challenges too late. In early May 1302, he formed a small army near Kortrijk and set out on a punitive expedition against Bruges and Ghent. The latter's town council, first sympathizing with the Liebaarts but now back in Leliaart hands, immediately sent a delegation to submit to de Châtillon. De Coninck marched to Ghent with some militiamen and tried to persuade the Gentenaars to stay on his side. He failed. De Châtillon rode on Bruges with a force of some 800 men, including 120 knights. Fearing French rage, the people of Bruges turned on the Liebaarts, who were banned from the town again. About 1,000 Liebaart supporters fled to Damme and Aardenburg. De Châtillon arrived in Bruges on May 17. Now controlled by Leliaarts, Bruges expected a peace-making delegation, but now feared that the French came to subdue them by the sword. Given de Châtillon's fierce demeanor and the fact that he hardly knew who

117

his friends and enemies were, the popularity of the Liebaarts rose rapidly over night.

Just before sunrise on May 18, 1302, the artisans of Bruges picked up their tools, awakened their burgher masters, and massacred them. The Liebaarts were strengthened by numerous exiles, including de Coninck and Breidel, who had secretly returned to the city during the night. Led by the weaver and the butcher, mobs rioted in the streets and murdered any Frenchman foolish enough to venture out of hiding. Numerous scores were settled in the chaos that descended on the city. Those unable to pronounce the Flemish slogan *Schild en vriendt* (shield and friend) with a perfect accent were put to death.[20] This chant, taken from a famous prayer used to beg God for assistance in battle, was chosen to differentiate Flemings from the French, as French speakers had a difficult time pronouncing it correctly.

The corpses of burghers and French soldiers lay in the streets and floated in the canals, which ran red with blood. Exactly how many Frenchmen and their Leliaart sympathizers were killed in this revolt, later known as the "Matins of Bruges" (*Brugse Metten*) or "Good Friday (*Goede Vrijdag*) of Bruges," is subject to widely varying claims. One source notes a few hundred killed and some 90 knights captured. Another speaks of 1,500 Frenchmen and their supporters killed.[21] Still others offer figures as high as 4,000. De Châtillon and Philip's devious chancellor Pierre Flotte escaped the city ironically by disguising themselves as commoners. A Liebaart magistracy was installed. The destruction of Bruges's fortifications was halted. The news spread rapidly and unrest erupted in most of Flanders, except Ghent.[22] Before the French could make a move, many of their allies in the Flemish elite were slaughtered.

Apart from the time of the day it occurred, the Matins of Bruges bore a distinct resemblance to the Sicilian Vespers of 1282, a massacre of some 2,000 French in Palermo. Backed by Pedro III of Aragon, this successful revolt against the repressive regime of Charles I of Anjou led to the end of Angevin power in southern Italy and later became the subject of an opera by Verdi.[23] But the result of the Matins was not merely a dynastic change. Whatever the actual death toll may have been, a revolution the likes of which no one living had known unfolded.

One unusual source of evidence about the events of 1302 is the Courtrai, or Oxford, Chest. Around 1909, this carved wooden chest was discovered at New College in Oxford, England where it is still kept. Its front panel, measuring 28 by 40.5 inches, depicts scenes from the Matins of Bruges (May 18) through to the aftermath of the Battle of Kortrijk (July 12). Commemorating the gains of the commoners, the chest was carved in Bruges by the guild of the *scrinewerkers* (chest-makers), probably in the winter of 1302. Given its detail, it is probable that the artist or artists may have taken part in some or all of the events depicted.[24]

The Matins of Bruges is illustrated with three men-at-arms decapitating another, perhaps in his bed. The soldiers wear mail coifs with skullcaps as helmets, protective gloves and small round bucklers. On the right edge of the carving, the image of a saint with a barrel-like offering box is shown. Nearby is a city gate.

The Courtrai Chest (© IRPA/KIK—Brussels).

The Matins of Bruges (© IRPA/KIK — Brussels).

The mayor and two aldermen are shown offering the keys of the city to the knights arriving on the next panel, which depicts the arrival of Guy of Namur and William of Gulik at Bruges. Guy and William are not carrying great helmets, as are the rest of their soldiers, but rather skullcaps with mail coifs. Guy of Namur is shown as a knight bearing a shield with a lion and a diagonal scalloped bar over it. William has a lion on his shield with a silver lily on its shoulder. Henry of Lontzen, who became marshal of the communal militia of Bruges, accompanies Count Guy's relatives. A soldier of the Bruges militia wears a skullcap with mail coif and a hauberk with gloves underneath his surcotte and is armed with a goedendag.

The Courtrai Chest also depicts a castle being attacked at this time. Its carvings show a French knight fighting against foot soldiers, three Flemish men-at-arms with goedendags and a man with an arrow in his chest at the feet of a crossbowman. This stronghold was probably Wijnendaal, or Wijnendaele, Castle, near Torhout on the Ostend Road. Following a Norse invasion, Count Robrecht "the Fries" of Flanders built an eight-sided wooden castle, which Count Guy had rebuilt in stone in 1278.[25] Male Castle near Bruges was also taken after a short siege. Most of Flanders rid itself of the French and the Leliaarts. "Popular" governments with a strong nationalist aspect replaced old oli-

The arrival of Guy of Namur and William of Gulik (© IRPA/KIK—Brussels).

garchies throughout Flanders and confiscated Leliaart property. The French held onto only a few strongholds such as Cassel and Kortrijk, while Ghent officially remained neutral.

The guilds rallied to meet the challenge they knew would come with vengeance. The city of Bruges carried most of the costs of the uprising. Expenses in the communal accounts were marked with entries like "to defend the country" and "to protect the land." De Coninck continued to help the Count's family lead the revolt against the French. Jan Breidel supplied William's army with meat, horses and oats for the coming campaign. Together William of Gulik and Pieter de Coninck led the people, one as representative of the Count, the other as representative of the commoners. A handful of nobles sided

The attack on Wijnendaal Castle (© IRPA/KIK—Brussels).

with commoners against their own class in a rare show of solidarity that transcended the language, class and upbringing of each.

Militia contingents from Bruges left for Kortrijk, a town in French hands still some distance from the border. Although most were guildsmen, many others joined the Flemish ranks. In addition to de Coninck and Breidel, other leaders emerged. An old Saxon chief, Eustace Sporkin, led the yeomen of Bruges. With the French victory in 1300 the van Sinte Baafs returned to Ghent, and the city government remained in Leliaart hands throughout the conflict to come. However, Jan Borluut returned from exile as far as Kortrijk and sent word that Gentenaars who wished to fight the French could join him there. His role as leader of the Ghent contingent in the coming battle made him a hero. Artisans from Leliaart-dominated Ypres soon joined him.

From the great Cistercian abbey of Ter Doest at Lissewege, Willem van Saeftingen rode south to join the fray with many others from Bruges' hinterland. As would soon be evident, the qualities of this quick-tempered giant of a man were far better suited to battle than to prayer. Elsewhere merchants left their stores, peasants deserted their fields, and monks abandoned their cubicles. Pooling their war chests, the guilds were able to hire some mercenary crossbowmen. Perhaps as high as 10 percent of Bruges' population headed for battle. After the Matins everyone realized that the rebellion was unique. It was no longer a quarrel between two lords, but an entire people resisting a king. They knew that their very survival, as well as Flanders' independence, depended on what would happen next.

5

The Battle

As evident in the many invasions throughout its later history, small, low-lying Flanders appears to be an easy target. However, the conditions and technologies of the early fourteenth century did not make success a foregone conclusion. Flanders' swampy terrain and rainy climate played an important defensive role. Originally joined, the counties of Flanders and Artois had been separated by inheritance, leading to the establishment of a more easily defensible southern Flemish frontier. The *Annals of Ghent* frequently mention the County's many marshes, as well as "a dyke between two marshes, protecting the County of Flanders and dividing it from the County of Artois."[1] The role of these geographical factors could be easily overlooked.

The conflict came to focus on the small textile town of Kortrijk (Courtrai in French) some 24 miles directly south of Bruges and roughly the same distance southwest of Ghent.[2] Archaeological evidence shows that the area around Kortrijk was inhabited around 1500 B.C., but no significant settlement existed there before the Roman period. In the first century A.D. a Gallo-Roman colony, Cortoriacum, grew on the southern banks of the Leie, or Lys, river near the crossroads of Tongeren-Cassel and Tournai-Oudenburg roads. Cortoriacum is the Latinized form of an older Celtic name. Surviving Frankish attacks, the town was an administrative center, or *municipium*, during Merovingian times. According to local legend, during this time St-Elooi founded a chapel, destroyed in the 800s, where Sint-Maarten's church would be built in the late 1200s. Later, one of Charlemagne's heirs, Charles the Bald, donated 30 hectares of land to St. Amand's abbey. The town's importance rose considerably. At the end of the ninth century, the Normans abandoned Ghent to establish their winter headquarters in Kortrijk, which apparently had been fortified by then. During the tenth century, a stone castle replaced the wooden stronghold. In 1190, Philip of Alsace gave the town its first privileges.

In the eleventh century Kortrijk developed into a textile manufacturing center. Unlike the wool-based economies of Bruges and Ghent, Kortrijk became a flourishing producer of linen and damask, as a result of excellent local conditions for flax cultivation. The Leie became known as the "golden river," due to its water's chalk-free chemical content, perfect for flax retting, the process whereby seed capsules are removed and fibers in the stalk are separated from its woody tissues through fermentation. As an inducement to encourage woolen weaving in the town, Countess Joan of Constantinople exempted settlers from the taille, or property tax.

> I, Joan, Countess of Flanders and Hainault, wish it to be known to all both now and in the future, that I and my successors cannot and ought not to take any tax or payment from the fifty men who shall come to live at Courtrai, for as long as they remain here, to work in the woolen industry from this day on. But their heirs, after the decease of their parents, shall serve me just as my other burgesses do. Given at Courtrai, in the year of the Lord 1224, on the feast of St. Cecilia.[3]

In the early thirteenth century Count Baldwin of Flanders founded Kortrijk's Gothic Church of Our Lady. The town was enclosed by a defensive wall, strengthened under Walter Van Nevele from 1270 to 1280 and later upgraded during the fourteenth and fifteenth centuries. In 1284, Count Guy granted a piece of land to beguines who had already been active in the town since 1238 and who had been endowed by Countess Joan four years later. Against the city wall and one of the ramparts of Kortrijk's castle, the newly built St. Elizabeth beguinage would be in the frontlines of the unfolding battle.[4]

124

5. The Battle

The Beguinage at Kortrijk.

The royal court in Paris reacted to the Matins of Bruges with fury. Philip the Fair dispatched his second cousin Count Robert II of Artois to the scene. Undoubtedly, the King felt that Robert would crush the growing unrest easily. Considered the best French knight and commander of his time, Robert was the second husband of Dame Agnes de Bourbon, a distant relative of Count Guy. Not only was his mother Beatrice Brabantine, but Robert had also spent part of his youth at Kortrijk Castle and knew Flanders well. His army formed around Arras by the end of June 1302 and confidently marched north to avenge the massacre at Bruges.

Concentrated around Kortrijk to besiege its castle, the Flemish army numbered between 8,000 and 10,500.[5] Several accounts suggest that the Flemish force was composed of 2,600 to 3,000 from Bruges led by William of Gulik, 2,400 to 2,500 from the Franc of Bruges[6] led by Guy of Namur, and 2,500 from East Flanders, of which 700 were from Ghent led by Jan Borluut, 500 from Ypres, and a reserve force of

125

500 led by John of Renesse, a nobleman from Flanders' northern neighbour, Zeeland, who had ad a quarrel with his lord and was hired along with other Zeelanders by the Flemings.[7] The *Annals of Ghent* state that there were no more than ten knights on the Flemish side.[8] The force from Bruges included 320 cavalrymen from the burgher class. However, knights, burghers and commoners alike were all to fight on foot. Some 60 trumpeters were designated to communicate orders during the heat of battle. In that era, trumpets signaled the saddling and mounting of horses, the formation of battlefield units, the collection of scattered troops, and the breaking of camp as well as the beginning of an attack, which was also denoted by bringing banners forward.[9]

As the gateway to Flanders from France, Kortrijk was of the utmost importance. The French, understanding this, marched there also. The town remained in the hands of its small French garrison, and before it could be liberated, scouts reported on July 2 that Artois' army had crossed the frontier. Less than a week of preparation and reinforcement remained before they would be upon the Flemings. The French army approached Kortrijk on July 8. On July 9, they camped two leagues south of Kortrijk's walls on a knoll known as Mossenberg (Mossy Mount) in what is now Kortrijk's suburb of Pottelberg. Having pillaged the countryside since entering Flanders, Artois' men took two days to assemble. They failed to relieve the town and concluded that battle on an open field was unavoidable. Kortrijk Castle's French defenders signaled that Groeningeveld (Groeninge plain), a field immediately east of town, would be suitable. Meanwhile, the Flemings camped north of the town.

Both armies rose early in the morning, but took a long time to prepare for battle. The French knightly formations needed much time to maneuver to their appointed positions. But the knights also wanted to exhaust the foot soldiers by forcing them to stay in battle order through the morning. This was noted by the battle's two most important chroniclers, a visiting Florentine merchant, Giovanni Villani, and a Brabantine priest named Louis van Velthem.[10] Both sides confessed their sins to priests and listened to their leaders' speeches and instructions. The Flemish force was strictly forbidden from taking any prisoners or booty, and violators were to be executed at once by their comrades in arms—rather unusual orders in medieval warfare. This may have been to concentrate the Flemings' attention on fighting. The battle was to be fought neither giving nor expecting mercy. After mass, each Fleming kissed a handful of earth to show his patriotism. Meanwhile Willem van Saeftingen, the monk of Lissewege, traded the horse he had brought with him from his abbey for a goedendag. After a breakfast of fish, eggs, mustard and sorrel, they joined ranks, standing as a phalanx before the enemy. Just before the battle, Breidel, de Coninck, two of de Coninck's sons and about forty others were knighted as reward for their services.

The Courtrai Chest shows the Flemish militias before the battle. The carvings show a priest giving absolution to a soldier, who is wearing a skullcap and a mail coif. Mail hauberks, which were very expensive, were rare. Most wear gloves strengthened with mail. All wear uniformly colored surcottes with the colors of their town or guild. Among the banners are those of Bruges's guilds of fullers, weavers, shippers, wine-measurers and wine-carriers. The range of arms includes pikes, goedendags, swords and falchions.

Chroniclers recorded that omens for their success were not lacking. A flock of doves flew over the Flemings while ravens wheeled over the heads of the French. Some accounts also note other bad omens: Artois' favorite hound was said to have attacked him that morning and his mighty war-horse Morel bucked him three times before he could mount it.[11]

The Flemish militias before the battle (© IRPA/KIK—Brussels).

The Golden Spurs of Kortrijk

The two armies met on Groeningeveld just east of Kortrijk's walls on July 11, 1302. Standing shoulder to shoulder, the Flemish infantry waited behind the marshy banks of Groeninge Beek (Groeninge Brook), which meandered around their east side to join the River Leie to the northeast. Behind them were, from west to east, the walls and moats of Kortrijk, the Leie, and Groeninge abbey. In front of them was the Grote Beek, or Great Brook, some three yards wide, connecting the moats with the Groeninge Beek. The brooks separated the sides on terrain very unfavorable for cavalry. All of the Flemings were dismounted. Wearing the visorless helmets of the militias, William of Gulik and Guy of Namur sent their horses to the rear and joined the Flemish ranks.[12] Although numerous pikes and handmade ball and chain weapons were deployed, the Flemings relied chiefly on their goedendags. This instrument proved effective in the capable hands of he guildsmen.

On the French side, thousands of heavily armored knights sat in their saddles. Philip the Fair had sent the best army he ever assembled to Flanders. Crossbowmen and peasant irregulars waited to assist. Beautiful horses, gleaming armor and colorful banners faced a ragged band of commoners on foot. The exact number of French is a subject of much dispute. At least 2,500 mounted knights and squires, 1,000 crossbowmen (some hired from as far as Spain and Genoa), 1,000 pike men and 2,000 other light infantry were organized into ten battles, which formed three larger units. Two units of four battles each were to attack. A third unit of two battles would form a reserve. This would add up to a force smaller than the Flemings'. Verbruggen also notes the numerical superiority of the Flemings.[13] The figure of 50,000 French quoted in some sources is quite ridiculous.[14] However, it is possible that up to 10,000 Frenchmen were engaged. Robert himself reportedly claimed before the battle that his forces "outnumber[ed] these men by half as many again."[15] As with many of his other judgments that day, this claim was almost certainly wrong. But no one doubted that the French force was far superior to the Flemings'. Robert's knights, drawn from France, Flanders, Brabant Hainault and Luxembourg, had years of war behind them. Many were experienced, battle-hardened veterans.

5. *The Battle*

But the army which faced the French at Kortrijk was not a peasant rabble but a well-ordered war machine. The aristocratic warriors of feudal Europe should have been disturbed by such developments, yet it was never doubted that armies of commoners would always be inferior to mounted knights on an open field of battle. This assumption was clearly reflected in the arrogant statements and behavior of Robert of Artois. Such attitudes, along with many other notions underlying feudalism, were to be upset that day.

Extending south from Groeninge Abbey, the men of East Flanders faced the knights of Lorraine and Saint-Pol over the Groeninge Beek. Knights from Normandy were immediately to the south. The center of the Flemish line, where the Grote Beek joined the Groeninge Beek, was held by the contingent from West Flanders. The exact location of Robert of Artois and his own knights is unclear. Some sources place Artois near Groeninge Abbey north of the knights of Lorraine.[16] Another probable position was closer to the center of the French lines, possibly north of the road to Oudenaarde near the point where the brooks met.[17] The southernmost Flemish unit was that from Bruges, which was confronted by the knights of Burlats, Brabant, Nesle and Trie, from west to east respectively. The men of Ypres were poised before the gates of Kortrijk Castle, guarding the Flemish rear. Knights from Clermont, Saint-Pol and Boulogne formed the French reserve, which positioned itself south of the Oudenaarde road. Renesse's Flemish reserve took up a position behind the lines in the center of the Flemish side. Crossbowmen stood in front of all units on both sides.

In the French camp a war council was held. Some bannerlords doubted the wisdom of a direct frontal attack, preferring to wait for the Flemings to attack, so that they could exhaust and disperse them more easily. But most of the French lords wished to defend their honor and attack, in order to teach the lowly army of guildsmen a lesson. In order to ascertain whether or not there were any great lords on the Flemish side who could be taken prisoner after the battle, and while waiting for his army to fully assemble, Artois sent a herald to inspect the enemy. After riding around the Flemings he reported to the Count:

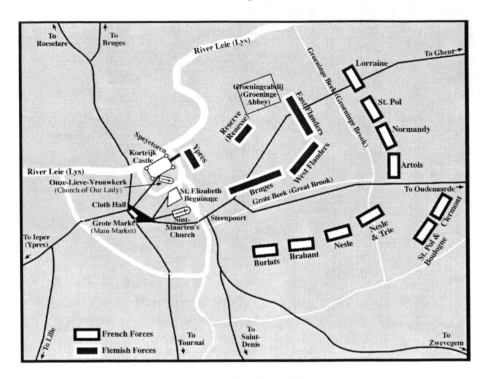

Map of the battlefield.

My Lord Count, I have seen nothing but rowdy peasants and weavers in army, and as I rode round the army I saw none of any importance save William of Juliers (Gulik) and my lord Guy (of Namur), a young knight who is the son of Guy of Dampierre. They are all on foot and have been posted along the banks of a river. We may not attack them from the rear. There too, I saw a shining banner — a lion rampant on a *field or*.[18]

The herald had seen well, for the golden lion banner was that of John of Renesse, considered to be one of the most competent knights of his time. What the scout apparently did not see was another small force led by William of Boenhem, who was to play an important role late in the battle. Boenhem joined the Flemings for two reasons: first he was a friend of Count Guy and second, as a Knight Templar he was aware of Philip the Fair's avaricious opposition to his order.

130

5. The Battle

Words of caution issued from the Brabantine camp. Godfrey, the uncle of Duke John II of Brabant, counseled Robert to move carefully. Unwilling to risk the 500 knights he had brought with him, Godfrey spoke to Artois. "It is my belief that we should most beware of the knight who bears the lion banner. That is my Lord John of Renesse; in all the world there are not six men who are his equals in military skill. Let me charge them on the morrow; they are only poor foot soldiers, and will be sore wearied by then."

Robert was outraged by these remarks. Rising in his stirrups he exclaimed, "Now thou drawest back Godfrey, and well I deem that it is thy purpose to flee and so thou seekest to guard thyself. Thy bearing misliketh me. We are mounted and they are on foot."

Repeating the much quoted knightly wisdom of his day, which equated a knight to ten foot soldiers, Artois continued, "A hundred horses are worth a thousand men. What then hast thou to fear? Turn and look; these valiant men will not abandon thee!"

> The knights' lofty concept of honour and duty is evident from the records of innumerable councils of war. Many times some nobles advised against a battle, but were overruled by a majority. Those who wanted to postpone the fighting to a more propitious time were frequently mocked because their courage was called into question. But every one of them, even those who did not want to fight, played their part bravely in the attack and were frequently killed, refusing to survive on the battlefield out of a sense of honour and military duty.[19]

On the Flemish side John of Renesse explained, "Do not allow the enemy to break through your ranks. Do not be afraid. Kill both man and horse. ... When the enemy attacks the corps of Lord Guy, we shall come to your help from behind. Anyone who breaks into your ranks, or gets through them, will be killed."[20]

While such instructions continued, the engagement began modestly along the banks of the Groeninge Beek around noon. Jean de Burlats, Grandmaster of the French crossbowmen, sent his archers forward to harass the Flemings. Behind a thick hedge along the road to Zwevegem, a company of Genoese archers spied some guildsmen.

131

Opening fire on them, the Italians gained an element of surprise. The Flemish crossbowmen took cover behind the large pavises held by their servants. Sending crossbowmen forward to weaken enemy lines was a common tactic employed at the beginning of many medieval battles. But as the crossbow bolts cut through the ranks of guildsmen, the French knights expressed consternation.

"Sire, sire," protested one. "If these villains do so much, the day will be theirs, and what share will the nobles have in the glory?"

Pierre Flotte, a shrewd law lord who had put on armor with no intention of going close to danger, suggested that Artois wait until the Genoese had driven the Flemings out of formation, giving the cavalry the honor or running down the fleeing enemy.

"By the devil, Pierre, you have still the wolf's skin," Robert responded, alluding to Flotte's common origins.

The crossbow bolts of both sides gained little. The Flemings ran out of arrows and the pressure from the French became too great. The Flemings withdrew out of crossbow range to their infantry lines, uncovering the front of their formation in the process. While retreating they cut the strings of their bows and threw them on the ground to make the anticipated charge of the knights more difficult. Robert assumed this to be a general retreat. By now French foot soldiers had advanced and were crossing the brooks. A trumpet was heard in the fields to the east. It was the armies of the counts of Saint-Pol and Boulogne coming to join Artois' formations. Seeing that the newcomers were enemies, the Flemings prepared for the worst. Crowding together, one against another, they closed ranks. The French standard was brought forward to signal the knights' first attack.[21]

To avoid obstructing a cavalry charge, the French commanders ordered their infantry to stand aside. Artois signaled his first wave to attack. Without waiting for their crossbowmen to demoralize the enemy further, the French left wing charged towards the Flemings. They were led by Rudolph (or Raoul) of Nesle, who has gone down in history as a three-fold traitor, for he was a Fleming, a direct descendent of Dietrich of Alsace, and a son-in-law of Count Guy. Various sources both claim and deny that the archers were trampled by their lords.[22] For the most part, the French infantry avoided being run over by their cavalry.

The knights dashed across the field, clearly unacquainted with the terrain. The Flemings had filled the many streams and ditches in front of them with brush to conceal the full extent of the marsh. They then barricaded themselves eight rows deep. Their front line alternated men with pikes and others with goedendags. The shaft ends of the pikes were stuck in the ground and stabilized by the pike men's feet to take the shock of the charge. The men with goedendags stood poised to club horses and knights as they were halted by the bristling line of pikes. Late thirteenth century Flemish infantry had learned to use the pike and goedendag in this way to discourage frontal attacks.

Most knights crossed the Grote Beek without too much trouble. However, the speed and close order of their attack was broken. Once across the brook they needed to re-form and charge again. But the distance between them and the Flemings was now too short to gain enough speed. Their charge produced a thundering crash, but the Flemings' formation did not break. The pikemen took the shock of the charge, while the men with goedendags finished the job. A few knights managed to push through the front line, but were immediately surrounded and killed. Within minutes, hundreds of horses and men were struggling in the mud, while the Flemings descended on them with their goedendags, first killing the horses, then their riders. In spite of their efforts the guildsmen were pushed north. Unfortunately for the French, the soil on the banks, though firmer than in the marsh, sank under the weight of the cavalry but was able to support foot soldiers.

On the Courtrai Chest, the Flemish line of battle is shown as a packed wall of pikes and goedendags with crossbows behind and the first slain horses lying on the ground in front. A French knight is shown stopped by a pike caught under his helmet and a sword driven into his horse's chest. Behind the pikes are crossbowmen and the rest of the town militias. Above fly the banners of Flanders, the towns and the guilds, including those of Henry of Lontzen, Pieter de Coninck and the carpenters', masons', blacksmiths' and brokers' guilds. The two large figures represent Guy of Namur with a pike in his hand and

The Flemish battle line (© IRPA/KIK—Brussels).

William of Gulik with a goedendag. The Lord of Sijsele, an enemy of Bruges and supporter of the French king, appears on the left. Depictions on the chest match the description given by Villani.[23]

The air resounded with battle cries. Soldiers in the height of battle often overcome their fears by fortifying themselves with battle cries. Such cries were powerful instruments of identification, unity and encouragement. In an age when uniforms were in their infancy, visual recognition of friend and foe was difficult at best.[24] A continuously shouted, predetermined cry enabled soldiers to recognize each other, particularly in the confusion and emotional upheaval of close combat. This was particularly the case during the battle of Kortrijk. The chosen battle cry of the Flemish was *Vlaendren die Leeu* ("Flanders the Lion"). This referred to the lion symbol of Flanders on the count's shield and signified that they fought for Flanders. The French cry was *Montjoie Saint-Denis*. The exact meaning of *montjoie* is unknown, but probably refers to heaps of stone used as beacons during the Crusades. Saint Denis was the patron saint of France. Later the *Oriflamme*, the most important French banner, was connected with the cry. This banner was kept in the abbey of Saint-Denis, where the French kings were buried. Hence the cry was a statement of faith in the *Oriflamme* and the protection of Saint-Denis.[25]

As desperately snorting destriers struggled to free themselves from the morass and Flemish goedendags took their toll on the first French assault, Count Robert persisted with his now questionable plan of operations. If he was at the north end of the field, he may not have seen

The Battle of Kortrijk as shown in a manuscript illumination in the Grands
Chroniques de France *(© Bibliothèque Nationale de France).*

what was happening. If he was in the center, he would have had a good
view of the action, but may have thought that the Flemish lines could
be forced with more knights. Still assuming knightly superiority, he
ordered a second charge, which included himself. Crossing the
Groeninge Beek was not difficult, but the Flemish lines again withstood

135

the shock. Piled on top of the first, the second attack, though more organized than the first, got bogged down as quickly. The guildsmen counterattacked, and most of the French were quickly unhorsed and killed. The field became a confused slaughtering ground thick with mud, bushes, bodies and stray horses, all preventing Artois' men from reorganizing.

Robert of Artois galloped to the front, and finding a low ditch, he called, "Let those who are faithful follow." Bounding over the obstacle, he found himself alone amid the Flemish ranks and quickly encircled by troops led by Guy of Namur. Slashing with his sword and tearing a banner to shreds, his foot slipped out of his stirrup. Facing him was a formidable opponent, Willem van Saeftingen, who felled his horse and pulled him from his saddle. As he cried surrender, the guildsmen shouted that they couldn't understand French. According to legend he also begged to save the life of his steed Morel. Before Guy of Namur could intervene both the French count and his horse had paid the supreme penalty for his arrogance.

While the knights attacked on the open field, the Ypres town militia prevented Kortrijk's garrison from forcing their way out of the castle's gates to attack the Flemish rear. Earlier, the garrison had burned houses to clear their line of fire. At that time the St. Elizabeth Beguinage was badly damaged. The Courtrai Chest shows the French garrison trapped inside the castle and trying to force a way out. From its tower a simplified form of the French flag and the banner of the castellan of Lens fly. Three Yprois men-at-arms carry falchions. One holds a buckler. Clearly showing that uniforms were worn, the Ypres town militia wears tunics with a double cross, the communal arms of their town. A large pavese with two crossbow bolts sticking in it shields the militiamen. The meanings behind some of the carvings are unclear. An unknown woman is shown lowered by a rope from a tower, behind which stands a trebuchet. Above the castle's entrance a barrel is suspended, perhaps to drop on possible intruders.

In the center of the Flemish lines, where the men of West Flanders were posted and where there was a bit more space to perform a better charge, the French almost managed to break through. The Flemish line almost collapsed in panic as the French knights pushed deep

5. The Battle

The militia of Ypres at the gates of Kortrijk Castle (© IRPA/KIK—Brussels).

into their lines. The reserve under John of Renesse quickly rushed in, threw back the enemy and repaired the wavering formation. Fierce close combat raged over the whole line. The French now had little room to maneuver. Once the knights lost any advantage they may have had, the Flemings pressed forward.

Having expressed his doubts about fighting around the brooks before the battle, Rudolph of Nesle advanced farther than anyone on Artois' side. But honor led him to commit the equivalent of suicide. He had chosen what he thought to be a winning side. He now knew he was wrong. The Middle Ages, unlike classical antiquity or modern times, has almost no illustrious suicides. Aggressive impulses among nobles were directed at others, rather than themselves. Both the code of chivalry and the Church considered taking one's life a sinful dishonor. But there are quite a few cases of knights and other nobles purposely endangering their lives in battles and tournaments. The

Chroniques de Flandre recount that Rudolph declared that "he no longer wanted to live when he saw all the flower of Christendom dead" and rushed headlong into the fray, preferring certain death to the humiliation of defeat.[26] Behind Rudolph lay Jacques de Châtillon and not far away was the body of Flotte, who got caught in the melee.

On the other side, things had not gone well for William of Gulik, who was carried from the field streaming with blood, having been knocked down by Godfrey of Brabant. To prevent panic, one of his squires buckled on his armor and returned to the thick of battle, impersonating the provost. In the end, William's wounds proved to be minor and it was Godfrey who was killed.

Denied of their leader, the French were in disorder. Shouting and jeering, the Flemings advanced in formation, first up to, then over the brooks. The men of Hainault, whose hearts were not truly on the French side, stood motionless facing the enemy but offered no resistance. As they retreated, they allowed their baggage to be carried away. Artois' army withdrew, shields hanging on their backs. Many escaping French foot soldiers were caught and killed by the Flemings. William of Boenhem led the men of Bruges out of the phalanx and chased the fleeing French, whose two battles of reserves, seeing the futility of a third wave, had taken to their heels. The battle had lasted more than three hours. Most casualties occurred near the brooks. Their banks were covered with the bodies of both men and horses. The most magnificent army of Europe had been virtually destroyed. Villani later wrote that this was "an almost impossible event."[27]

When it became clear that the French were losing, some Brabantine lords and Flemish knights fighting for the French tried to change sides by shouting "Vlaendren die Leeu." The knights on the Flemish side would normally have not differed noticeably from their French opponents. However, to fight on foot the Flemish knights were required to remove their spurs. Furthermore they almost certainly did not wear all of their armor, particularly their heavy maille chausses, which would have been cumbersome. The differences must have been apparent. Guy of Namur ordered all those who wore spurs killed. No prisoners were spared. Flemings looted the French camp at Pottelberg. Van Velthem, reported that the forces of Boenhem pursued the French for almost eight miles through Zwevegem and St. Denijs to Dottignies. The fortunate were able to make it to Tournai by night.[28]

> From the towers of the church of Notre Dame of Tournai, of the abbey of St. Martin and of the city, they could be seen fleeing along the roads, through hedges and fields, in such numbers that no one who had not seen it would believe it ... in the outskirts of the city and in the villages there were so many starving knights and foot-soldiers that it was a frightful sight. Those who managed to find food outside the town bartered their equipment for it. All that night and the next day those who came into the city were so terrified that many of them could not even eat.[29]

That night the Flemings stood guard over the battlefield. In the thinking of the day, a battle was won only when the victorious army could hold the field until the next morning. Hence, not until next day was the booty gathered. The final segment of the Courtrai Chest depicts the collection of loot. Showing a body ripped open, it illustrates how vicious and bloody the battle had been. The dead were stripped of their gilded spurs, thus the engagement was dubbed "The Battle of the Golden Spurs."[30]

Exactly how many French knights were killed is open to question. Today many Flemings assert a claim of 2,000. Although some figures tend to be inflated, it is probable that French noble deaths exceeded a thousand. Along with de Nesle, Flotte, de Châtillon and

The collection of loot on the morning after the battle (© IRPA/KIK—Brussels).

Artois, the dead included de Nesle's brother Guy, Godfrey of Brabant, Jean de Burlats, Renaud de Trie, the Count of Aumale, the Count of Eu, the Lord of Tancarville, both marshals of France, some sixty barons and other lords, hundreds of knights and more than a thousand squires. After the battle some 500 to 700 spurs were mounted on the walls of the nearby Church of Our Lady. Others were sent to William of Gulik's church in Maastricht.[31] The number of French archers and foot soldiers killed was never recorded, but was undoubtedly high. Similarly, accounts of Flemish losses are also sketchy. Verbruggen states that "the victors lost only a few hundred dead."[32] However, the significance of the battle went far beyond mere statistics. For the first time in history, an army of common foot soldiers defeating a major force of knights had confirmed a popular revolution.

Seven days later Pope Boniface VII was wakened from his sleep when the unbelievable news of the Flemish victory arrived in Rome. No doubt, the pontiff had mixed feelings about such tidings. The divinely-ordained world which he, at least in theory, presided over had been overturned. On the other hand, the power and legitimacy of his

A Prick Spur from Kortrijk (Photograph by A. G. Pauwels, © Stedelijke Musea Kortrijk).

archrival Philip the Fair had been called into question. Rome celebrated. Also aware of its significance, another famous Italian of the era, Dante Alighieri, referred to the approach of the battle in his *Purgatory*.[33]

It was standard protocol for units of a communal militia to meet approaching dignitaries outside of a city to lead them in a ceremonial entry. When the victors of Kortrijk made their ceremonial entry into Ghent on July 14, 1302, observers noted that "anyone who could carry a bow went out to meet them."[34] John of Namur was received in Ghent as its prince and held power in Flanders until the return of his younger brother Philip of Thiette from Italy in May 1303.[35] The Leliaart councils of Ghent and Ypres were overthrown within days of the battle, and the corporate and political rights of their craft guilds were expanded to match the extensive rights of those in Bruges. To say that these new regimes were democratic would be exaggerating. But they did include a broader segment of the propertied classes than their predecessors had. Although Bruges' guilds were not given specific seats on their city council, a fuller became the new mayor, and thirteen new aldermen included nine who were probably guildsmen not in previous administrations.[36]

In the autumn of 1302, a satirical gospel, mostly concerning the battle, was popular in Bruges. It was intended for an audience of the generally anti–French local clergy, who, despite the attitudes of their superiors, seem to have enjoyed irreverent humor. The Passion takes the form of an epic full of puns, with Robert of Artois and Pierre Flotte against Pieter de Coninck. It begins with a standard liturgical "in that time" and ends with the French, like the Magi, returning "home by another way." Referring to Charles of Valois, Philip IV's brother, *Pater Noster, qui est in caelis* (Our Father, who is in heaven), became *frater meus, qui est infelix* (my brother, who is unhappy). With a pun on the words Pater/Pieter, Robert of Artois asks de Coninck not to kill him: "Father/Peter, let this cup pass from me."[37]

John of Namur began a deliberate policy of linking his family's interests to the cities. On August 1, 1302, he granted Bruges a charter prohibiting higher rents and inheritance taxes and granting perpetual freedom from all tolls.[38] Bruges, Ghent and Ypres were given greater power over the hinterland beyond their city walls. He also enhanced the power of the guilds. Numerous guilds later claimed to have received corporate privileges in around 1302. Weavers, butchers, fullers, shearers, mercers, coopers, shrine workers, brokers, smiths, fishmongers and others were formally recognized as corporations. Among the privileges guaranteed or reaffirmed in numerous documents were absolute hereditary mastership, legislative and judicial powers and the right to have militias, courts, seals and council seats. To entice foreign merchants back to Flanders, John and Bruges' city government gave a charter to the brokers, which fixed the rate owed on various goods subject to brokerage.[39]

A heady confidence surged through Flanders. One boast claimed that a Fleming with his goedendag would dare to fight two knights on horse. In shock, Philip the Fair dispatched royal commissioners throughout his realm to find townsmen and rich peasants willing to pay for ennoblement.[40] He required all commoners possessing wealth in goods or property over a certain amount to serve in the army for four months.[41] Meanwhile rumors swept France that the Flemings had ejected King Philip and crowned a weaver as King Peter. It was evidently based on de Coninck's name, which means Peter King.[42]

The battle entered mythology as a milestone in Flanders' national struggle, as the first major battle in which urban infantry defeated noble cavalry. Even the banners used that day in 1302 remain. The County of Flanders had a black lion on a golden field as its flag. This banner is still found in the flags of Belgium's Flemish Region and its province of East Flanders. It is also used as the symbol of the Flemish nationalist movement, although the historic county and modern region are not nearly the same. The old Duchy of Brabant, now split between the Netherlands and Belgium, was symbolized by a golden lion on a black field. Carried by the duke's men on the French side at Kortrijk, it still serves as the arms of Belgium and the Dutch province of Northern Brabant. This banner was also the flag and arms of the Belgian province of Brabant until it was partitioned in January 1995 and still forms the basis of the flags of the new provinces of Flemish Brabant and Walloon Brabant. The red-yellow-black colors of the Belgian flag are directly derived from the Brabantine banner. Also still in use, the arms of Bruges features a blue lion with red claws and a golden tongue, wearing a golden crown and collar with a cross. Its field consists of five red bars on white. The city of Ghent then and now used a white lion on a black field. The lion had golden nails, a red tongue, a golden crown and a golden collar with a cross attached to it. The lion theme has clearly been very strong. Found in some early illuminations, a flag containing the black lion of Flanders, the white lion of Ghent, and a blue lion with golden needles, tongue and nails on a red field probably belonged to Ghent's weavers' guild.[43]

The Battle of the Golden Spurs shattered French hopes of annexing Flanders. Except for brief periods of occupation, Germanic Flanders was never to be part of France again. But the road ahead would not be easy. Guy of Dampierre remained imprisoned in France and Philip the Fair's ambitions were only temporarily stalled. The battle was won, but the now over-confident commoners hardly realized that the war was not over.

6

The Aftermath

The attentions of Bruges went far beyond the recent victory. Often having their own compounds or palaces, merchants from sixteen nations were represented in the city, half from Italy. Among the wealthiest natives were inn-keepers, particularly the van der Beurs (Beurse) family. Thus the name Beurs features prominently in economic history. Traders arranged deals and exchanged papers in their inn, which was steps away from the Poortersloge and the Genoese and Florentine compounds. This process was formalized in 1302 as the world's first *bourse*, or stock exchange, one of the key institutions of the modern economy.[1]

With urban production and new modes of doing business came a need to organize time more efficiently. Manufacturing and the discipline it evoked owe much to the medieval perfection of the mechanical clock. While sundials, hourglasses and waterclocks were used in antiquity, mechanical clocks are more recent, first appearing in China and later the Middle East. For centuries clocks were more for astronomical and astrological purposes than for telling the time. Large mechanical clocks began to appear in European cities early in the 1300s. Behavior changed profoundly. Before the clock, people based their work, meals and sleep on the sun or on the toll of church bells, whose rough timing remained a mystery to all beyond the clergy. Clocks divided time into regulated units, in which "time took on the character of an enclosed space: it could be divided, it could be filled up, and it could even be expanded by the invention of labor-saving instruments."[2] The mechanical efficiency of this abstract time became the new rhythm of life.

For all its sophistication, Flanders suffered from some very old problems. Piracy in the English Channel became a persistent problem from the 1290s and would continue to trouble diplomacy, trade and shipping through the early 1400s. Understandably upset at being left alone in 1297, the counts generally ignored English claims against Flemish pirates, who were rarely punished more severely than having to restore the value of the stolen property. In 1306 two English merchants were authorized to seize Flemish goods at Boston to compensate for a robbery at sea. The English also seized Flemish boats that they caught dealing with the Scots. In December 1310 an entire Flemish fleet was burned at Grauzon in Brittany. The large number of Flemings residing in England by the late thirteenth century were disliked intensely. Eight Flemings and Brabantines, as well as some Italians, Provençals and Germans, were prosecuted in 1298 for using a hostel to conceal customs violations.[3] Attacks on Flemings in London in 1311 and 1312 caused many to leave for other English ports.

Meanwhile, the war with Philip the Fair continued. Between 1302 and 1304 French armies retreated from the Flemings several times. Fueled by increases in population and prosperity, enthusiasm in Flanders ran high. The victory at Kortrijk had given the Flemings confidence in their own youthful powers. They even mounted offensives against Hainault and Holland, the French king's weaker allies.[4]

Not present at Kortrijk, Philip the Fair took the initiative and personally led a campaign in September 1302. Urged on by William of Gulik, the Flemish communal militias wanted to take the offensive and attack the royal army. But the French king made no attempt to drive the Flemings out of good positions at Vitry on September 17 and Flines on September 22. Not daring to risk a frontal attack and hand-to-hand combat, the French feigned charges in front and tried to flank the militias. In both cases, they found that the Flemings formed a crown-like

configuration, protected on all sides by a hedge of pikes and goedendags. On two other occasions retreats almost turned into panic.
However, at Arques on April 4, 1303, French knights began to retreat
in good order. When William of Gulik saw this, he prepared his militia infantry for attack. Then the knights halted and feigned attack,
leading the Flemings to rearrange themselves for a defensive battle.
The French retreated again. William advanced, and again the knights
stopped. After doing this five or six times to keep the Flemings at a
distance, the French army was able to withdraw to the well-fortified
town of St. Omer. On July 10, 1303, the Flemings offered battle again.
But the Constable of France withdrew his army rather than fight the
militias in an open field. Kortrijk was not forgotten.

Also in 1303 the Flemings besieged Tournai in a 47-day campaign.
When the Flemings finally retreated, they covered their infantry with
a band of cavalry and a smokescreen, made by burning the straw huts
they had camped in. When the French knights tried to attack they col-
lided with the Flemish rear guard and suffered heavy losses.[5]

On the night of March 20, 1304, Zeelanders and Flemings, led by
Guy of Namur, surprised the Frisians and Hollanders on the island of
Duiveland. They inflicted a heavy defeat on William of Avesnes, count
of Holland. Although unable to take the fortified town of Zierikzee,
they occupied most of Holland until a rebellion chased them south
again.[6]

Philip the Fair led another campaign against Flanders in 1304.
Departing from Arras, he was prevented by Flemish militias from passing through the Pont-à-Vendin gap on the direct route to Flanders. He
then made a detour via Tournai, and tried to take the bridges over the
Marcq at Bouvines and Pont-à-Tressin, but failed again. However, he
managed to reached Faumont on August 11. The Flemings advanced
toward his camp. Parleys were held on August 14, 15 and 16, but Philip's
supply wagons were in difficulties, and the Flemings held a strong position with marshes in front and behind them, so he decided to move
on Pont-à-Vendin again. Early on the morning of August 17, the Flemings advanced to the village of Mons-en-Pévèle and forced the King to
halt. After knighting many squires, Philip divided his troops into 15

divisions and tried to tire the battle-eager Flemings by waiting out the day. That evening, the Flemings made a surprise attack on the French camp south of the village. Always in the first lines of battle, William of Gulik entered deep into the enemy lines, where according to legend he drank from the king's cup in the royal pavilion. Philip barely escaped death, thanks to his bodyguards, who tore off his surcotte decorated with lilies so that he could not be recognized. Thus members of the royal retinue rescued Philip, many sacrificing their lives in the process.[7] However, it would appear that such acts of courage were rare. Panicking French knights fled their camp in whole battles, some never to return to the battlefield.[8]

> Public opinion in France could not understand that brave knights sometimes had to flee when they were defeated. In such a case, the nobility was considered suspect, or else was openly accused of treason. Such accusations were made after the defeat at Courtrai. The nobles were said to have behaved treasonably in September 1302 during the retreat of the royal army. They were again accused of treason when the knights fled in panic at Mons-en-Pevele.[9]

This retreat took them out of range of the Flemings, where Philip was able to re-form most of his units at a safe distance.[10] The king advanced to give battle and personally led his reserve. The Flemings were winning when the contingents of Ghent, Ypres and Kortrijk left the field, a pattern that would recur in future engagements. The French held the field and so were proclaimed the victors, but were too damaged to pursue the Flemish militias.[11] After the battle, William of Gulik was never found, a fact which fed legends that one day he would return to lead his country to victory when it needed him most. Not yet thirty years old, he became Flanders' knight in shining armor.

Flemish reverses at this indecisive battle led the Count to seek a settlement. After a new Flemish army appeared before Lille, negotiations were opened that led to the peace of Athis-sur-Orge of June 1305. Although the urban privileges of Flanders were confirmed, the treaty obliged the Flemings to pay an enormous indemnity within four years and a perpetual rent of £20,000 (half of which was to go to the count), provide the king with 600 soldiers, and destroy the fortifications of the major cities. Bruges was compelled to send 3,000 citizens on pilgrimages as a punishment for the Matins. The Leliaarts who had been damaged due to their loyalty to the king would be compensated. All Flemings over 14 years of age, including the Count, were to swear eternal fidelity to the king. Until the peace was fulfilled, the Count pledged the castellanies of Lille, Douai and Béthune and the castles of Kortrijk and Cassel to the king.[12]

Having returned for a short visit to Flanders in 1304, Count Guy of Dampierre died in captivity at Compiègne in France before the treaty was signed. His beloved daughter Philippa died in Paris the next year. Despite some romantic stories suggesting he was present at Kortrijk, Robert of Béthune was only released from prison around the time of his father's death. As the new count, he was granted two major concessions from the French king. He was justifiable before his peers rather than before parlement, and Holland/Hainault was not included in the peace, leaving him free to pursue his war in Zeeland against the Avesnes.[13]

Militarily Flanders was not defeated. The cities refused to accept such an unfavorable treaty, accusing the Count and his family of complicity with the French. No guildsman had been part of the negotiations. Plagued by mass migrations of refugees from the instability, the cities had incurred enormous debts from the war. This led to forced loans and high taxes. Dissension also arose in the Count's family. Robert of Béthune showed little independence until 1309, but his eldest son Louis I of Nevers opposed all concessions with France. Philip the Fair had confiscated Louis's fiefs in France and a court of peers jailed the Count's son in 1311. He escaped to Imperial Flanders.[14]

The alliance of convenience between the Count and the towns disintegrated. Almost none of the provisions agreed at Athis-sur-Orge ever saw the light of day. Eventually under the Treaty of Pontoise of July 11, 1312, Lille, Douai, Orchies and Béthune were annexed to the French royal domain. The Five Cities became three, but the total incorporation of Flanders was no longer a question.

Although the old families once again ruled the major cities by

1312, the burghers never held the great powers of their predecessors again. The guilds had invested themselves with new privileges, and infighting among the victors followed. The prosperity of Flanders declined during a century of revolutionary unrest.

After the Battle of the Golden Spurs, Jan Breidel moved into the confiscated home of a Leliaart. He was given a number of profitable positions and was active in municipal politics, including a number of violent incidents. Though he never sought any higher office, a variety of surviving documents indicate that he was one of Bruges's wealthiest citizens up to his death sometime between 1328 and 1331. Like Breidel, de Coninck also took over the home of a Leliaart. He became an alderman in Bruges and was granted an annual pension of £1000 by the Count.[15] Although he did not occupy another official post, he continued to support the commoners and influence policy as a popular radical leader. However, he chose the side of the Count during a popular revolt in 1321 and was required to leave the city. He died in 1332 or January 1333.[16]

The hot-tempered Willem van Saeftingen apparently found abbey life dissatisfying. He severely wounded Ter Doest's abbot and cruelly killed its aged cellarer in a rebellion of lay brothers against the monastery's authorities. He fled to the tower of the Church of Our Lady in Lissewege, which was besieged by monks and men of the village. Hearing this news, Jan Breidel, a son of Peter de Coninck and about eighty well armed men from Bruges put the besiegers to flight, rescued Willem and took him to their city where he lived the rest of his life. Although he did not belong to Bruges by birth, he was in favor with the city, as a result of his record at Kortrijk.[17] This was one of many cases in which military prowess in the fight against the French could get support for virtually any kind of behavior.

Public order was never a strong suit in medieval Flanders. Social class and "nationalism" have frequently been cited as the cause of Flanders' internal discord during this era. However, family honor, political control, private ambition, and the tendency for killing to beget more killing provide much stronger explanations. Conditions were confused, particularly in the cities. The burghers of the major cities were immune from prosecution outside of their home cities, even for offenses committed outside the walls. Such a state of affairs was sure to be abused. In Ypres in late November 1303 seven aldermen and councilors were killed by mobs for collecting an unauthorized tax. Forty-four persons were executed for murder and five for robbery. Significantly, Ypres' agreement to accept the verdict was made under the seals of the town and five guilds: the weavers, fullers, shearers, butchers and fishmongers. Each guild was to choose a captain from its members to keep the peace.[18]

The ousted Leliaarts were allowed to return to Ghent under the terms of Athis-sur-Orge. The old feuds immediately reemerged. The son of the bailiff murdered by Jan Borluut in 1294 failed in two attempts to kill Borluut but finally got him on a third as he left a drinking bout in the town hall in December 1305. The usual penalty for murder was a pilgrimage to some distant location and the payment of blood money. But severity of punishment was based on the social standing of the person killed and whether the deed had been done during or outside of a truce. Both sides agreed that the aldermen and count should arbitrate. On June 10, 1306, a settlement to end the feud was announced. The Borluuts were required to send fifteen men on pilgrimages and the van Sinte Baafs twelve. The Borluuts paid slightly more in blood money and personal injury claims, while the Sinte Baafs paid more judicial fines. Because his victim was not a landed man of the city, Jan Borluut's shocking murder of Jan Staes was atoned by his family with a simple money payment. The families were collectively responsible for carrying out the terms.[19]

A cutthroat atmosphere prevailed. One Gentenaar Leliaart who profited greatly from the Flemish rebellion was Wasselin Haec, who fled to Paris after 1302. Once a Liebaart, Haec amassed great wealth after being entrusted with the confiscation of Liebaart property in France.[20]

Flanders suffered further setbacks. From the 1290s the English began raising duties on wool exports, driving up the prices of Flemish cloth. By that time, the drapers of Ypres were buying wool directly in England. Late in his reign, Philip the Fair annexed the county of

Champagne to his royal domain and tried to bring Flanders to its knees by severely restricting the fairs. Flemish textile exports reached their peak in the late thirteenth century and started to decline. The wool trade recovered rapidly between 1302 and 1315, but then long-term decline set in.[21] The Hundred Years War, together with the increasing importance of the sea routes from Italy to the Low Countries after 1277, caused the grand fairs to decline by the mid–1300s. Thus the role of Flemish merchants in the French wine trade to Flanders and England declined. Trade fairs never disappeared, but they became little more than regional markets at which farm produce and livestock were sold. Merchants now started to operate out of offices in all major European cities and no longer traveled about. Economic adversity, accompanied by political and social unrest, was to mark the rest of the fourteenth century. The economic rise of England also forced changes. Flanders remained hopelessly dependent on imports at a time when war, famine and plague were profoundly disrupting trade patterns.

Meanwhile, events on the other side of Europe swept the continent into controversy. Boniface VIII's papacy ended in a tragic conflict between Rome and Philip the Fair. In the papal bull *Ad Clericos* Boniface had asserted that no cleric should pay taxes to a king without papal consent. Philip counteracted by issuing an edict banning the export of currency. After the publication of the even stronger bull *Unam Sanctam*, which asserted papal dominance over monarchs, a campaign against the Pope swept France. Fearing that a possible excommunication could give his enemies within France an excuse to foment rebellion, Philip went on the offensive. Boniface was labeled a usurper, a murderer and even a heretic. Leading these attacks, zealous and unscrupulous Guillaume de Nogaret spoke out against the Pope at the Assembly of the Louvre on March 12, 1303. Since Pierre Flotte's death at Kortrijk, he had emerged as Philip's chief advisor. Allied with Florentine banker Musciatto de Franzesi and the head of the Ghibelline party, Sciarra Colonna, de Nogaret went to Italy with a band of armed men, who together with Sciarra Colonna and his followers attacked and captured the aged Pope Boniface VIII in his palace in Anagni on September 7, 1303. After one of de Nogaret's men struck the Pope, the townspeople of Anagni rallied to Boniface's aid and surrounded the palace. After a few tense days under siege, de Nogaret released Boniface because he realized he would never be able to get the Pope out of the village. The Pope immediately excommunicated Philip with the Papal Bull *Super Solio* of September 20, 1303. Boniface died a bitter man in Rome on October 11.[22]

Early in 1304, de Nogaret explained his actions to the king, and received considerable property as a result. Philip even sent him as his emissary to the new pope, Benedict XI, who refused to absolve Philip from the excommunication. However, Benedict's reign lasted only two years. His successor, a Frenchman, Bertrand de Got, Archbishop of Lyons, who reigned as Clement V, backed down from his predecessor's intransigent position and dissolved the excommunication in 1311. Clement promptly appointed a number of French cardinals, but was unable to establish himself among the angry Romans. He was unable to travel to Rome even for his election. Philip saw a golden opportunity to dominate the papacy and pressured the Pope, now critically ill with cancer, to move to France. Not wanting to appear a puppet of the French king by moving to Paris, Clement took his huge court to Avignon on the Rhône in southern France in 1309. Technically an enclave of the Holy Roman Empire, Avignon was a reasonable compromise, given his desire to ultimately relocate to Rome.

Clement never left Avignon, and a French-dominated College of Cardinals would name his successors for another 54 years, a period known as the "Babylonian Captivity" of the Church. Ultimately, this state of affairs provoked the Great Schism, a forty-year struggle within the church between popes in Rome and rival antipopes in Avignon. Not surprisingly, the English, Flemings and most Italians supported the pope in Rome, while the French, Spanish and Scots sided with the Avignon claimant. Finally, a Spaniard was elected and moved the papal court back to Rome. Not long thereafter, Italians regained their monopoly on the papacy. Dissatisfaction with the Church was widespread. In England this manifested itself in John Wyclif's calls for reforms in 1376 and the Peasants' Revolt of 1381. At a time of many other crises, the faithful found little harmony in their mother church.

The Golden Spurs of Kortrijk

With the Church neutralized, Philip the Fair moved against his other enemies. In 1306, he expelled the Jews from France and confiscated their wealth. He then confiscated the assets of the Lombards, Italian bankers in France. However, his greatest rivals were within the inner sanctum of Christendom: the Knights Templar. Originally founded to protect pilgrims going to the Holy Land, after the Crusades the Templars had grown to be a hidden empire within Europe. Philip's financial difficulties may have led to their downfall, as he owed them money due to the huge expenditures of trying to expand his realm. His proceeds from looting the Jews and Lombards was insufficient to cope with his debts. Once again the French king cast an envious eye on a rival's powerful influence and considerable wealth. And once again Guillaume de Nogaret played a decisive role in his lord's schemes. At Maubuisson on September 22, 1307, Philip issued a warrant for the arrest of the Templars, which was executed on October 12. The Knights were accused of all manner of crimes, ranging from sorcery to heresy to debauchery to losing the Holy Land to the infidel.[23] De Nogaret personally arrested the Knights of the Temple in Paris. He directed the trials that ended with the execution of the order's Grandmaster Jacques de Molay and the other leading Templars in 1314. That same year de Nogaret tried to justify the condemnation of the Templars by announcing plans for a new crusade, the expenses of which were to be defrayed by the confiscated property of the order.[24]

From the stake on which he was burned Jacques de Molay swore that Pope Clement V would die within forty days and that Philip would not see in the end of the year. His prophecies proved mysteriously accurate. The pope died on April 20, 1314. De Nogaret died later in that year. On November 29, Philip the Fair was mortally injured in a hunting accident at his birthplace, Fontainebleau. Little did he realize how easily his lifetime of scheming would be undone. The empire he had devoted himself to establishing was to be attacked from all quarters.

Philip's death marked the beginning of a decline in the French monarchy's power. Philip's heir, Louis X, "the Quarrelsome" (1314–16), faced discontent among the nobles. Among these was Robert of

6. The Aftermath

Béthune, who had begun to adopt a more independent posture towards Paris after 1309. However, the Count's cause never gained the level of urban support it had in 1302. Furthermore, troubles continued to split the Count's family. Robert of Cassel, the Count's younger son, made trouble over his presumed exclusion from the succession and was bought off with a rent of £10,000 secured to Imperial Flanders.

Bruges remained the most anti-royal of the cities, while Ghent and the other towns made separate treaties with the French. The peace of Arras in July 1313 placed Kortrijk under French rule as a guarantee. In 1314 Robert broke off dealings with the French, ejected them from Kortrijk and besieged Lille. In 1315 Louis X allied himself with Hainault for an invasion of Flanders. But heavy rains made troop movements impossible. The Flemish cities opened negotiations, which led to the Treaty of Paris of September 1, 1316, which confirmed the status quo but intensified the Flemish cities' financial obligations. The Leliaart and Liebaart (now known as Klaewaart) parties revived. Most Leliaarts exiled in 1302 now returned to Flanders.

Multiple disasters struck Flanders from 1315 to 1317. Europe's climate had generally been favorable during the thirteenth century. But then it began to change. Harvests were poor after 1310, and the rains which stopped the invasion of Flanders in 1315 also wiped out that year's harvest. The result was a Europe-wide famine, which was most severe in the highly populated southern Low Countries. Grain reached twenty-four times its normal price. In the first known mass transport of food from southern to northern Europe, Italian merchants brought grain to Flanders. The magistrates of Bruges sold the imported grain at cost, first to their citizens and then to others. The next year the weakened population was decimated by an epidemic. This pestilence was made worse by the crowded conditions of the cities and the fact that Europeans had not dealt with a major epidemic for some 400 years. 2,800 Yprois and 2,000 Brugeois were carried from the streets to mass graves.[25] The growth of Flemish towns stabilized and even dropped in some places.

On Louis X's death, Salic law was invoked to prevent his daughter from succeeding to the throne. His brother, Philip V, "the Tall," replaced him. In 1319 Robert of Béthune prepared to attack Lille, but the Gentenaars spoiled his campaign by refusing to send their militia across the Leie. The next year the "Regime of the Captains" restored Leliaart rule in Ghent. On May 5, 1320, a second Treaty of Paris renewed Robert of Béthune's tie to the French crown and arranged the marriage of his grandson and eventual successor, Louis of Nevers (the Younger), to Philip V's daughter Marguerite. Troubles between Philip and prominent French nobles distracted the French from Flanders. However, Philip was soon succeeded by Charles IV, "the Fair," who reigned only six years (1322–28), during which Robert of Béthune died in 1325.

In 1323, a rebellion, backed by Bruges, broke out in the Westhoek region of maritime Flanders under a local leader, Niklaas Zannekin. Forced to evacuate Ypres, Louis of Nevers was captured at Kortrijk and handed over to the Brugeois. The rebels then chose his uncle, Robert of Cassel, as regent. Meanwhile the militia of Ghent remained faithful to the captured Louis and recognized John of Namur as regent. The rebels attacked Oudenaarde, then defeated the Gentenaars at Deinze on July 15. John of Namur defended Ghent successfully against them with only Oudenaarde and Aalst as allies. Count John and the city of Ghent agreed not to make separate peaces with Bruges and the rebels. Ghent was placed under the medieval equivalent of martial law. Restrictions on the movements of traders and an economic embargo of the rebel areas were announced. The rebels surrounded the city and imposed a blockade in retaliation. Ambassadors from Ghent went to Paris, and the French king then forbade all trade with Flanders. The count's forces were confined to the city, except for 200 crossbowmen and 3,000 levies who were used for raids beyond the city's walls. Plundering was forbidden. Count John's plans succeeded in loosening the grip of Ghent.[26]

The rebellion culminated in a battle near Cassel in August 1328. The rebels from Westhoek overextended themselves by trying to push southwards to surprise their foes. An impressive French army, composed of ten battles with 177 banners, advanced to attack Zannekin's forces. With reinforcements it finally totaled 196 banners.[27] The King's forces charged. "The French thought that they were riding to their deaths, or at least that they would lose their horses in a charge against the crown-formation of Zannekin's closely packed troops. They opened up their own encircling formation to let the Flemings get away, and so to kill them more easily."[28] Despite the fears of the French, the coastal rebels were crushed and Zannekin was killed. Bruges was punished with severe fines for its support of the rebels.

One of the difficulties facing Flemish forces through this era was their inability to activate and concentrate all or even most of their forces at the same time. At Kortrijk in 1302, only troops from part of the county were present. Ghent was noticeably absent. At Arques in 1303, only the Westhoek militias fought. Zierikzee and Mons-en-Pévèle occurred roughly at the same time. Hence, all Flemish forces were again unable to go into action at the same time on one field of battle. Finally, at Cassel in 1328 again only Westhoek forces fought.[29]

With the death of all of Philip the Fair's sons, none of whom had heirs of their own, the crown passed by noble election from the main line of the Capetians to Charles's cousin Philip VI of the cadet house of Valois. Almost immediately, the ambitious Edward III of England claimed the French throne by right of his mother Isabella, daughter of Philip IV. Having little sense of "Englishness," most of the English nobility spoke French and traced their power and lineage to French sources. Edward was no exception. This succession crisis, along with long-running disputes over English-ruled Gascony and Aquitaine, trade rivalries over Flanders, civil war in Brittany, French aid to the Scots and English aid to the Flemings, led to an intensification of a conflict already two centuries old.

Flanders featured prominently in these struggles. The new count of Flanders, Louis of Nevers, made Flanders virtually a French province, causing many Flemish weavers and shipbuilders to emigrate to England. An uprising swept the county, leaving Louis with only the city of Ghent under his control. French king Philip VI of Valois responded to the count's pleas for help by invading Flanders and defeating the Flemings at Ypres. Edward III then intervened, as Flanders' freedom was now seen as vital to England's prosperity.[30] In 1336 Count

Louis arrested all Englishmen in Flanders. In retaliation Edward seized Flemings in England and banned the export of English wool. As Flemish looms fell silent, Ghent rebelled under Jacob van Artevelde, a rich burgher, who made a treaty with England. Joined by Bruges and Ypres in 1337, van Artevelde effectively ruled Flanders until his death nine years later. Louis de Nevers sought the protection of Philip VI, while van Artevelde played a dangerous game of intrigue between France, who was still Flanders' official overlord, and England, the source of its livelihood. The spark which set off the long conflict later known as the Hundred Years War was the coronation of Edward III of England as king of France in Ghent. Beginning in 1337, this conflict would comprise dozens of starts and stops and numerous noble maneuvers before ending in 1453.

Marching from Valenciennes on the Flemish border, 12,000 English soldiers and German mercenaries attacked Cambrai on September 20, 1339, and advanced into France. However, Edward failed in this campaign after Philip VI bribed the dukes of Brabant and Gueldres, the count of Hainault and the margrave of Juliers to support him. French armies returned to Flanders

Philip VI responded to the English claims by mobilizing the Norman fleet, hoping to repeat William the Conqueror's success. However, he made the mistake of dismissing two squadrons of Italian galleys, who in 1338 had given him the mastery of the Channel. His fleet consisted of two hundred heavy ships, encircled by barges, arranged in three divisions. In the Zwin estuary, the head of which then extended as far as Bruges, 25,000 men were waiting to invade England when Edward III pre-empted their attack. Despite the lesson given to Philip Augustus, and against the advice of the Genoese Barbavera, who wished to fight at sea, French admiral Quiéret had anchored between Damme and Sluis. On June 24, 1340, an English fleet of some 250 ships, commanded by Morley and Fitzalan, attacked the French in this restrictive waterway. Surrounded by the English fleet by sea and Flemish pillagers on land, the French sailors were pressed against great dikes, described by Dante in his *Inferno*. The fire of 12,000 English archers crushed Quiéret's force, while only 400 French crossbowmen could reply. The French fleet failed to break out and lost 190 ships and 20,000 men. With the Channel under England's thumb, Philip's invasion plans were abandoned.[31]

Though smaller than France in population, The English had better, more mobile troops, better leadership at the outset, a more efficient government, and thousands of booty-hungry soldiers eager to enrich themselves with a campaign in France. They scored significant early victories. Along with Sluis in 1340, Crécy followed in 1346 and Calais the following year. The Count of Flanders, Louis of Never, was among the dead at Crécy. His son, Louis of Male became the new count.

The Black Death halted the war for three years. Arriving in Sicily with Genoese sailors in 1347, Black Death ravaged Europe, decimating Flanders in 1349 before sweeping through Russia by 1351. At least a quarter of the continent's population fell victim.

In 1350 Philip VI died and was succeeded by Jean II, who was defeated and captured by Edward, the Black Prince, at Poitiers in 1356. The Dauphin Charles, serving as regent during John's imprisonment, attempted to reassert greater royal control through the French parliament, the Estates-General. Led by merchant Etienne Marcel, the Estates-General attempted a series of reforms. By 1358 widespread opposition led to civil war and a rebellion known as the Jacquerie.

In 1360 the Treaty of Brétigny brought peace with England, but gave up large territories south of the Loire in return for Edward III's renunciation of his claim to the French throne. In 1363 Philip the Bold, son of Jean II, became Duke of Burgundy, while his brother Charles V, "the Wise," succeeded his father in 1364. Although he failed to annex Brittany, he and the able Bertrand du Guesclin, Constable of France, were successful in reconquering most of English occupied territories, defeating the Spanish, regaining control of the English Channel after a naval battle at La Rochelle, and restoring some power of the crown. But he was succeeded by Charles VI, "the Mad," who was insane after 1392. Violent aristocratic quarrels led the powerful, independent-minded duke of Burgundy to ally himself with the English.

Another phase of the war began. Edward the Black Prince sacked Limoges in 1370. Three years later, the duke of Lancaster and son of

Edward III, John of Gaunt, led a new English invasion of France. "Gaunt" is in fact a variation of "Ghent," to which he had ancestral ties. In 1374 John of Gaunt returned to England to take charge of the government. Edward III was now in his dotage and his heir, the Black Prince, was deathly ill. The prince died in 1376, at the age of 45, and his son was crowned Richard II after his grandfather's death in 1389. Assuming power at age 22, Richard II campaigned to subdue Ireland and married seven-year-old Princess Isabella of France. By 1398 Richard proclaimed himself absolute ruler. Following John of Gaunt's death, his oldest son, Henry of Bolingbroke, landed in Yorkshire, rapidly gained support, deposed Richard II and became Henry IV of England.

Meanwhile, Philip van Artevelde, son of Jacob, had hoped to ally Ghent with England, but no English aid was forthcoming, and a French army was dispatched north once again to assert the king's influence. Again the Flemings marched south with their banners and goedendags. The two forces met near the village of Westrozebeke, a few miles from Passchendaele, where another of history's great battles would unfold in the First World War. The Flemings were confident, while the French were anxious. Even the king's constable felt compelled to resign for the day. Another royal defeat in Flanders would have meant that the world of chivalry would be "dead and lost in France."[32] On top of all of this, it was raining.

Van Artevelde, who had already defeated the count of Flanders, was eager for a fight. Like the Flemish commanders at Kortrijk, van Artevelde ordered his army to take no prisoners other than the king himself, adding "for he is but a child who acts only as instructed. We shall bring him to Ghent and teach him to speak Flemish."[33] On the morning of November 29, 1382, the two sides moved towards each other in a thick mist. This time both sides were on foot. Flemish crossbows and bombards opened up on the French ranks, while the French advanced with their pole weapons. The French center almost gave way but gradually the king's forces were able to compress their enemy's formation. The Flemings were unable to maneuver their pikes and goedendags, while the French hacked away at their solid mass with axes and lances. Van Artevelde was unable to maintain control as the French counterattack turned into a rout. Along with his legendary banner-bearer, a woman named Big Margot, he was trampled by his own forces. Indeed, after the battle many Flemish bodies were found without wounds, suffocated in their mass formation. Once it was apparent that their victory was assured, the French knights mounted their horses to finish the job.

Following the engagement at Westrozebeke, Kortrijk was sacked mercilessly, even though Count Louis of Male begged on his knees for mercy on the town. When Charles VI heard of the golden spurs on the church wall, he demanded an indemnity and burned the town.[34] Virtually every house was ransacked and many citizens were carried away for ransom. The repression also included 224 executions in Bruges. Despite their great victory, the French never took Ghent. Soon the Royal House of France and the overlords of Flanders would part ways. Count Louis of Male's son Philip succeeded to the thrones of both Flanders and Burgundy in 1384. Known as Philip the Bold, he would mold an independent empire from his holdings and conquests extending from Holland to Switzerland.

In 1415, Henry V of England won the Battle of Agincourt and with the help of the Burgundians overran northern France, including Paris. Forced on the French, the Treaty of Troyes made Henry V regent of France and disinherited the French heir. The English king married Charles VI's daughter Catherine of Valois and was to succeed to the French throne on Charles's death. Both kings died in 1422, Henry before Charles. Henry's nine-month-old son Henry VI was proclaimed king of France in Paris, while Charles VI's son was simultaneously proclaimed king at Bourges as Charles VII. The power of the French monarch was at an all-time low. However, the victories of Joan of Arc encouraged the French. Gradually the conquests of the English were won back. At great expense, most of central France was fortified, making it more difficult for the English to live off the land. Meanwhile the conduct of the English in France drove the Burgundians back into the French camp. The 1435 Treaty of Arras restored relations between the French and Burgundians. Paris was recaptured in 1436. By the war's end in 1453, only Calais remained in English hands.

The Golden Spurs of Kortrijk

The last great medieval war, the Hundred Years War was not just a war between kings, but also between lesser nobles pursuing their own personal agendas. Neither side really won. Both sides exhausted themselves, sometimes to the point of provoking civil wars, but a sense of nationhood pervaded both kingdoms by the war's end. Gunpowder, standing armies and patriotism came to the fore in this conflict.

Though gaining many powerful enemies early in his reign, Louis XI, who succeeded Charles VII in 1461, did much to bolster French royal power. He fomented rebellions in Flanders against Burgundian rule and won back Normandy. He blocked the schemes of Charles the Bold, who was killed at the Battle of Nancy in 1477. He seized Burgundy and Artois, but was frustrated by the marriage of Charles the Bold's daughter Mary of Burgundy to Archduke Maximilian of Austria, who thereby acquired the Burgundian Netherlands (modern Belgium and the Netherlands) for the Habsburgs. Mary of Burgundy's daughter, Margaret of Austria, was engaged to be married to Louis's infant son, the future Charles VIII. But a dynastic dispute led to the breaking of the engagement, and France had to cede Franche-Comté to Austria in compensation. Eventually the royal houses of Burgundy, Spain and Austria melded into the House of Hapsburg. Meanwhile, the Valois line ruled France to the end of the 1500s. For centuries, French kings and Hapsburg emperors, each claiming to be the heirs of Charlemagne, would struggle for dominance. In the course of the latter's attempts to encircle and contain France, Flanders became part of the Spanish Netherlands, later the Austrian Netherlands.

Fourteenth century Bruges remained one of the most prosperous cities in Europe. Its 40,000 citizens were a major market in their own right. Its manufacturers boasted advanced technical skills, and their products grew increasingly refined. Large volumes of textiles produced in rural Flanders, Brabant and Artois were exported entirely through Bruges. In 1340, a fifth of its population was employed as tailors, skilled craftsmen or utensil makers. Another quarter was active in wholesale trade, in finance and as broker-hoteliers.[35] Bruges was a major international center with an advanced financial system.

6. The Aftermath

Wool and sheepskins, lead and tin were imported from England and Scotland. Hides, wood, copper, dried and pickled fish, pitch and potash from the Baltic were offered for sale by the German Hansa. Wine was imported from France, the Rhine and Italy. The Iberian Peninsula provided oranges and lemons, leather, wool, iron ore and sugar, while the Italians traded in luxury products, spices and other goods. Many of the imported products were processed in Bruges. The city was also the point of contact between the Mediterranean world (Italy, Spain and Portugal) and the north (Flanders, England and the Hanseatic League). The international presence in Bruges took on an added dimension towards the end of the fourteenth century with the dynastic fusion of the County of Flanders and the Duchy of Burgundy.[36]

Particularly important in the constant inflation, speculation and currency debasement of the fourteenth century, moneychangers and bankers cooperated with the city's broker-hoteliers to provide financial services to traders, including current accounts, deposits, transfers, long- and short-term loans and investments, and even banknotes for local use. The use of letters of exchange rather than cash became the norm. Italian bankers were particularly prominent. Not surprisingly, trade in Bruges focused around the Beursplein, where the Genoese, Florentine and Venetian communities had their headquarters and the Van der Beurse family ran their inn.

When taken over by the Burgundians in the fifteenth century, Flanders was still one of the most prosperous regions of the Low Countries, despite its tribulations. The reasons for this are complex:

There was overpopulation and economic distress, but there is no direct evidence linking this to a decline of the Flemish textile industry. Flanders did not even come close to having a monopoly of the international trade in woollen cloth. The drop in the overseas trade was not as catastrophic as it would necessarily have been if the Flemish economy had been as dominated by export textiles as was once thought. The wealth and political power of the Flemish nobility was declining, but the urban elites remained very rich. Much Flemish cloth was sold on an internal market swollen by overpopulation, as evinced by statutes of Ypres and Ghent forbidding their citizens to buy cloth except that of the home city. Although the city governments of the fourteenth century seemed to be under a different impression, textiles were not the only source of wealth for Flanders. The grain trade, peat exports, brokerage and other forms of manufacture were also important. Furthermore, although the textile industries of the large cities were declining, it is not at all certain that Flanders taken as a whole produced less cash value in cloth in 1400 than in 1300,...[37]

The counts also placed their finances on a different footing. They no longer resorted to forced loans in emergencies as they had in the 1200s. A count's income had long ceased to be dependent on his domain. New tolls and commercial revenues brought him less than two other sources: taxes known as aids, which had to be levied with the consent of the Five, later Three Cities and the Transport of Flanders, the rent paid to the counts as a result of their agreement with Philip the Fair, which became his first regular source of income apart from the domain. "The rate of assessment [of the Transport] was supposedly assigned on the basis of the ability of each unit to pay; the very fact that such an assessment was attempted shows that the counts had much more sophisticated records of local income and property holding than have survived. The Three Cities in combination paid nearly two-fifths of the Transport assessment, with Bruges the richest and Ypres, at about two-thirds Bruges's rate, the poorest; but since the cities and the count by then were the real government of Flanders, with other groups having little power, it is likely that they were in fact underassessed."[38]

After 1302, economic growth slowed and the guild system had to face new and harsher conditions. Many guilds restricted admission and promotion and lowered costs, quality, working conditions and contributions to charity. They took work from smaller guilds and defended their monopolies, by violence if necessary. But the situation did not improve. Warfare, the Black Death and even the weather contributed to rapid economic decline. Stability and concern for the common good had traditionally been favored over efficiency and profit. The system was designed to be cooperative rather than competitive. Now it was neither.

When markets began to shrink after 1350, many long-distance

merchants began to bypass the guilds by manufacturing their own products to lower their costs. Hence, Flanders saw the birth of the putting-out system of manufacturing. This mode of production was rooted in a complex network of subcontracted labor. Merchants distributed raw fiber to spinners, weavers and fullers scattered throughout the town in hundreds of households, often visited by inspectors. They would then collect the finished cloth, pay the artisan a fee, and sell the final product at a profit. Common in the production of candles, clocks, pewter, clothing and hats, as well as woven cloth, this mode of production would be Europe's principal form of manufacturing until the Industrial Revolution of the early nineteenth century.

Some merchants concentrated equipment in a warehouse or "factory" and hired workers for wages only. The old production quotas and concept of a just price were abandoned. This system was primarily for processes consisting of several steps or dealing with heavy materials. It eventually developed into the centralized factory system which characterized the Industrial Revolution and which remains prevalent in our post-industrial era. Not surprisingly, Belgium followed closely behind Britain in industrialization in the 1800s.[39]

The craft guilds fought these proto-capitalistic developments, but were defeated.[40] The new bosses were not as civic-minded as the old and urban life deteriorated. Living standards dropped. Until the 1700s, much production was moved to the countryside, where the manorial system disappeared. The medieval structure of social classes was replaced by the modern concept of economic classes. Wealth was concentrated in fewer hands. Although class wars persisted in many places, most guilds eventually disappeared. However, some held on for centuries, especially in retail trade and small-scale services. Guilds of butchers and bakers continued until the appearance of supermarkets and shopping centers after World War II. Labor unions were inspired by the artisan brotherhoods of the Middle Ages. Modern professional organizations for occupations ranging from medicine to plumbing drew their roots from medieval guilds.

Originating from the guilds, the urban militias foreshadowed the rise of mass armies. In the mid–1300s Flemish communal armies were even stronger than in the early years of the century. It is possible that in 1304 Flanders had at least 20,000 or 24,000 men under arms in Zeeland and along the French border. The Transport of Flanders fixed the number of soldiers to be sent by every town, based on taxation. An army of 10,000 consisted of 1,520 men from Bruges, 1,384 from Ghent, 1,333 from coastal Flanders and 1,072 from Ypres. In 1340 Bruges and Ghent sent large armies to serve Edward III. The total strength of the Bruges militia was 8,280 men and Ghent 5,455. At Cassel in 1328 at least 3,185 Flemings from the Westhoek alone were killed of a force that could have numbered 8,000. The Flemings had three such forces at the time.[41]

The political configurations of Western Europe changed rapidly in the 1300s. In the 1338 Declaration of Rense, the electors of Holy Roman Empire declared the empire independent of the papacy. That same year the Empire allied itself to England by the Treaty of Koblenz. The Golden Bull of 1356 provided the Holy Roman Empire with a new constitution, in which seven electors were mandated to choose future emperors. Meanwhile, the English removed the pope's power to give English benefices to foreigners in 1351, and two years later, the English Parliament forbade appeals to the pope with the Statute of Praemunire.

Much happened in the fourteenth century beyond the rather narrow confines of the struggles in what is now labeled Western Europe. Southern Europe continued to be a trendsetter for the continent. The Italian poet Petrarch was born two years after the Battle of the Golden Spurs, while Geoffrey Chaucer began work on his Canterbury Tales by 1387. The Renaissance approached. John I founded the Avis Dynasty in Portugal in 1382. His son Prince Henry the Navigator, also the grandson of John of Gaunt, paved the way for tiny Portugal to become a major maritime power by establishing a naval institute at Sarges in 1439. In the north, the Teutonic Knights defeated the Poles in 1333. In the Peace of Kalish, which followed ten years later, Poland, once Europe's largest country in area, was cut off from the Baltic Sea, signaling its gradual partition. Farther west, seventy-seven Hanse towns joined in the Confederation of Cologne to oppose Denmark. The 1370

6. *The Aftermath*

Peace of Stralsund established the Hanseatic League's right to veto Danish kings. By 1397 the Union of Kalmar united Norway, Denmark and Sweden under King Eric of Pomerania.

While an unstable Europe passed through difficult times, elsewhere great powers emerged that outshone even the greatest of Christendom's monarchies. Defeating the Serbs at Kossovo in 1389, the Ottoman Turks conquered all of Asia Minor by 1390 and Bulgaria by 1396. The fall of Constantinople followed 52 years later. Building an empire on three continents, Turkey would be a major power until the First World War. In 1363 Mongol leader Tamerlane (Timur the Lame) began his conquest of Asia, ultimately becoming king of Samarkand in 1369. Five years later, a rebellion led by Chu Yuan-chang overthrew the Mongols in China and ushered in the Ming Dynasty, which lasted until 1644. Laying the foundations of India's great Mughal Dynasty, Tamerlane went on to ravage the Sultanate of Delhi in 1398. Meanwhile Mansa Musa, king of Mali from 1307 to 1332, presided over a vast, wealthy West African empire, while in 1325 the Aztecs founded Tenochtitlan (now Mexico City).

In Europe, the Age of Faith had yielded to a new era of doubt. The world was a larger place than the medieval mind had imagined. The old restraints on excess and violence were thrown off. The knighthood did not protect. Indeed, indebted nobles came to be a scourge, thieving land and abusing their subjects. Appropriately, one source describes this phenomenon as "fur collar crime."[42] The guild system was shaken with discord and unfathomable economic difficulties. A worldly Church seemed more interested in its internal politics than in guiding the way to God. The population, depleted by the Black Death and oppressed by their masters, were all too ready to question. Discord, war and pestilence had taken their toll.

7

The Legacy

Much can still be found which evokes the era of the Battle of the Golden Spurs. Instability following the battle did not stop Kortrijk's development.[1] Sometime before 1307, weavers built a covered market on Kortrijk's main square. By 1313 Kortrijk's castle was again occupied by the French. The Flemish cities rebelled against Count Louis de Nevers, who sought the refuge of Kortrijk's fortifications in 1323. In order to protect the town from invading troops from Bruges, the Count ordered buildings around the town burned. Unfortunately the wind blew the flames inside the walls and much more was destroyed.

Opposing the count, who supported France, Ghent, led by Jacob van Artevelde, brought Kortrijk under its authority in 1337. During the Hundred Years' war, both Kortrijk and Ghent supported England. In 1340 the French attacked Kortrijk, which was the base for about 1,000 soldiers from Ghent. In 1366, Philip of Artois, Bishop of Tournai, approved the construction of a refuge for pilgrims and wanderers with a chapel in St-Elooi's house, site of St-Elooi's church today. Supporting Ghent in another revolt against the Count, Kortrijk became a military center in 1380.

Gentenaar leader Philip van Artevelde conquered much of the County in 1382 and, assuming the powers of a count, changed Kortrijk's laws. The French troops attacked the town as an ally of Ghent.

The Golden Spurs of Kortrijk

On November 27, 1382, Kortrijk was destroyed after the battle of Westrozebeke. It was rebuilt in 1386. One victim of this destruction was thirteenth century Sint-Maarten's church, which was rebuilt at the beginning of the fifteenth century. Its pointed tower was added after its original tower was wrecked in 1682. Built in Gothic style, it is noted for its baptistery, Baroque pulpit, 49-bell carillon, paintings by Flemish masters, and finely sculpted Burgundian white stone Way of the Cross.

Construction in the town continued in 1401 with the completion of the Inghelborchtoren, the second Broel tower, and the bridge over the Leie connecting it with the earlier Speyetoren, which had been built before the battle. Surviving to the present, these towers, the oldest remaining parts of the town's fortifications, have had different functions over time, first as gates, then as powder magazines, and later as a museum. On the bridge linking them stands a statue of Saint Nepomucenus, patron of the drowned. Following its destruction in 1382, Kortrijk's Town Hall was rebuilt and expanded from 1417 to 1420 in Brabant Gothic style. A new castle was built in 1430. By 1440, Kortrijk had 5,317 inhabitants. Around 1445, historian Philippe de Comines (or Commynes) was born near Kortrijk.

Conflicts over the replacement of magistrates in Ghent spilled over into Kortrijk in 1449 and 1450. Kortrijk chose its own magistrates but was not supported by the other Flemish cities. Two years later Ghent attacked Kortrijk, which by the end of the century was a highly fortified town. Kortrijk's Town Hall was built in 1526 in a late gothic-renaissance style with a façade decorated with statues of the counts of Flanders. Laws were enacted in its upstairs Council Hall, while the Aldermen's Chamber on the ground floor was used as a court. Both chambers have sixteenth century mantelpieces, stained glass windows and murals. By 1530 the town had 6,920 inhabitants, which increased to 10,540 by 1571.

Flemish painter Roelandt Savery was born in Kortrijk in 1576. But the late 1500s would be known more for the destruction of art than its creation. From March 1578 to February 1580, Kortrijk was caught up in the fervor of the Reformation as part of the Dutch Republic.

7. The Legacy

The Broel Towers are the symbol of Kortrijk. The Speyetoren on the right was already built when the battle occurred. The Inghelborchtoren, on the left, was finished in 1401.

Opposing the decoration of churches as sacrilegious, the fanatical Protestant Calvinist movement did much damage to the town. Both the Church of Our Lady and Sint-Maarten's church were vandalized. On February 27, 1580, arch–Catholic King Philip II of Spain forgave the town, which ended its Protestant ties and reaffirmed its ties to Spain and the Hapsburgs. Damaged buildings were eventually repaired, and the town's Bruges gate was built in 1589.

During the peaceful first half of the seventeenth century, the textile industry and commerce and construction related to it experienced great development. The town spread on both sides of the Leie. Religious institutions also flourished. Consisting of some 40 small houses and chapels, the current structures comprising Kortrijk's Beguinage date from this period. Near its entrance, a statue of Countess Joan of Constantinople, the Beguinage's founder, stands in the middle of a small lawn. Today, the last Beguine and a couple of aged ladies still live there. The stepped gabled house where the Superior lived is now a museum dedicated to the Beguinage's history and life.

Kortrijk saw multiple occupations by the French during the wars of the late seventeenth and early eighteenth centuries. In 1647, the city fortifications were strengthened and the French built a citadel, which was reconstructed in 1690. The ponds, which formed part of the medieval moat system between the old town and Overbeke, became unnecessary. In September 1675, King Louis XIV of France had his governor, Pertuis, destroy the medieval walls and fill in the moats, then in a disastrous state. Houses soon filled the areas where the fortifications had been. Façades dating from this period bear much influence of Louis XIV style.

Provisions in the Treaty of Regensburg between France and Spain in August 1684 led to the destruction of the town's other strategic structures. As a result of war and uncertainty the town's population dropped to 9,865 by 1698. However, growth eventually returned. In 1761 Jozef Van Dale founded a school for young people in Budastraat. New fortifications were built in 1794 after an attack by French revolutionary troops. Four years later the city was recorded to have 14,027 inhabitants.

Many public buildings were built during the Dutch occupation from 1817 to 1830. Sister Anna Planckaert founded a small women's community and a school for poor girls in Onze-Lieve-Vrouw parish in 1814. Later in 1845, she founded the town's first elementary school. With its 1827 completion the Bissegem's Gate became Willem's Gate, the last town gate built. Kortrijk had 19,036 inhabitants at the time of Belgium's independence from the short-lived Kingdom of the United Netherlands in 1830. In 1839 the Ghent-Kortrijk railway was officially opened. The station was situated outside the town center between the Lille and Tournai gates. The town was connected by river and canals to the coast, and to Antwerp and Brussels. The year 1911 saw the town's first street lighting.

Sited close to the heavy fighting around Ypres, Kortrijk became a German headquarters in World War I. The town was badly damaged by Allied bombing in the Second World War. Out of 11,102 houses, 1,625 houses and 225 other buildings were destroyed, including the covered medieval marketplace, the cemetery chapel, railway station and library. Sewers, streets, telephone, electricity and gas services were also severely damaged. As a result, the Belfry is the only remaining part of the medieval Cloth Hall. The figures, "Marten" and "Kalle," still strike the bells, while from its peak an eighteenth-century statue of the god of trade, Mercurius, looks down on the marketplace. Appropriately, behind the Belfry is the town's war memorial.

The Market Square around the Belfry is believed to have been the site of Kortrijk's Roman forum. Fragments of Roman tiles were discovered in the northern part of the square. A covered market was built around the belfry in 1411, but was destroyed in 1550 and replaced by 22 houses. The houses on the Market Square are in various styles. A combination of classical, roccoco and modern façades are the result of the destruction brought by wars.

Another victim of the 1944 bombing was *De Guldensporenslag*, a romanticized painting of the Battle of the Golden Spurs done by Nicaise De Keyser in 1836. Showing the death of Robert of Artois, the painting's style was nineteenth century, rather than fourteenth. While it could hardly be viewed as a historical document in any real sense, it is evidence of the enduring cult which developed around the battle. Measuring 16 by 20 feet, this huge masterpiece was exhibited in Kortrijk's Cloth Hall from 1841 until its destruction. Fortunately, a good preliminary study survived in a city museum.

The oldest surviving building in town, the Church of Our Lady, was part of Kortrijk's fortifications, built to bolster the now vanished castle. Its façade and two towers date back to the second half of the thirteenth century. A chapel was built by Louis of Male in honor of Saint Catherine about 1370 but destroyed in 1382 after the battle of Westrozebeke, when the French removed the spurs that had been nailed to the walls in 1302. The church was rebuilt in the style of the 1400s. In 1578, the Iconoclasts destroyed the interior, which was repaired in fifteenth century Baroque style. More recent golden spurs were hung on the ceiling behind the main altar. To the right in the front of the church, the Chapel of the Counts displays mural paintings of the "Forestiers" and the counts of Flanders. Near an alabaster statue of

Surrounded by market halls until bombed in 1944, Kortrijk's Belfry now stands alone in the middle of the town's Market Square.

7. The Legacy

Saint Catherine, Anthony Van Dyck's *Erection of the Cross* towers over a late Baroque altar. Beside the church is an excavated section of the town's medieval wall and moat. On a lawn behind the church stands a statue of Guido Gezelle, Flanders' greatest poet and vicar of the church in the 1870s.

Kortrijk's Broel Museum contains an important collection of paintings and drawings by Roelandt Savery and works by other Kortrijk artists. Linked with this gallery under the administration of the Stedelijke Musea Kortrijk is the Groeningeabdij Museum, where Kortrijk's history is traced. Its collection of sixteenth to eighteenth century damask is world-famous and its ceramics are considered the most important in Belgium. Appropriately, this museum devotes a room to the Battle of the Golden Spurs. In the center of this room a large scale-model depicts the battle's beginning. Early fourteenth century artifacts include a goedendag head, dagger, catapult projectile, paving tile and gilded bronze spur. Accompanying these are a mold of the Courtrai Chest, photographs of miniatures of the battle, the tombstone of King Sigis and a statuette of a warrior. The walls are decorated with *The Foundation of Groeninge Abbey* and *The Origin of Our Lady of Groeninge* by unknown masters.[2]

Locally grown flax was historically the basis of the town's fame as a center of carpet and linen production. Belgium's National Flax Museum, located just outside of town in an old Flemish flax farm, with 26 displays traces the evolution of flax cultivation as it was practiced in centuries past.

Years of rebuilding saw the growth of a prosperous community. Belgium's first pedestrianized shopping streets were established in Kortrijk in 1963. A 3,0000 square meter congress palace, built in 1967 near the E17 motorway, became a regular venue for international expositions. A new music academy and a BRT radio and television facility were finished in 1970. Since 1965, Kortrijk has been the site of a campus of the Catholic University of Leuven. On May 5, 1972, the campus opened its philosophy and literature faculty. By 1997 the population within the town's boundaries stood at 75,600. With its many suburbs, Greater Kortrijk has 310,000 inhabitants.

The Golden Spurs of Kortrijk

History looms large in Kortrijk. Louis XIV, the Duke of Wellington, King William of the United Netherlands, Kaiser Wilhelm II and the all of Belgium's sovereigns have visited the town. But an eye has been kept on the future also. Kortrijk's economy has diversified since the Second World War. Light industries have developed, including engineering, electronics, jewelry manufacture and printing. Kennedy Park, with its futuristic glass buildings, is reserved for important firms. With five museums, eleven libraries, four hospitals, a small airport, several hotels, numerous cafés and many industries settled in and around the town, Kortrijk's prosperity is evident everywhere. Ironically, cross-border connections with France are particularly strong.

Kortrijk's historic sites have seen much recent restoration. On March 9, 1983, the Broel towers, considered symbols of the town, were classified as one of Kortrijk's 35 protected monuments and buildings. In 1989 the local authorities oversaw much needed restorations of the Church of Our Lady, Belfry and other old buildings, using the town's own resources.

The Groeningeveld, the field where the battle was fought, is covered by the growing town today. However, set just beyond the center, near the place where the men of Bruges faced the first charge, a peaceful park breaks the busy movement of the town. A gateway into the park tells visitors the significance of the site. At the end of a shady lane, two shining gilded monuments commemorate the battle. One, designed by Godfried Devreese for the battle's 600th anniversary in 1902, depicts the Virgin of Flanders holding the Lion of Flanders. The second, more recent, monument consists of two giant shiny prick spurs propped against each other.

For the 700th anniversary of the Battle of the Golden Spurs, the Kortrijk campus of the Catholic University of Leuven has organized a four-day conference focusing on the year 1302 and the aftereffects of the battle. The City Museums and Public Library of Kortrijk, along with the City Archives of Bruges, have also sponsored an exhibition on the events of 1302.[3]

While modern Kortrijk provides many insights into the era of the Battle of the Golden Spurs, no place captures the Middle Ages better

The battle monuments at Groeningeveld in Kortrijk.

than Bruges.[4] The city's center retains much captivating medieval charm. Rich in artistic and architectural treasures, its quiet canals and handsome step-gabled buildings have attracted numerous visitors, who amble along its cobbled streets and glide by in canal boats. The city's great glory and great tragedy casts a shadow that cannot be effaced by tour buses, souvenir shops and love-struck honeymooners.

Bruges's fortifications were bolstered by gates added in the century after the battle. Four of the city's nine gates survive to this day, including the Ezelpoort (built 1369–70), the Gentpoort (built 1361–63 and rebuilt 1401–06), the Kruispoort (built 1366–68 and rebuilt 1401–06) and the Smedenpoort (built 1367–68 and rebuilt 1615). The Poertoren, which stands by the Minnewater, is Bruges's only remaining defensive tower. Built in 1398, it was used as a gunpowder magazine from the fifteenth century onwards. The medieval waterhouse on Hendrik Consciencelaan also survives, along with a dozen almshouses.[5]

The crises of the fourteenth century ended with the dynastic

The Kruispoort, one of Bruges surviving medieval gates.

merger of Flanders and Burgundy in 1384. Facilitating commercial contacts from Portugal to Poland, Bruges would remain the most important trade center north of the Alps throughout the Burgundian period. Cloth production was partly replaced by luxury goods, banking, and non-textile crafts such as diamond-cutting. Prosperity increased. The city's beauty and luxury impressed travelers. Art and culture flourished as never before. But this revival ended with the sudden death of Mary of Burgundy in 1482. A revolt against her widower Maximilian of Austria meant that Bruges suffered political uncertainty and military occupation for a decade. Prosperity disappeared along with the Burgundian court and the foreign traders.

In the early sixteenth century Bruges recovered to an extent. But the city had clearly lost its leading role to Antwerp and remained important as only as a provincial center with a flourishing art sector and a modest maritime reputation. Then, by the middle of the century, disaster struck. Bruges's access to the North Sea, the Zwin, had silted up to the point that ships could no longer approach the city. Trade routes shifted and the cloth industry declined. The forces of nature which had made the city a perfect harbor destroyed it five centuries later. Division from the Netherlands during the Reformation led to further decline. The focus of European trade moved from Bruges to Antwerp, then to London and Amsterdam in the sixteenth and seventeenth centuries.

The Industrial Revolution hardly disturbed the city, which had become a ghost of its former self. By 1850 Bruges was the poorest city in newly established Belgium. The upper and middle classes spoke French, while the illiterate masses knew only their local Flemish dialect. But the Flemish Movement successfully reestablished the language of the majority in literature and public life. Guido Gezelle, the most important Dutch-speaking poet of the 1800s, was a native of Bruges and resident of Kortrijk.

Ironically, a French language novel made Bruges famous again. Published in 1892, *Bruges-la-Morte* by Georges Rodenbach describes a sleeping, seemingly dead, but mysteriously charming city.[6] Europeans, particularly the Britons, began to put Bruges on the itineraries of their "grand tours." Around this same time, a new seaport was built on the nearby coast at Zeebrugge, though it did not achieve full prosperity until the last quarter of the twentieth century. Trade and some manufacturing developed. But Bruges would remain a haven for art lovers, honeymooners and tourists. Ironically, the silting of the Zwin and Bruges's other calamities ultimately saved the city from the destruction and redevelopment seen elsewhere throughout the continent. Historians, artists, and Bruges's millions of visitors are eternally grateful for the city's strange salvation by its misfortunes. Its sleepy decrepitude meant that the city was of little interest to either side during the two world wars. The First World War missed the city completely. Only Bruges's port Zeebrugge suffered any significant damage during the Second World War. Unlike Coventry or Leuven or Cologne, Bruges remains a medieval jewel, an entire city caught in a time warp like nowhere else on earth.

In the Burg, the Town Hall and Basilica of the Holy Blood still evoke the age of knightly chivalry and unending guild strife. The first stone of Bruges's Town Hall was laid in 1376, shortly before the beginning of the Burgundian period. Serving as a model for similar buildings throughout Flanders and Brabant, both its interior and exterior reflect the power enjoyed by the city at the time of its construction. Its façade balances the sober style of the fourteenth century with the exuberance of the fifteenth. The Gothic Hall, or council chamber, of this medieval masterpiece resounds with the spirit of the Groeningeveld. Full length depictions of Jan Breidel, Pieter de Coninck and Willem van Saeftingen dominate the front of the chamber, while a mural showing the return of the men of Bruges from the battle covers one side wall.

Nearby, the Belfry stands in the old marketplace. Considered Belgium's finest, it was immoralized by Longfellow's poem "The Belfry of Bruges." The tallest tower of its time, it still dominates the city. Its carillon has rung out the hours for nearly seven and a half centuries. In front of the Belfry stands a statue of Jan Breidel and Pieter de Coninck designed by Brussels sculptor Paul de Vigne in 1887. Local architect Louis Delacenserie produced the base, which depicts the Matins and the Battle of the Golden Spurs.

A mural showing the return of the men of Bruges dominates an entire wall in the main chamber of Bruges Town Hall.

The unveiling of this statue was accompanied by the sort of political controversy that would have made the butcher and the weaver feel at home. In fact it was unveiled twice, first by the liberal Breidel Committee on July 11, 1887 and then by the Municipal Breydel and De Coninck Committee on August 15, 1887. Festivities on the second occasion included speeches in French by both King Leopold II and Burgomaster Visart de Bocarme, which provoked protest by even the most mildly nationalistic Flemings, who deeply resented that French had been decreed the official language of Belgian public life in 1885.[7]

Over the centuries, Bruges became renown for its art. The Church of Our Lady supplemented its architectural beauty with masterpieces ranging from the tombs of Charles the Bold and Mary of Burgundy to Michelangelo's marble *Virgin and Child* to Anthony Van Dyke's *Christ on the Cross*. Facing the church, the medieval Hospital of St. John now houses a museum of the works of fifteenth century painter Hans

181

Memling, the most renowned being the *Shrine of St. Ursula*, a reliquary decorated with paintings illustrating the legend of the saint. Nearby, the Groeninge and Gruuthuse and Brangwyn museums form a complex of world renowned collections of art and antiques.

Virtually none of the Wijngaard Beguinage's original features remain. The stone and whitewashed buildings and peaceful rectangular common of grass, trees and daffodils seen today date from a later age. Today few Beguines still live in Belgium; only the community of St. Amandsberg near Ghent is important. Elsewhere beguinages have been converted into convents, student dormitories or housing for the elderly. Those in Kortrijk, Bruges, Ghent, Diest, Oudenaarde, Leuven, Lier and Dendermonde are also tourist attractions. Like Kortrijk's St. Elizabeth Beguinage, the Wijngaard has a museum illustrating the life of the Beguines.

Many canals were covered or filled in over the years. The Pandeitje, in the center of Bruges, was filled in 1768. The Kraanrei, the

The entrance to the Wijngaard Beguinage at Bruges.

approach to the famous, but long-gone, crane, was covered over in three stages from 1787 to 1856. On the north the filling of the Komvest in 1897 interrupted the city's encirclement by waterways. In the 1600s, a new town dock, the Handelskom, was excavated at Dampoort, near termination of a canal linking Bruges with Ostend (and later with Zeebrugge) just outside the city's defenses. Parts of Bruges's defenses were incorporated into the eighteenth-century canal linking Ghent with Ostend. In particular, a canal known as the Coupure, dating from 1751, was dug to reduce the length of the journey across town between Dampoort and the Ghent canal. Today no commercial ships sail Bruges's inner canals, which are now exclusively used for open tourist boats, run by five families, each with four boats.[8]

Despite the alterations of history, treasures continue to be uncovered from Bruges's thousands of medieval sites. In 1974, remnants from the 1300s were found in the façade of a house at Hoogstraat 36, enabling the original front to be reconstructed. Hidden by a more recent stepped gable, even more striking fourteenth century remains with fine murals, including ones of St. George and the dragon and allegorical portrayals of the ten virtues, were found in 1994 at Spinolarei 2.[9]

Bruges is Cultural Capital of Europe in 2002. Its 115,000 inhabitants have many reasons to celebrate.[10] The year 2002 marks the 700th anniversary of both the Battle of the Golden Spurs and the world's first stock exchange. The future is also borne in mind. After January 2002, twelve European countries will share the euro as their common currency. It is no accident that Bruges holds a special place in the European Union. Indeed, the city's importance in European history lies particularly in its "Europeanization" of the medieval economy. It was the pivot point, where English wool and Byzantine silk were traded and Florentine bankers and Hanseatic merchants made their deals. Strolling through the streets of Bruges, one can easily see the city's long-standing connections with the rest of the European continent. Around every corner, names remind one of distant lands: Noorweegse (Norwegian) Kaai, Spaanse (Spanish) Loskaai, Spanjaardstraat (Spaniard Street), the Oosterlingenplein, the English Convent, the Genoese Lodge, the Austrian warehouses, the trading houses of the Venetians and Florentines and the coat of arms of Peter of Luxembourg over the Customs House. The Van der Beurse's inn, where the first stock exchange traded, is now a branch of the Roeselare Bank on Vlamingstraat. Not surprisingly, the city's renowned College of Europe is educating young people to promote European unity. Bruges also hosts the International Hanseatic Days of Modern Times in 2002. Begun in 1980, this annual event is a four-day cultural festival in which more than 100 northern European cities participate in concerts, conferences, processions and other events.[11]

Bruges's outer harbor, Damme, suffered a similar decline and revival. By the beginning of the fifteenth century the silting of its harbor on the Zwin meant that vessels had to unload their cargo onto lighters at Sluis. The wine trade moved to Zeeland and the herring monopoly to Sluis. By 1616 Damme lost its function as a harbor completely and became a garrison town with a defensive wall in the form of a seven-pointed star. During the wars of Louis XIV, Damme regularly changed hands and was occupied by Scots, Irishmen, Frenchmen, Walloons, Spaniards and Englishmen. At its high point a town of 20,000, Damme dwindled to its present status of a small village extending barely beyond two streets.

Once famed for commerce, Damme also became famous in the literary world. In the second half of the 1200s, the "father of Dutch poets," Jacob van Maerlant, lived and wrote here.[12] The greatest Flemish poet of the Middle Ages, he wrote a large body of works in styles varying from chivalrous romances adapted from French and Latin sources to strophic poems of a didactic and moralizing nature, including a treatise on politics, a versified natural history and a rhymed Biblical history. Van Maerlant's most extensive work is the *Spiegel Historiael* (Mirror of History), a rhymed chronicle of the world, translated from the *Speculum Historiale* of Vincent of Beauvais and dedicated to Count Floris V of Holland. Begun in 1283, but unfinished at the poet's death, this work was continued by Philip Utenbroeke and Louis van Velthem, the latter being the author of the best contemporary account of the Battle of Kortrijk.[13] Later Damme would be immortalized as the home of Tijl Ulenspiegel, the fictional hero of numerous tales and novels. More

7. The Legacy

Today, Damme is famed for its many restaurants.

than six miles from the sea today, Damme along with the nearby villages of Hoeke, Oostkerke, Lapscheure, Moerkerke and Sijsele form a
quiet rural community of 10,000 inhabitants scattered over a large
area. One of Belgium's most picturesque villages, Damme now has a
reputation as a destination for day-trippers seeking fine restaurants,
cozy shops and unparalleled polder scenery.[14]

Nearby Lissewege is also one of West Flanders most charming villages.[15] Decorated with flowers, its picturesque medieval watercourse
runs through the old village center. Two impressive thirteenth century monuments are well worth a visit: Our Lady's Church in the marketplace and the monumental barn of the abbey. A bronze statue of
Willem van Saeftingen by Jef Claerhout (1988) stands in the marketplace near the Church of Our Lady. From April to September one can
climb the church's tower for a wonderful view of the surrounding
countryside and coast. Also from the 1200s, Ter Doest's monumental
tithe barn is the only evidence of the flourishing medieval abbey south

Lissewege is bisected by its narrow medieval canal.

of the village. This unique monument with its façade of Gothic blind-niches and buttresses and its beautiful oak beamed interior remains open to the public, even though it is still used as a barn. In the 1600s the abbey's farm, pigeontower and tiny roadside chapel were rebuilt in the style of that era.

Unlike Bruges, Ghent remained prosperous by shifting its economy from textiles to shipping. However, the closing of the Scheldt estuary during the Wars of the Reformation brought commercial decline, not to be reversed until the revival of cloth production during Belgium's nineteenth century industrial revolution. The setting for negotiations ending the War of 1812, Ghent remained important through the ages.

Today Ghent has a population of 225,000 and remains the largest city in what was the County of Flanders.[16] Though the city is a leading industrial and population center and a major inland port, much of its historic center remain intact. Like Bruges, it was largely bypassed

186

A canal in Ghent, viewed from the Castle of the Counts.

in the two world wars. Its imposing Castle of the Counts of Flanders, fine Belfry, elegant Cloth Hall and many beautiful churches still stand watch over the canal-laced town. Guildhalls still line the Graslei and Korenlei on the city's most central canal. A statue of Jacob van Artevelde, done by Petrus de Vigne-Quyo in 1863, stands in the middle of Ghent's Vrijdagmarkt, where much of the city's medieval discord unfolded. One of the greatest works of art ever created, Van Eyck brothers' *The Adoration of the Mystic Lamb* also known as the Ghent Altarpiece, is on view in the magnificent Cathedral of Sint Baaf's. Though not as dependent on tourism as Bruges, Ghent is visited by tens of thousands annually, particularly during its ten-day summer festival, the Gentse Feesten.

For the present-day inhabitants of Flanders, the Battle of the Golden Spurs is more than just a distant incident in their long history. Though pre-dating nationalism, the Flemings at Kortrijk fought for their *Patria Flandrensis* and thereby saved not only their county, but the entire Low Countries from absorption into France.

The Golden Spurs of Kortrijk

The present Region of Flanders is not quite comparable with the historic county. The county of Flanders became part of the Burgundian Empire, together with Brabant and Limburg. Officially a feudal dependency of the Holy Roman Emperor, Brabant was a virtually independent duchy, ruled from Leuven, until its absorption by the Burgundians in 1430. This Burgundian period forged the Dutch-speaking areas of the Southern Netherlands together and formed the foundations of modern Flanders, which includes the provinces of Antwerp, Limburg and parts of Brabant, as well as East and West Flanders. When the kingdom of Belgium emerged in 1830, it was divided into a Dutch-speaking North and French-speaking South.

The confrontation between modern Belgium's two linguistic groups, Dutch-speaking Flemings and French-speaking Walloons, is fueled by the memory of Groeningeveld. The cult of the Battle of the Golden Spurs started very soon after the event and continues today. Successive medieval, humanist and romantic historians endowed the battle with a national quality and embedded it, as a historiographical myth, into the Flemish collective memory. Throughout the region, the names of people and places related to the battle reappear in the names of events, streets, scout troops, sports teams, a bicycle race, a marathon and even a comic strip. In 1973 the Cultuurraad van de Nederlandse Cultuurgemeenschap chose July 11 as the official National Holiday of Belgium's Flemish Community, thereby promoting the Battle of the Spurs as a symbol of Flemish identity and recognizing a primary reason why most present day Belgians speak Flemish (Dutch) and their country is not part of France. For today's Flemish nationalists, the haughty Robert of Artois has become the stereotypical Frenchman. They are prone to recall the time when their humble weavers crushed their snobbish enemies, but seldom mention the years of mob rule and decline which followed, when history showed that arrogance knows no language and intolerance stops at no borders.

Nevertheless, Kortrijk was remarkable. Throughout virtually the whole of recorded history, the plains of Flanders have been key invasion routes for all who have sought dominance in Europe. Topography has cursed the Flemings. The unbroken flatness of their land

7. The Legacy

brought Roman legions; Frankish, Viking and Hun raiders; Burgundian, Spanish and Austrian knights; French revolutionaries; British tommies and German panzers. Kortrijk was one of a very few times in which the inhabitants of Flanders were actually able to repel an invader by themselves.

Militarily, the battle was one of the earliest milestones on the road to a new type of warfare in which the status of the common foot soldier was enhanced and the myth of invincibility cultivated by the knighthood exploded. The superiority of cavalry had been unquestioned form the time of the Visigoths' victory over the Romans at Adrianople in 378. While the Byzantine Empire resisted the Turkish advance, Western Europe's fragmented and unstable states developed feudalism, a new social order obsessed with defense organized by nobles. The use of the stirrup spread west from Persia after the seventh or early eight century, from where it spread to the Arabs, Byzantium and France. It was widely assumed that the stirrup was decisive in the growing importance of knightly cavalry, although this view is now disputed.

Precursors to Kortrijk can be found in two smaller engagements. In 1176 at Legnano an army of the Lombard League, consisting of infantry armed with spears accompanied by cavalry, defeated the all-cavalry force of Frederick Barbarossa. On September 11, 1297, almost five years before Kortrijk, William Wallace's Scottish army of predominantly foot soldiers defeated an English army under the Earl of Surrey at Stirling Bridge. But while these surprising turns of events shocked many, Kortrijk was felt much further afield. The defeat of a knightly army by only foot soldiers went against all accepted wisdom. The French assumed that Kortrijk had been a coincidental departure from the normal and that it was the marsh or the leadership of Robert of Artois and not the guilds responsible for their defeat.

However, in the century following the Battle of the Golden Spurs, infantry was reappraised. Despite the fact that their strategic and tactical leadership at Kortrijk was outstanding, the Flemish triumph was not repeated.[17] At Cassel in 1327 and again at Westrozebeke in 1382 they suffered heavy losses, though it must be added that the former was due to a complete demoralization by crossbowmen and the latter

189

because of the tight inflexibility of the guildsmen's formation. However, elsewhere the lessons of Groeningeveld were evident. In 1306, a year after the capture and execution of William Wallace, a Scottish revolt against English rule succeeded and Robert the Bruce was crowned king of Scotland. Edward I died marching north to crush Robert in 1307. In an engagement similar to Kortrijk in many ways, pike-wielding Scots demolished the army of his successor, Edward II, at Bannockburn in 1314. Scotland remained independent for several centuries. A year after Bannockburn a numerically inferior Swiss force, armed with halberds, pikes and crossbows, defeated an Austrian army combining cavalry and infantry at Morgarten, and in 1319 the peasants of Ditmarschen crushed the knights of Holstein. In England the lords learned their lesson, and at Halidon Hill, Edward III routed the Scots by copying their tactics. The long bow became England's national weapon. Crecy and Poitiers have gone down in the history of the Anglophone world as turning points, no doubt because there were no English at Kortrijk.

Traditional military histories have maintained the idea that cavalry dominated the battlefield until the introduction of gunpowder. More recent scholarship ties English successes during the Hundred Years War to the power of the longbow and its tactical deployment. However, Kelly DeVries powerfully argues that neither of these views is accurate, that it was infantry rather than archers that transformed warfare between Kortrijk (1302) and Neville's Cross (1346).[18]

On much of the European continent, unbending aristocracies continued to rely on mounted knights and ill-used mercenary crossbowmen. But in Switzerland, the value of patriotic citizen-soldiers was fully realized. At Laupen in 1339, a Swiss formation more akin to the Macedonian phalanx than to any medieval battle order savagely defeated mounted Austrians who outnumbered them three to one. At Sempach in 1386 Austrians using pikes dismounted to face the Swiss on foot. Though the Swiss only narrowly prevailed, their country was freed of Hapsburg rule forever. A year later Portuguese peasants triumphed over knights at Aljubarrota. In the words of Barbara Tuchman, it was the age of "the common soldier armed with a pike and a motive."[19] Europe's commoners were effective in fighting their over-lords, "because they were not wed to glory nor bound to the horse."[20] Warfare would never be the same.

The French nobility learned little from Kortrijk and were vulnerable to English infantry tactics in the Hundred Years War. Numerous medieval chroniclers decried the knights for their pride. But heavy cavalry was still often successful. Mounted knights and their fearsome destriers could strike fear into infantry. Success or failure depended on whether the foot soldiers could narrow their front or the knights could flank their opponents. But horses are not tanks and should not be overestimated when confronted with well-organized, disciplined infantry. Improved armor simply led to heavier swords and pole weapons. Combinations of infantry, cavalry, archers and early cannons—the style of Edward III—proved very effective in balancing increasingly complex engagements. As the Middle Ages drew to a close, the importance of such combined forces grew.

The transition from cavalry to infantry was eventually overshadowed by the even greater revolution spawned by the introduction of gunpowder. While Kortrijk was the earliest sign of a new type of warfare, the use of guns and armored wagons by the Czechs in the Hussite Wars of 1419–1436 marked the finale of the long era in which mounted warriors dominated. Even the French lords grudgingly accepted these changes, which had cost them so much. This is apparent at Westrozebeke. The transition was not painless, for chronicles mention incidents where commanders forced knights to dismount for combat under penalty of death.[21] At Morat (Murten) in 1476 and at Nancy the following year, the French employed Swiss mercenaries as infantry and used them in combination with cavalry to defeat the Burgundians.

The battle on Groeninge plain remains an illustration of two important features of warfare which have endured to this day. Firstly, that the foot soldier, particularly the specialist, must never be written off as unimportant; and secondly, that soldiers who are committed to an ideal, be it patriotic or opportunistic, have an unmeasurable advantage over those who fight out of obligation, whether to a feudal lord

The Battle of Aljubarrota as shown in a manuscript illumination in the Chroniques de Jean Froissart *(© Bibliothèque Nationale de France).*

or to a modern nation-state. In these respects, the military consequences of the battle blend with the social.

Late medieval Flanders was not a slave society, nor was it free. Surrounded by strange sights, sounds and smells, twenty-first century people would feel oppressed in such a structured, collective society that knew little standardization and even less privacy. Undoubtedly, we would also miss the technologies we depend on. But the modern world owes much to the era of the Matins and Groeningeveld.

The late medieval experience profoundly changed attitudes about the very nature of humanity itself. Stratified as it was into those who fight, those who work and those who pray, people were clearly unequal. But medieval societies believed that every man and woman was a unique creation of God and the possessor of God's gift of a soul. An oft-quoted passage from the Gospel according to St Luke notes that laborers are worthy of their hire.[22] In other words, work had to be bought, not simply taken from a person. "The idea of contract occupied a central role in many aspects of medieval society. ... The taker of wages had some rights under the prevailing concepts of contract, and they were free at least as day laborers, to take their capacity for work where it suited them."[23] The Church, particularly the monks, asserted that work was not demeaning and that human beings did not lose their dignity through labor, an attitude unique in the world at that time. Taking this principle further, the masses of Flanders rejected the idea that they were somehow inferior because they had to work with their hands.

Similarly, they rejected the notions that God intended a few to rule over the many and that ordinary people should have no say in what happened to them. The uprising in Flanders originated from the grassroots, without noble provocation. Only when it became widespread did the Count's relatives and a handful of other nobles join in. The Flemings put the principle of popular sovereignty into practice, rebelling against their lords, gaining charters, and in some cases setting up independent states. Along with the Swiss, they were the most successful. Ball, Wyclif, Hus and others tried. William of Ockham argued that concepts such as justice, truth and beauty were constructed by common consent. The British Parliament, Switzerland, the Althing of Iceland, and a few other democratic institutions have survived into the modern era, but most were swept away by the rising tide of absolutism. However, the American and French revolutions of the late eighteenth century owe much to the medieval era. Indeed they simply continued what Flemings, Swiss, Scots and others had begun.

Medieval sensibilities encouraged respect for law, which though frequently violated by rulers persevered as a reminder for all. Early evidence of this is the code of chivalry, which regulated the warrior class, and the Benedictine Rule, which has governed monastic life from the early Middle Ages to the present. Scholars such as Albertus Magnus and Thomas Aquinas emphasized that there were universal, divinely prescribed laws that humans could not set aside. By the dawn of the 1500s Niccolò Machiavelli was compiling his advice on how rulers could acquire, maintain and enhance political power. Two centuries earlier such advice would have hardly mattered in the rigidly hierarchical Age of Faith. Known to be molded by classical Greece and Rome, America's Founding Fathers were also influenced by the experience of the medieval city and its contradictory tendencies towards both factionalism and oligarchy. Indeed, modern constitutionalism began with the city charters of Flanders and northern Italy.[24]

The Battle of the Golden Spurs is not a mere detail in history. In the spirit of the early fourteenth century, one can see the roots of capitalism, socialism, labor unions, Protestantism, the world economy, the nation-state and the Industrial Revolution. Flanders stood in the forefront of a new era of mass politics, mass production and mass armies. For better or worse, a modern world approached that would be far beyond the imaginations of those who faced their foes across the Groeninge Beek seven hundred years ago.

Notes

1— Metropolis in the North

1. Population statistics are from Geirnaert, N. and Vandamme, L. *Bruges: Two Thousand Years of History* (Bruges: Stichting Kunstboek, 1996), pp. 25, 28; Bairoch, P. Batou, J. and Chèvre, P. *La Population des Villes Européenes de 800 à 1850* (Geneva: Librarie Droz, 1988); DeLong, J.B. and Shleifer, A. *Princes and Merchants: European City Growth Before the Industrial Revolution* (Berkeley: University of California, 1995) http://econ158.berkeley.edu/Refereed_Articles/Princes_and_Merchants/Princes.html; Rempel, G. *Guilds and Commerce* (Springfield, MA: Western New England College) http://mars.acnet.wnec.edu/~grempel/courses/wc1/lectures/24guilds.html (for Florence, London and Cologne); de Sutter, J. *De Liebaart* http://home.tiscalinet.be/liebaart/index.htm; and de Vries, J. *European Urbanization, 1500–1800* (Cambridge, MA: Harvard University Press, 1984).

2. Geirnaert, N. and Vandamme, L. *Bruges: Two Thousand Years of History* pp. 20–21.

3. *Bruges: More Than an Art City* (Bruges: Bryggia/BMG Interactive, 1997) CD-ROM format.

4. Geirnaert, N. and Vandamme, L. *Bruges: Two Thousand Years of History* p. 25.

5. A short history and a description of the difficulties of modern linen manufacture can be found at *The Linen House* (Brussels) http://www.thelinenhouse.com/learninglinen.asp.

6. Gies, J. and F. *Cathedral, Forge and Waterwheel* (New York: Harper Collins, 1994) p. 50.

7. For urban political and economic bodies: Clare, J. D. (ed.) *Fourteenth Century Towns* (London: Random House, 1993); DeLong, J. B. and Shleifer, A. *Princes and Merchants: European City Growth before the Industrial Revolution*; Nicholas, D. *Medieval Flanders* (London: Longman, 1992); Pirenne, H. *Early Democracies in the Low Countries* (New York: Harper Row, 1963); and Pirenne, H. *Medieval Cities* (Princeton: Princeton University Press, 1969).

8. Kemble, J. M. *The Saxons in England* (London: Quaritch, 1876) Vol. II, p. 533, reprinted in Cave, R. C. and Coulson, H. H. *A Source Book for Medieval Economic History*, p. 207.

9. A good comparison of Bruges and Florence is provided by Ingersoll, R. *Medieval Cities, Bruges and Florence* (Rice University, 1995) http://www.owlnet.rice.edu/~arch343/lecture9.html.

10. Hills, R. L. *Richard Arkwright and Cotton Spinning* (London: Priory Press, 1973) p. 15.

11. For material on the history of the loom, Gans, P. J. "The Horizontal Loom" *Medieval Technology Pages* http://scholar.chem.nyu.edu/~tekpages/loom.html.

12. Geirnaert N. and Vandamme, L. *Bruges: Two Thousand Years of History* pp. 34–6; De Sutter, J. *De Liebaart*; and De Roover, R. *Money, Banking and Credit in Medieval Bruges* (London: Routledge, 2000).

13. De Sutter, J. *De Liebaart*, also de Romans, H. *On Markets & Fairs* at http://www.fordham.edu/halsall/source/1270romans.html.

14. De Sutter, J. *De Liebaart*.

15. Knox, E.L. *Medieval Society*, http://orb.rhodes.edu/textbooks/westciv/medievalsoc.html (1999).

16. Fagniez, G. (ed.) *Documents Relatifs à l'Histoire de l'Industrie et du Commerce en France* (Paris: Alphonse Picard et Fils, 1898), Vol. I., p. 97; reprinted in Cave, R.C. and Coulson, H.H. (eds.) *A Source Book for Medieval Economic History*, p. 222.

17. De Sutter, J. *De Liebaart*.

18. Garcia, W.F.W. *The Golden Falcon* "Winter's Bloom" http://www.pillagoda.freewire.co.uk/CRECY.htm.

19. Nelson, L. *Regional Specialization* (University of Kansas, 1997) http://www.ukans.edu/kansas/medieval/108/lectures/eleventh_century_economy.html.

20. Hohenberg, P. *A Primer on the Economic History of Europe* (New York: Random House, 1968) p. 29.

21. Descriptions of guilds are from: Boissonnade, P. *Life and Work in Medieval Europe* (New York: Harper Row, 1964); Clare, J.D. (ed.) *Fourteenth Century Towns* (London: Random House, 1993); Epstein, S.A. *Wage Labor and Guilds in Medieval Europe* (Chapel Hill: University of North Carolina Press, 1991); Gies, J. and F. *Life in a Medieval City* (New York: Harper Row, 1981); Strayer, J.R. *On the Medieval Origins of the Modern State* (Princeton: Princeton University Press, 1973); Pirenne, H. *Early Democracies in the Low Countries*; and

Notes—Chapter 1

Pirenne, H. *Medieval Cities*. Web sites used in this section are: Betcher G.J. *Date and Composition of The Book of Margery Kempe* (Iowa State University) http://www.public.iastate.edu/~gbetcher/ 373/guilds.htm; Knox, E.L. *Medieval Society* http://orb.rhodes.edu/textbooks/westciv/medievalsoc.html (1999); Munro, J. *The Symbiosis of Towns and Textiles: Urban Institutions and the Changing Fortunes of Cloth Manufacturing in the Low Countries and England, 1280–1570* (Toronto: University of Toronto, 1998) Working Paper Number Ut-Ecipa-Munro5–98-03; *Topics in Western Civilization: Ideals of Community and the Development of Urban Life, 1250–1700* (New Haven: Yale University, 1986) Vol. III, http://www.cis.yale.edu/ynhtl/curriculum/guides/1986/3/; Panagakis, B., Marszalek, C. and Mazanek, L. *Guilds* (Buffalo Grove, IL: 1997) http://renaissance.district96.k12.il.us/guildhall/guilds/guilds.html; Nelson, L. *The Rise of Capitalism* (University of Kansas: 1997) http://www.ukans.edu/kansas/medieval/108/lectures/capitalism.html; and Rempel, G. *Guilds and Commerce* (Western New England College) http://mars.acnet.wnec.edu/~grempel/courses/wc1/lectures/24guilds.html.

22. Knox, E.L. *Medieval Society*.

23. Epstein, S.A. *Wage Labor and Guilds in Medieval Europe*, pg. 4.

24. *Ibid.*, pg. 3.

25. Scheid, T. and Toon, L. *City of Women* (High School for the Performing and Visual Arts) http://library.thinkquest.org/12834/text/marketplace.html.

26. Geirnaert, N. and Vandamme, L. *Bruges: Two Thousand Years of History* pp. 29–30.

27. Aspeslag, P. *Chapel of the Holy Blood Bruges* (Oostende: Van Mieghem, 1988).

28. Geirnaert N. and Vandamme, L. *Bruges: Two Thousand Years of History*, p. 29.

29. *Ibid.* pp. 40–1.

30. An interesting look at Flemish beguinages is provided in Simons, W. "The Beguine Movement in the Southern Low Countries: A Reassessment" *Bulletin de l'Institut Historique Belge de Rome*, which appears at http://matrix.divinity.yale. edu/MatrixWebData/Simonsc.txt.

31. Court, A. *Baedecker's Belgium* (London: Jarrold and Sons, 1993) pp. 82–3.

32. Bennett, P. (trans.) *Beguinage "The Vineyard" Brugge* (Oostende: Van Mieghem, 1988).

33. Most of this material on Lissewege was acquired from the town's pamphlet: anonymous, *Lissewege* (Lissewege: VVV-Lissewege, undated).

34. *Lissewege* (Lissewege: VVV-Lissewege, undated) and Dendooven, L. *De Abdij Ter Doest te Lissewege-Brugge* (Lissewege: Uitgeverij Groot Ter Doest, 1994–99).

35. Geirnaert, N. and Vandamme, L. *Bruges: Two Thousand Years of History* pp. 28–9.

197

36. Tilley, A. *Medieval France: A Companion to French Studies* (London: 1922) pp. 154–60.

37. Ross, D. *Britain Express* http://www.britainexpress.com/History/Feudalism_and_Medieval_life.htm; also Healey, T. *History of Costume* (London: MacDonald Educational Ltd., 1997); Oliver, J. *Costume Through the Centuries* (London: Oliver & Boyd Ltd., 1963); and Lester, K. M. *Historic Costume* (Peoria IL: Chas. A. Bennet Co., 1956).

38. Gans, P.J. *Medieval Technology Pages* http://scholar.chem.nyu.edu/~tekpages/ (2000) and Wilkinson, P. *Building* (New York: Alfred A. Knopf, 1995), especially pp. 20–1.

39. The city paid for every third tile. Geirnaert N. and Vandamme, L. *Bruges: Two Thousand Years of History*, p. 27.

40. Geirnaert N. and Vandamme, L. *Bruges: Two Thousand Years of History*, p. 27.

41. A good presentation on pottery in medieval Flanders is at De Sutter, J. *De Liebaart*, http://home.tiscalinet.be/liebaart/index.htm.

42. Davison, M.W. *Everyday Life Through the Ages* (London: Reader's Digest Assn. Ltd., 1992) p. 367.

43. Emerson, K.L. *Writer's Guide to Everyday Life in Renaissance England* (Cincinnati: Writer's Digest Books, 1996) and Macmillan, F. "A Trencher Quencher" *Wine Day* (7 December 1999); Henisch, B.A. *Fast & Feast: Food in Medieval Society* (University Park PA: Pennsylvania State University Press, 1985); and also http://www.globalgourmet.com/food/wineday/1999/wd1299/wd120799.html.

44. An excellent short history of sausages appears at: de Develyn, K. *Sausage History* http://www.geocities.com/Athens/Acropolis/4756/sausages.htm.

45. This recipe can be found at De Sutter, J. *De Liebaart*, http://home.tiscalinet.be/liebaart/index.htm.

46. Numerous academic, commercial and popular sources on the history of food are available at http://www.pbm.com/~lindahl/food.html.

47. Willis, T. *Feasting and Fasting in Medieval England* http://www.millersv.edu/~english/homepage/duncan/medfem/feast.html.

48. Boissonnade, P. *Life and Work in Medieval Europe* (New York: Harper & Row, 1964), p. 186; also Delort, R. *Life in the Middle Ages* (New York: Ed. Lausanne, 1972), p. 140

49. Geirnaert N. and Vandamme, L. *Bruges: Two Thousand Years of History* p. 27.

50. *Ibid.*, pp. 27–8.

2 — The Overlords

1. Population statistics are from Geirnaert, N. and Vandamme, L. *Bruges: Two Thousand Years of History* (Bruges: Stichting Kunstboek, 1996) pp. 25, 28; Bairoch, P. Batou, J. and Chèvre, P. *La Population des villes européenes de 800 à 1850* (Geneva: Librarie Droz, 1988); DeLong, J.B. and Shleifer, A. *Princes and Merchants: European City Growth before the Industrial Revolution* (Berkeley: University of California, 1995) http://econ158.berkeley.edu/Refereed_Articles/Princes_and_Merchants/Princes.html; Rempel, G. *Guilds and Commerce* (Springfield, MA: Western New England College) http://mars.acnet.wnec.edu/~grempel/courses/wcl/lectures/24guilds.html (for Florence, London and Cologne); de Sutter, J. *De Liebaart* http://home.tiscalinet.be/liebaart/index.htm; and de Vries, J. *European Urbanization, 1500–1800* (Cambridge, MA: Harvard University Press, 1984).

2. Geirnaert, N. and Vandamme, L. *Bruges: Two Thousand Years of History*, pp. 20–21.

3. *Bruges: More Than an Art City* (Bruges: Bryggia/BMG Interactive, 1997) CD-ROM format.

4. Geirnaert, N. and Vandamme, L. *Bruges: Two Thousand Years of History* p. 25.

5. A short history and a description of the difficulties of modern linen manufacture can be found at *The Linen House* (Brussels) http://www.thelinen-house.com/learninglinen.asp.

6. Gies, J. and F. *Cathedral, Forge and Waterwheel* (New York: Harper Collins, 1994) p. 50.

7. For urban political and economic bodies: Clare, J. D. (ed.) *Fourteenth Century Towns* (London: Random House, 1993); DeLong, J. B. and Shleifer, A. *Princes and Merchants: European City Growth before the Industrial Revolution*; Nicholas, D. *Medieval Flanders* (London: Longman, 1992); Pirenne, H. *Early Democracies in the Low Countries* (New York: Harper Row, 1963); and Pirenne, H. *Medieval Cities* (Princeton: Princeton University Press, 1969).

8. Kemble, J. M. *The Saxons in England* (London: Quaritch, 1876) Vol. II, p. 533, reprinted in Cave, R. C. and Coulson, H. H. *A Source Book for Medieval Economic History*, p. 207.

9. A good comparison of Bruges and Florence is provided by Ingersoll, R. *Medieval Cities, Bruges and Florence* (Rice University, 1995) http://www.owlnet.rice.edu/~arch343/lecture9.html.

10. Hills, R. L. *Richard Arkwright and Cotton Spinning* (London: Priory Press, 1973) p. 15.

11. For material on the history of the loom, Gans, P. J. "The Horizontal Loom" *Medieval Technology Pages* http://scholar.chem.nyu.edu/~tekpages/loom.html.

12. Geirnaert N. and Vandamme, L. *Bruges: Two Thousand Years of History*,

pp. 34–6; De Sutter, J. *De Liebaart*; and De Roover, R. *Money, Banking and Credit in Medieval Bruges* (London: Routledge, 2000).

13. De Sutter, J. *De Liebaart*, also de Romans, H. *On Markets & Fairs* at http://www.fordham.edu/halsall/source/1270romans.html.

14. De Sutter, J. *De Liebaart*.

15. Knox, E.L. *Medieval Society* http://orb.rhodes.edu/textbooks/westciv/ medievalsoc.html (1999).

16. Fagniez, G. (ed.) *Documents Relatifs à l'Histoire de l'Industrie et du Commerce en France* (Paris: Alphonse Picard et Fils, 1898), Vol. I., p. 97; reprinted in Cave, R.C. and Coulson, H.H. (eds.) *A Source Book for Medieval Economic History*, p. 222.

17. De Sutter, J. *De Liebaart*.

18. Garcia, W.F.W. *The Golden Falcon* "Winter's Bloom" http://www.pillagoda.freewire.co.uk/CRECY.htm.

19. Nelson, L. *Regional Specialization* (University of Kansas, 1997) http:// www.ukans.edu/kansas/medieval/108/lectures/eleventh_century_economy.html.

20. Hohenberg, P. *A Primer on the Economic History of Europe* (New York: Random House, 1968) p. 29.

21. Descriptions of guilds are from: Boissonnade, P. *Life and Work in Medieval Europe* (New York: Harper Row, 1964); Clare, J.D. (ed.) *Fourteenth Century Towns* (London: Random House, 1993); Epstein, S.A. *Wage Labor and Guilds in Medieval Europe* (Chapel Hill: University of North Carolina Press, 1991); Gies, J. and F. *Life in a Medieval City* (New York: Harper Row, 1981); Strayer, J.R. *On the Medieval Origins of the Modern State* (Princeton: Princeton University Press, 1973); Pirenne, H. *Early Democracies in the Low Countries*; and Pirenne, H. *Medieval Cities*. Web sites used in this section are: Betcher G.J. *Date and Composition of The Book of Margery Kempe* (Iowa State University) http://www.public.iastate.edu/~gbetcher/373/guilds.htm; Knox, E.L. *Medieval Society* http:// orb.rhodes.edu/textbooks/westciv/medievalsoc.html (1999); Munro, J. *The Symbiosis of Towns and Textiles: Urban Institutions and the Changing Fortunes of Cloth Manufacturing in the Low Countries and England, 1280–1570* (Toronto: University of Toronto, 1998) Working Paper Number Ut-Ecipa-Munro5–98-03; *Topics in Western Civilization: Ideals of Community and the Development of Urban Life, 1250–1700* (New Haven: Yale University, 1986) Vol. III, http://www.cis.yale. edu/ynhtl/curriculum/guides/1986/3/; Panagakis, B., Marszalek, C. and Mazanek, L. *Guilds* (Buffalo Grove, IL: 1997) http://renaissance. district96.k12.il.us/guildhall/guilds/guilds.html; Nelson, L. *The Rise of Capitalism* (University of Kansas: 1997) http://www.ukans.edu/kansas/medieval/ 108/lectures/capitalism.html; and Rempel, G. *Guilds and Commerce* (Western New England College) http://mars. acnet.wnec.edu/~grempel/courses/wcl/lectures/24guilds.html.

22. Knox, E.L. *Medieval Society*.

23. Epstein, S.A. *Wage Labor and Guilds in Medieval Europe*, pg. 4.

24. *Ibid.*, pg. 3.

25. Scheid, T. and Toon, L. *City of Women* (High School for the Performing and Visual Arts) http://library.thinkquest.org/12834/text/marketplace.html.

26. Geirnaert, N. and Vandamme, L. *Bruges: Two Thousand Years of History*, pp. 29–30.

27. Aspeslag, P. *Chapel of the Holy Blood Bruges* (Oostende: Van Mieghem, 1988).

28. Geirnaert N. and Vandamme, L. *Bruges: Two Thousand Years of History*, p. 29.

29. *Ibid.* pp. 40–1.

30. An interesting look at Flemish beguinages is provided in Simons, W. "The Beguine Movement in the Southern Low Countries: A Reassessment," *Bulletin de l'Institut Historique Belge de Rome*, which appears at http://matrix.divinity.yale.edu/MatrixWebData/Simonsc.txt.

31. Court, A. *Baedecker's Belgium* (London: Jarrold and Sons, 1993) pp. 82–3.

32. Bennett, P. (trans.) *Beguinage "The Vineyard" Brugge* (Oostende: Van Mieghem, 1988).

33. Most of this material on Lissewege was acquired from the town's pamphlet: anonymous, *Lissewege* (Lissewege: VVV-Lissewege, undated).

34. *Lissewege* (Lissewege: VVV-Lissewege, undated) and Dendooven, L. *De Abdij Ter Doest te Lissewege-Brugge* (Lissewege: Uitgeverij Groot Ter Doest, 1994–99).

35. Geirnaert, N. and Vandamme, L. *Bruges: Two Thousand Years of History* pp. 28–9.

36. Tilley, A. *Medieval France: A Companion to French Studies* (London: 1922) pp. 154–60.

37. Ross, D. *Britain Express* http://www.britainexpress.com/History/Feudalism_and_Medieval_life.htm; also Healey, T. *History of Costume* (London: MacDonald Educational Ltd., 1997); Oliver, J. *Costume Through the Centuries* (London: Oliver & Boyd Ltd., 1963); and Lester, K. M. *Historic Costume* (Peoria IL: Chas. A. Bennet Co., 1956).

38. Gans, P.J. *Medieval Technology Pages* http://scholar.chem.nyu.edu/~tekpages/ (2000) and Wilkinson, P. *Building* (New York: Alfred A. Knopf, 1995) especially pp. 20–1.

39. The city paid for every third tile. Geirnaert N. and Vandamme, L. *Bruges: Two Thousand Years of History* p. 27.

40. Geirnaert N. and Vandamme, L. *Bruges: Two Thousand Years of History*, p. 27.

41. A good presentation on pottery in medieval Flanders is at De Sutter, J. *De Liebaart-* http://home.tiscalinet.be/liebaart/index.htm.

42. Davison, M.W. *Everyday Life Through the Ages* (London: Reader's Digest Assn. Ltd., 1992) p. 367.

43. Emerson, K.L. *Writer's Guide to Everyday Life in Renaissance England* (Cincinnati: Writer's Digest Books, 1996) and Macmillan, F. "A Trencher Quencher" *Wine Day* (7 December 1999); Henisch, B.A. *Fast & Feast: Food in Medieval Society* (University Park PA: Pennsylvania State University Press, 1985); and also http://www.globalgourmet.com/food/wineday/1999/wd1299/wd120799.html.

44. An excellent short history of sausages appears at: de Develyn, K. *Sausage History* http://www.geocities.com/Athens/Acropolis/4756/sausages.htm.

45. This recipe can be found at De Sutter, J. *De Liebaart-* http://home.tiscalinet.be/liebaart/index.htm.

46. Numerous academic, commercial and popular sources on the history of food are available at http://www.pbm.com/~lindahl/food.html.

47. Willis, T. *Feasting and Fasting in Medieval England* http://www.millersv.edu/~english/homepage/duncan/medfem/feast.html.

48. Boissonnade, P. *Life and Work in Medieval Europe* (New York: Harper & Row, 1964) p. 186; also Delort, R. *Life in the Middle Ages* (New York: Ed. Lausanne, 1972) p. 140.

49. Geirnaert N. and Vandamme, L. *Bruges: Two Thousand Years of History*, p. 27

50. *Ibid.*, pp. 27–8.

51. Gans, P.J. "The Stirrup Controversy," *Medieval Technology Pages.* http://scholar.chem.nyu.edu/~tekpages/texts/strpcont.html (1999) An excellent academic enquiry into the stirrup's role was also pursued by John Sloan on the discussion list mediev-l@ukanvm.cc.ukans.edu as part of the thread "The Stirrup Controversy," October 5, 1994.

52. McKay, J.P., Hill, B.D., and Buckler, J. *A History of Western Society* Vol. I (New York: Houghton Mifflin, 1999), pp. 247–9; Le Goff, J. *Medieval Civilization, 400–1500* (London: Blackwell, 1990); and Nelson, L. *The Rise of Feudalism* http://www.ukans.edu/kansas/medieval/108/lectures/feudalism.html.

53. Nelson, L. *The Rise of Feudalism.*

54. Cheney, E.P. (trans.) *University of Pennsylvania Translations and Reprints* (Philadelphia: University of Pennsylvania Press, 1898) Vol. 4, No. 3, p. 3.

55. Ross, D. *Britain Express* http://www.britainexpress.com/History/Feudalism_and_Medieval_life.htm.

56. "The Legacy of the Horse" *International Museum of the Horse* — http://www.imh.org/imh/kyhpl2a.html.

57. McKay, J.P., Hill, B.D. and Buckler, J. *A History of Western Society* Vol. I, pp. 284–5; and White, L. *Medieval Technology and Social Change* (Oxford: Clarendon Press, 1962) pp. 59–63.

58. Material on Paris in this era is largely from Benveniste, M.-C. *Paris At*

The Time of Philippe Auguste (Paris: Ecole Multimedia, March 1999) http://www.philippe-auguste.com/uk/index.html; Cole, R. *A Traveler's History of Paris,* (New York: Interlink Books, 1994); and Fierro, A. and Laffont, R. *Histoire et dictionnaire de Paris* (Paris: 1996).

59. The best studies of Paris's medieval walls are Bonnardot, A. *Dissertations archéologiques sur les anciennes enceintes de Paris* (Paris: 1851); and Berry, M. and Fleury, M. *L'Enceinte et le Louvre de Philippe-Auguste* (Paris: Délagation à l'Action Artistique de la Ville de Paris, 1988).

60. Benveniste, M.-C. *Paris at the Time of Philippe Auguste.*

61. *Ibid.*

62. *Ibid.*

63. Large sections of the *Livre de la Taille* appear in Geraud, H., *Paris sous Philippe-le-Bel* (Paris: Crapelet, 1837).

64. *Paris: Urban Sanitation 1200—1789* http://www.op.net/~uarts/krupa/.

65. Parent-Duchatelet, A.J.-B. *La Prostitution dans la ville de Paris, considérée sous le rapport de l'hygiène publique, de la morale et de l'administration; ouvrage appuyé de documents statistiques* (Paris, J.-B. Baillière, 1857) 2 vols.

66. Laures, R. *A Medieval Response to Municipal Pollution.* Paper presented to the Mid-America Conference on History, 17–19 September 1992 (University of Kansas, Lawrence, KS).

67. *Paris: Urban Sanitation 1200—1789* http://www.op.net/~uarts/krupa/.

68. For material on Philip IV: Duby, G. *France in the Middle Ages: 987–1460* (Oxford: Blackwell, 1991) pp. 261-8; and Law, J., *Fleur de Lys* (New York: McGraw-Hill, 1976).

69. Cambrai, BM, Mss. 422, fol. 20v.

70. Brehier, L. "Guillaume de Nogaret" *The Catholic Encyclopedia* Vol. XI (New York: Robert Appleton, 1911).

3 — The Deadly Politics of Medieval Flanders

1. Verbruggen, J.F. *The Art of Warfare in Western Europe During the Middle Ages* (Woodbridge UK: Boydell, 1997) pp. 149-150.

2. Tilley, A. *Medieval France: A Companion to French Studies,* p. 155.

3. Verbruggen, J.F. *The Art of Warfare in Western Europe During the Middle Ages,* p. 166.

4. Figures in this and the two following paragraphs come from De Sutter, J. *De Liebaart* and Verbruggen, J.F. *The Art of Warfare in Western Europe During the Middle Ages.*

5. De Sutter, J. *De Liebaart.*

6. Museums and other collections have few weapons dating before 1350. Materials such as wood, wrought iron, horn and flax rope deteriorated with

time. Important, but not infallible sources of information are accounts of weapon deliveries, accounts of battles, works of art and archaeological finds. See DeVries, K. *Infantry Warfare in the Fourteenth Century* (Rochester NY: University of Rochester Press, 1998); Rothero, C. *Medieval Military Dress: 1066 to 1500* (Poole, UK: Blandford, 1983); Verbruggen, J.F. *The Art of Warfare in Western Europe During the Middle Ages*; and De Sutter, J. *De Liebaart.*

7. De Sutter, J. *De Liebaart* and Jones, B. "The Crossbow in the Medieval Period." *The* Beckonin.g http://www.gci-net.com/~users/W/wolfsoul/medieval/crossbow/cross_l_v_c.html (14 April 2001).

8. De Sutter, J. *De Liebaart.*

9. Verbruggen, J.F. *The Art of Warfare in Western Europe During the Middle Ages*; pp. 170–1.

10. *Ibid.*, pp. 149–50.

11. Bland, C.C.S. (trans.) *The Autobiography of Guibert, Abbot of Nogent-sous-Coucy* (London: George Routledge & Sons, Ltd., 1925), pp. 152–64. Abridged and reprinted in Barnard L. & Hodges T.B. *Readings in European History* (New York: Macmillan, 1958), pp. 111–4.

12. de Lepinois, E. & Merlet L. (eds.); *Cartulaire de Notre-Dame de Chartres* (Chartres: Garnier, 1863) Vol. II, pp. 56–62.

13. Verbruggen, J.F. *The Art of Warfare in Western Europe During the Middle Ages*, p. 150.

14. Tilley, A. *Mediaeval France: A Companion to French Studies*, pp. 154–60.

15. Verbruggen, J.F. *The Art of Warfare in Western Europe During the Middle Ages*, p. 27.

16. *Ibid.*, p. 347.

17. *Ibid.*, p. 346.

18. *Ibid.*, pp. 346–7.

19. *Ibid.*, pp. 32–3.

20. "The Legacy of the Horse" *International Museum of the Horse* http://www.imh.org/imh/kyhpl2a.html.

21. von Aue, H. (trans. Thomas L. Keller). *Garland Library of Mediaeval Literature* (New York: Garland, 1987) Vol. 12, Series B, No. 9070.

22. Verbruggen, J.F. *The Art of Warfare in Western Europe During the Middle Ages*, pp. 28–9, 32.

23. Information on knightly dress and armor is from De Sutter, J. *De Liebaart,* and Rothero, C. *Medieval Military Dress: 1066 to 1500.*

24. Information on medieval horses is from "The Legacy of the Horse" *International Museum of the Horse* — http://www.imh.org/imh/kyhpl2a.html.

25. Rothero, C. *Medieval Military Dress: 1066 to 1500*, p. 138.

26. Verbruggen, J.F. *The Art of Warfare in Western Europe During the Middle Ages*, p. 103.

27. *Ibid.*, p. 329.

28. *Ibid.*, pp. 25–7.

29. *Ibid.*, p. 25.

30. *Ibid.*, p. 176.

31. *Ibid.*, p. 51.

32. Nicholas, D. *Medieval Flanders*, pp. 180–85; Pirenne, H. *Histoire Belgique* (Brussels: Maurice Lamertin, 1922–29), Vol. I, pp. 389–90.

33. Vandermaesen, M. "Vlaanderen en Henegouwen onder het Huis van Dampierre 1244–1384," *Algeme Geschiedenis der Nederlanden* (Utrecht: 1982), pp. 403–10; Pirenne, H. *Histoire Belgique*, Vol. I, pp. 389–435; also Nowé, H. *La Bataille des Eperons d'Or* (Paris: La Renaissance du Livre, 1945).

34. Nicholas, D. *Medieval Flanders* p. 183.

35. *Ibid.*

36. *Ibid.*, p. 182.

37. Most information on these events comes from inquests held after the rebellion. See Nicholas, D. *Medieval Flanders* pp. 181–5.

38. Doudelez, G. "La Révolution communale de 1280 à Ypres," in Mus, O., and van Houtte, J.A. *Prisma van de Geschiedenis van Ieper* (Ieper: Stadsbestuur, 1974), pp. 188–294.

39. Nicholas, D. *Medieval Flanders* p. 182.

40. *Ibid.*, p. 184.

41. *Ibid.*, p. 181.

42. de Smet, A. "De Klacht van de 'ghemeente' van Damme in 1280: Enkele gegevens over politieke en sociale toestanden in een klein vlaamse stad gedurende de tweede helft der XIIIe eeuw," *Bulletin de la Commission Royale d'Histoire* Vol. 115 (1950), pp. 1–15; also Verbruggen, J.F. "Beschouwingen over 1302," *Annales de la Société d'Emulation de Bruges*, Vol. 93 (1956) p. 41.

43. Wyffels, C. "Nieuwe Gegevens Betreffende een XIIIde Eeuwse 'Democratische' Stedelijke Opstand: De Brugse 'Moelemaye' (1280–81)," *Bulletin de la Commission Royale d'Histoire*, Vol. 132 (1966), pp. 37–142.

44. Godding, P. *Le Droit privé dans les Pays-Bas méridionaux du 12e au 18e siècles* (Brussels: Palais des Académies, 1987), p. 57.

45. Marechal, J. "Het Weezengeld in de Bruge stadfinancien van de middeleeuwen" *Annales de la Société d'Emulation de Bruges*, Vol. 82 (1939), pp. 1–41.

46. van Werveke, H. *De Gentsche Stadsfinancien in de Middeleeuwen* (Brussels: Paleis der Academiën, 1934), pp. 27 & 199 ff.

47. Garcia, W.F.W. *The Golden Falcon* Chap. 5 Winter's Bloom. http://www.pillagoda.freewire.co.uk/CRECY.htm.

48. I use the terms "Leliaart" and "Liebaart" throughout this work as these forms are currently used in Dutch/Flemish. However, the medieval era's unstandardized spellings have led to the use of numerous alternatives. For example, Liebaart appears as Libaart, Liebaert, Liebaard, Libaard, Liebaerd and Libaerd.

An introduction to these usages is found at De Sutter, J. *De Liebaart* http://home.tiscalinet.be/liebaart/index.htm.

49. Prevenier, W. "Motieven voor Leliaardsgezindheid in Vlaanderen in de Periode 1297–1305," *De Leiegouw*, Vol. 19 (1977), pp. 277–85; Prevenier, W. "La Bourgeoisie en Flandre au XIIIe siècle," *Revue de l'Université de Bruxelles* (1978), no. 4, p. 423.

50. Blockmans, W.P. *Een Middeleeuwse Vendetta: Gent 1300* (Houten: De Haan, 1987), p. 75.

51. Märtens, R. *Weltorientierungenund wirtschaftliches Erfolgsstreben Mittelalterlicher Großkaufleute: Das Beispiel Gent im 13 Jahrhundert* (Cologne: Böhlau, 1976), p. 244–51.

52. Verbruggen, J.F. "Beschouwingen over 1302," pp. 38–40; see also de Smet, J. "Brugse Leliaards Gevlucht te Sint-Omaars van 1302 tot 1305," *Annales de la Société d'Emulation de Bruges* Vol. 89 (1957), pp. 146–52.

53. Nicholas, D. *Medieval Flanders*, p. 199.

54. *Ibid.*

4 — The Matins

1. Gilliat-Smith, E. *The Story of Bruges* (London: J.M. Dent & Co., 1901), p. 137.

2. Vandermaesen, M. "Vlaanderen en Henegouwen onder het Huis van Dampierre 1244–1384," p. 405; Pirenne, H. *Histoire Belgique*, Vol. I, pp. 396–7.

3. Monier, R. *Institutions centrales du Comté de Flandre du IXe siècle à 1384* (Paris: 1943), p. 8.

4. Nicholas, D., *Medieval Flanders*, pp. 187–88; Pirenne, H. *Histoire Belgique*, Vol. I, p. 399; Nowé, H. *La Bataille des Eperons d'Or*, pp. 36–7.

5. Nicholas, D., *Medieval Flanders*, p. 188; Pirenne, H. *Histoire Belgique*, Vol. I, p. 401; Lloyd, T.H. *The English Wool Trade in the Middle Ages* (Cambridge: Cambridge University Press, 1977), p. 75; Vandermaesen, M. "Vlaanderen en Henegouwen onder het Huis van Dampierre 1244–1384," pp. 406–7.

6. Nicholas, D., *Medieval Flanders*, p. 189; Pirenne, H. *Histoire Belgique*, Vol. I, pp. 403–4; Nowé, H. *La Bataille des Eperons d'Or*, pp. 9–10; Monier, R. *Institutions centrales du Comté de Flandre du IXe siècle à 1384*, p. 100.

7. Lloyd, T.H. *The English Wool Trade in the Middle Ages*, p. 74; and Lloyd, T.H. *Alien Merchants in England in the High Middle Ages* (Cambridge: Cambridge University Press), p. 101.

8. Pirenne, H. *Histoire Belgique*, Vol. I, pp. 406–7; Nowé, H. *La Bataille des Eperons d'Or*, p. 44; Lloyd, T.H. *The English Wool Trade in the Middle Ages*, p. 82.

9. Nicholas, D., *Medieval Flanders*, p. 189.

10. De Sutter, J., *De Liebaart*.

11. Vandermaesen, M. "Vlaanderen en Henegouwen onder het Huis van Dampierre 1244–1384," p. 408; Prevenier, W. "Motieven voor Leliaardsgezindheid in Vlaanderen in de Periode 1297–1305," pp. 274–7.

12. Gilliat-Smith, E., *The Story of Bruges* (London: J.M. Dent & Co., 1901), p. 143.

13. Johnstone, H. (ed. & trans.). *Annales Gandenses: Annals of Ghent* (London: Thomas Nelson, 1951), p. 13.

14. Pirenne, H. *Histoire Belgique* Vol. I, p. 414; and Prevenier, W. "La Bourgeoisie en Flandre au XIIIe siècle," p. 425.

15. Gies, F. & J. *Women in the Middle Ages* (New York: Harper Perennial 1978) pp. 187–90. Also useful on the era's apparel are Healey, T. *History of Costume*; Oliver, J. *Costume Through the Centuries*; and Lester, K.M. *Historic Costume*.

16. Gilliat-Smith, E. *The Story of Bruges* (London: J.M. Dent & Co., 1901), p. 144.

17. Nicholas, D., *Medieval Flanders*, p. 192; Johnstone, H. (ed.) *Annales Gandenses*, p. 28; and Nowé, H. *La Bataille des Eperons d'Or*, pp. 65–6.

18. Geirnaert N., and Vandamme, L. *Bruges: Two Thousand Years of History*, pp. 38–9.

19. Pirenne, H. *Histoire Belgique* Vol. I, pp. 416–17; Bovesse, J. "La Régence comtale namuroise en Flandre: juillet 1302–mai 1303," *Liber Buntinx*, pp. 139–40; and Nowé, H. *La Bataille des Eperons d'Or*; p. 65.

20. Other variants of this spelling is *Scilt ende Vrient* and *Schild en Vriend*.

21. Geirnaert N., and Vandamme, L. *Bruges: Two Thousand Years of History*, p. 32.

22. Pirenne, H. *Histoire Belgique* Vol. I, pp. 418–19.

23. Runciman, S. *The Sicilian Vespers* (Cambridge: Cambridge University Press, 1958).

24. An excellent description of the Courtrai Chest, with photographs of its details is provided at De Sutter, J. *De Liebaart* http://home.tiscalinet.be/liebaart/index.htm. Other sources on the Chest include Dewilde B., Pauwels A., Verbruggen J.F., and Warlop E. "De Kist van Oxford," *De Leiegouw* Vol. XXIII (1980), pp. 163–256; Gilmour B., and Tyers I. "Courtrai Chest: Relic Or Recent," *Papers of the Mediaeval Europa Brugge 1997 Conference*, Vol. V, pp. 17–26; Hall E.T. "The Courtrai Chest from New College, Oxford, Re-Examined," *Antiquity*, Vol. 61, no. 231 (March 1987), pp. 104–107; Marijnissen R.H. En Van De Voorde G., "De 'Chest of Courtrai,' een Vervalsing van het Pasticcio-Type," in *Mededelingen van de Koninklijke Academie voor Wetenschappen, Letteren en Schone Kunsten van België*, Klasse Schone Kunsten, Vol. XL (1978), no. 3, pp. 1–17; and Verbruggen J.F. "De 'Chest of Courtrai,' Een Oorspronkelijk Getuigenis Over 1302," in *Belgisch Tijdschrift voor Militaire Geschiedenis*, Vol. XXIII, no. 7 (1980), pp. 585–608.

25. In 1578 Wijnendaal castle was destroyed by the *Geuzen* (Protestants). Napoleon destroyed it again, after which it became an army barracks. In 1833 it was bought by banker J.P. Matthieu, who rebuilt it.

5 — The Battle

1. Johnstone, H. (ed.) *Annales Gandenses,* pp. 34, 37.

2. Material on early Kortrijk comes from Maddens, N. *De Geschiedenis van Kortrijk* (Tielt, Belgium: Lannoo, 1990); Willen, L. *Cyber-Kortrijk* http://www. ccim.be/courtrai/korten4.htm; and *The Belgian Travel Network* http://www. trabel.com/kortrijk/kortrijk-buildingstour.htm.

3. Espinas, G. and Pirenne, H. (eds.) *Recueil de documents relatifs à l'histoire de l'industrie drapière en Flandre* (Brussels, 1906), p. 648; reprinted in Cave, R.C. and Coulson, H.H. *A Source Book for Medieval Economic History*), p. 374. Also found at http://www.fordham.edu/halsall/source/1224Exmptail.html.

4. *Begynhof St. Elisabeth Kortrijk* (Kortrijk: Committee for Initiative of the Kortrijk Region, undated).

5. Verbruggen, J.F. *The Art of Warfare in Western Europe During the Middle Ages,* p. 166.

6. The Franc or Castellany of Bruges consisted of the northern two-thirds of modern West Flanders province, including the Bruges Free Land around the city, much of coastal Flanders and part of Zeeland (now in the Netherlands).

7. de Sutter, J. *De Liebaart;* and van Velthem, L., "Spiegel Historiael," in *Documents Illustrating the History of Belgium* Vol. I (Brussels: Ministry of Foreign Affairs, April 1978).

8. Johnstone, H. (ed.) *Annales Gandenses,* pp. 28–9.

9. Verbruggen, J.F. *The Art of Warfare in Western Europe During the Middle Ages,* p. 85.

10. Verbruggen, J.F. *The Art of Warfare in Western Europe During the Middle Ages,* pp. 179–80.

11. Gilliat-Smith, E. *The Story of Bruges* (London: J.M. Dent & Co., 1901), p. 156.

12. Verbruggen, J.F. *The Art of Warfare in Western Europe During the Middle Ages,* p. 192.

13. Verbruggen, J.F. *The Art of Warfare in Western Europe During the Middle Ages,* p. 284.

14. Tilley, A. *Mediaeval France: A Companion to French Studies,* p. 160; and also Willen, L. *Cyber-Kortrijk* http://perso.wanadoo.fr/karaya/courtrai.htm. Gilliat-Smith also uses exaggerated figures.

15. Gilliat-Smith, E. *The Story of Bruges* (London: J.M. Dent & Co., 1901), p. 155.

16. The relief map at Kortrijk's Groeningeabdij Museum shows Artois in this position.

17. de Sutter, J. *De Liebaart.*

18. van Velthem, L., "Spiegel Historiael" in *Documents Illustrating the History of Belgium* Vol. I (Brussels: Ministry of Foreign Affairs, April 1978), pp. 106.

19. Verbruggen, J.F. *The Art of Warfare in Western Europe During the Middle Ages*, p. 56.

20. van Velthem, L. *Spiegel Historiael (1248–1316)* Vander Linden, H. (ed.) (Brussels: 1906–38) Vol. II, pp. 303–6; and Johnstone, H. (ed.) *Annals Gandenses*, p. 33.

21. Verbruggen, J.F. *The Art of Warfare in Western Europe During the Middle Ages*, p. 106.

22. Gilliat-Smith, E. *The Story of Bruges*; Nowé, H. *La Bataille des Eperons d'Or*; and Verbruggen, J.F. *The Art of Warfare in Western Europe During the Middle Ages.*

23. Villani, G., *Historie Fiorentine*, in Muratori, L.A. (ed.) *Rerum Italicarum Scriptores*, Vol. 13.

24. The Flemish guilds did use uniforms, but undoubtedly many wore clothes that hardly distinguished them from any other commoner.

25. De Sutter, J. *De Liebaart.*

26. Minois, G., Cochrane, L. (trans.) *Voluntary Death in the Western World* (Baltimore: Johns Hopkins University Press, 1998).

27. Villani, G., *Historie Fiorentine*, in Muratori, L.A. (ed.) *Rerum Italicarum Scriptores.*

28. van Velthem, L., "Spiegel Historiael" in *Documents Illustrating the History of Belgium* Vol. I, pp. 107.

29. le Muisit, G.; Lemaître, H. (ed.) *Chroniques et annales* (Paris: Société de l'histoire de France, 1905), pp. 67–8.

30. Not to be confused with Henry VIII's Battle of the Spurs at Guinegate in 1513.

31. Gilliat-Smith, E. *The Story of Bruges* (London: J.M. Dent & Co., 1901), p. 160.

32. Verbruggen, J.F. *De Slag der Gulden Sporen* (Antwerp: Standaard, 1952) p. 302.

33. Dante Alighieri, *Purgatorio* Canto XX, v. 46.

34. Verbruggen, J.F. *The Art of Warfare in Western Europe During the Middle Ages*: p. 175.

35. Pirenne, H. *Histoire Belgique* Vol. I, p. 420–1; Bovesse, J. "La Régence comtale namuroise en Flandre: juillet 1302–mai 1303," pp. 140–2.

36. Verbruggen, J.F. "Beschouwingen Over 1302," p. 43; Prevenier, W. "La Bourgeoisie en Flandre au XIIIe siècle," p. 425.

37. Nicholas, D. *Medieval Flanders*, p. 194

38. Nicholas, D., *Medieval Flanders*, p. 202.

39. *Ibid.* and Verbruggen, J.F. "Beschouwingen Over 1302," pp. 44–9; Bovesse, J. "La Régence comtale namuroise en Flandre: juillet 1302–mai 1303," pp. 143–8.

40. Bloch, M. *Feudal Society* (Chicago: University of Chicago Press, 1971), pp. 324–5.

41. Tilley, A. *Mediaeval France: A Companion to French Studies*, p. 160.

42. Pirenne, H. *Histoire Belgique* Vol. I, p. 425.

43. Sache, I. *Flags in 14th Century Flanders*, http://www.crwflags.com/fotw/flags/be-vl-14.html (April 2001).

6 — The Aftermath

1. Marechal, J. *Geschiedenis van de Brugse Beurs* (Bruges: 1949); Geirnaert N., and Vandamme, L. *Bruges: Two Thousand Years of History*; and De Roover, R. *Money, Banking and Credit in Medieval Bruges*.

2. Dohrn-van Rossum, G. and Dunlap, T. (trans.) *History of the Hour: Clocks and Modern Temporal Orders* (Chicago: University of Chicago Press, 1996); and Mumford, L. *The Lewis Mumford Reader* (New York: Pantheon Books, 1986), p. 328.

3. Lloyd, T.H. *Alien Merchants in England in the High Middle Ages* pp. 13–24, 53.

4. Verbruggen, J.F. *The Art of Warfare in Western Europe During the Middle Ages*: p. 341.

5. *Ibid.*, pp. 222–4.

6. *Ibid.*, p. 286

7. *Ibid.*, p. 69

8. Johnstone, H. (ed.) *Annales Gandenses*, p. 75

9. Verbruggen, J.F., "De Slag bij de Pevelenberg," *Bijdragen voor de Geschiedenis der Nederlanden* Vol. VI (1952), p. 189; and Six, G. "La Bataille de Mons-en-Pévèle," *Annales de l'Est et du Nord* Vol. I (1905), p. 226.

10. Verbruggen, J.F. *The Art of Warfare in Western Europe During the Middle Ages*, p. 97.

11. Verbruggen, J.F. "De Historiografie van de Guldensporenslag," *De Leigouw* Vol. 19 (1977), p. 245.

12. Pirenne, H. *Histoire Belgique*, Vol. I, pp. 432–3.

13. *Ibid.*, pp. 427–9 and Nicholas, D., *Medieval Flanders*, p. 195.

14. Nicholas, D., *Medieval Flanders*, p. 196.

15. Verbruggen, J.F. "De Historiografie van de Guldensporenslag," p. 272.

16. Geirnaert N., and Vandamme, L. *Bruges: Two Thousand Years of History*, pp. 38–9

17. Johnstone, H. (ed.) *Annales Gandenses*, pp. 9–12; and Dekker, C. and Kruisheer, J.G. "Een rekening van de abdij Ter Doest over het jaar 1315," *Bulletin de la Commission Royale d'Histoire* Vol. 133 (1967), pp. 282–6.

18. Diegerick, I.L.A. (ed.). *Inventaire Analytique et Chronologique des Chartes et Documents Appartenant aux Archives de la Ville d'Ypres* (Bruges: Vandecasteele-Werbrouck, 1853–68) Vol. I, pp. 184–5, 190–4.

19. Nicholas, D. *Medieval Flanders*, p. 201

20. Märtens, R. *Weltorientierungenund wirtschaftliches Erfolgsstreben Mittelalterlicher Großkaufleute: Das Beispiel Gent im 13 Jahrhundert*, pp. 244–51.

21. Nicholas, D., *Medieval Flanders*, p. 204.

22. A good contemporary account of events in Anagni is provided in Beck, H.G.J. (trans.) "William of Hundlehy's Account of the Anagni Outrage," *Catholic Historical Review* Vol. 32 (1947), pp. 200–1.

23. Barber, M.C. "The Trial of the Templars Revisited," The Whichard Lecture at East Carolina University, Greenville, North Carolina (Fall 1999), published in Nicholson, H. (ed.) *The Military Orders* Vol. II, "Welfare and Warfare" (Aldershot, 1998), pp. 329–42

24. Brehier, L. "Guillaume de Nogaret," *The Catholic Encyclopedia* Vol. XI (New York: Robert Appleton, 1911).

25. This was a population loss of about 10 percent and 5 percent respectively. See Nicholas, D. *Medieval Flanders* pp. 206–8; Prevenier, W. *et al.*, "Tassen crisis en welvaart: Sociale Veranderingen, 1300–1482," *Algeme Geschiedenis der Nederlanden* (Utrecht: 1982) Vol. IV, p. 56; Lucas, H.S. "The Great European Famine of 1315, 1316 and 1317," *Speculum* Vol. V (1930), pp. 343–77; van Werveke, H. "La Famine de l'an 1316 en Flandre et dans les régions voisines," *Revue du Nord* (1959), pp. 5–14; van Werveke, H. "Bronnenmateriaal uit de Brugse stadsrekeningen betreffende de hongersnood van 1316," *Bulletin de la Commission Royale d'Histoire* Vol. 125 (1959), pp. 431–510.

26. Verbruggen, J.F. *The Art of Warfare in Western Europe During the Middle Ages*, pp. 309–11.

27. *Ibid.*, p. 76.

28. *Ibid.*, p. 47.

29. *Ibid.*, p. 169.

30. In one year alone, Edward received more than £80,000 from duties levied solely on wool, almost all of which was exported to Flanders. See Garcia, W.F.W. *The Golden Falcon*, Chap. 5 — Winter's Bloom. http://www.pillagoda.freewire.co.uk/CRECY.htm.

31. Tilley, A. *Mediaeval France: A Companion to French Studies*, pp. 154–78.

32. Tuchman, B. *A Distant Mirror: The Calamitous 14th Century* (New York: Knopf, 1978) p. 390.

33. *Ibid.*

34. Verbruggen, J.F. "De Historiografie van de Guldensporenslag," pp. 245–72.

35. Geirnaert N. and Vandamme, L. *Bruges: Two Thousand Years of History*, pp. 34–5.

36. *Ibid.*

37. Nicholas, D. *Medieval Flanders*, p. 206.

38. *Ibid.*, p. 186.

39. Bairoch, P. "International Industrialization Levels from 1750 to 1980," *Journal of European Economic History* (Fall 1982), p. 294.

40. Nelson, L. *The Rise of Capitalism*, http://www.ukans.edu/kansas/medieval/108/lectures/capitalism.html.

41. Verbruggen, J.F. *The Art of Warfare in Western Europe During the Middle Ages*, p. 167.

42. McKay, J., Hill, B.D., and Buckler, J. *A History of Western Society* Vol. I, p. 400.

7 — The Legacy

1. Material on Kortrijk since the battle comes from Maddens, N. *De Geschiedenis van Kortrijk*; Willen, L. *Cyber-Kortrijk* http://www.ccim.be/courtrai/korten4.htm; and *The Belgian Travel Network*. http://www.trabel.com/kortrijk/kortrijk-buildingstour.htm.

2. *Visitor's Guide to the Groeningeabdij Kortrijk* (Kortrijk: Stedelijke Musea Kortrijk, undated).

3. Details are available at http://www.brugge2002.com/programmatie/index_en.shtml.

4. Excellent guidance to Bruges for both scholars and travellers is provided by Geirnaert N. and Vandamme, L. *Bruges: Two Thousand Years of History* (Bruges: Stichting Kunstboek, 1996); and also Bruges' official web sites, http://www.brugge.be/toerisme/en/index.htm & http://www.brugge.com/.

5. Geirnaert N. and Vandamme, L. *Bruges: Two Thousand Years of History*, pp. 27–8.

6. Rodenbach, G. *Bruges-la-Morte* (London: Atlas, 1993).

7. Geirnaert N. and Vandamme, L. *Bruges: Two Thousand Years of History*, p. 38.

8. *Ibid.*, pp. 22–3.

9. *Ibid.*, p. 36.

10. Census 1997.

11. Details are available at *Brugge 2002* http://www.brugge2002.com/historiek2002/index_en.shtml.

12. Remy, A.F.J. "Jacob van Maelant," *The Catholic Encyclopedia* Vol. IX (New York: Robert Appleton, 1910).

13. The "Spiegel Historiael" was published in modern times by de Vries and Verwijs of Leyden in 1857–63 and by Davidsfonds-Clauwaert in 1997.

14. Van Meldert, R. *Damme, boekendorp* at http://www.ping.be/~pin10181/dammeinform.htm (October 2000).

15. *Lissewege* (Lissewege: VVV-Lissewege, undated); Dendooven, L. *De Abdij*

Ter Doest te Lissewege-Brugge (Lissewege: Uitgeverij Groot Ter Doest, 1994-99); and Lissewege's official web site, http://lissewege.gq.nu/.

16. Census 1997.

17. Verbruggen, J.F. *The Art of Warfare in Western Europe During the Middle Ages*, p. 52.

18. DeVries, K. *Infantry Warfare in the Fourteenth Century* (Rochester: University of Rochester Press, 1998).

19. Tuchman, B. *A Distant Mirror: The Calamitous 14th Century*, p. 77.

20. *Ibid.* p. 592.

21. Koch, H.W. *Medieval Warfare* (London: Bison, 1982) pp. 134–5.

22. *The Gospel of Luke*, Chapter X, verse 7.

23. Epstein, S.A. *Wage Labor and Guilds in Medieval Europe*, pg. 4.

24. Strayer, J.R. *On the Medieval Origins of the Modern State* (Princeton: Princeton University Press, 1973).

Bibliography

Books

Aue, Hartmann von. *Garland Library of Medieval Literature* trans. Thomas L. Keller (New York: Garland, 1987) Vol. 12, Series B, No. 9070

Bairoch, Paul, Batou, Jean and Chèvre, Pierre. *La Population des villes euro-péenes de 800 à 1850* (Geneva: Librarie Droz, 1988)

Baldwin, John. *Philippe-Auguste et son gouvernement* (Paris: Fayard, 1991)

Bernard of Clairvaux. *Life and Works of St. Bernard, Abbot of Clairvaux* trans. Samuel J. Eales (New York: Benziger Bros., 1912), 2 vols.

Blockmans, W. P. *Een Middeleeuwse Vendetta: Gent 1300* (Houten: De Haan, 1987)

Boissonnade, P. *Life and Work in Medieval Europe* (New York: Harper Row, 1964)

Bonnardot, Alfred. *Dissertations archéologiques sur les anciennes enceintes de Paris* (Paris: 1851)

Braunfels, Wolfgang. *Monasteries of Western Europe* (New York: Thames & Hudson, 1993)

Bunson, Matthew E. *Encyclopedia of the Middle Ages* (New York: Facts On File, 1995)

Carson, Patricia. *The Fair Face of Flanders* (Ghent: E. Story-Scientia, 1969)

Cave, Roy C., and Coulson, Herbert H. (eds.) *A Source Book for Medieval Economic History* (Milwaukee: Bruce Publishing, 1936; reprinted New York: Biblo & Tannen, 1965)

Clare, John D. (ed.) *Fourteenth Century Towns* (London: Random House, 1993)

Cole, Robert. *A Traveler's History of Paris* (New York: Interlink Books, 1994)

Court, Alec. *Baedecker's Belgium* (London: Jarrold and Sons, 1993)

De Bruyne, Arthur. *De Guldensporenslag* (Leuven: Davidsfonds, 1952)

Bibliography

De Gryse, Piet. *Glossarium Armorum Nederlandse Uitgave* (Brussels: Legermuseum, 1998)

Delbrück, Hans. *Medieval Warfare* (Lincoln: University of Nebraska Press, 1990)

Delfos, Leo. *1302 door Tijdgenoten Verteld* (Bruges: Uitgeverij Patria, 1932)

_____. *Het Avontuur van de Liebaards* (Tielt, Belgium: Lannoo, 1952)

De Meester, Jules. *Onze Helden van 1302* (Bruges: Ed. Duclos, 1902)

De Roover, Raymond. *Money, Banking and Credit in Medieval Bruges* (London: Routledge, 2000)

De Vries, Jan. *European Urbanization, 1500–1800* (Cambridge, Mass: Harvard University Press, 1984)

DeVries, Kelly. *Infantry Warfare in the Fourteenth Century* (Rochester NY: University of Rochester Press, 1998)

Dohrn-van Rossum, Gerard. *History of the Hour: Clocks and Modern Temporal Orders*, trans. Thomas Dunlap (Chicago: University of Chicago Press, 1996)

Duby, Georges. *France in the Middle Ages: 987–1460* (Oxford: Blackwell, 1991)

Durant, Will. *The Renaissance: A History of Civilization in Italy from 1304 to 1576 A.D.* (New York: Simon & Schuster, 1953).

Edge, David and Paddock, John Miles. *Arms and Armour of the Medieval Knight* (New York: Random House, 1993)

Emerson, Kathy Lynn. *Writer's Guide to Everyday Life in Renaissance England* (Cincinnati: Writer's Digest Books, 1996)

Epstein, Steven A. *Wage Labor and Guilds in Medieval Europe* (Chapel Hill: University of North Carolina Press, 1991)

Fagniez, Gustave (ed.). *Documents relatifs à l'histoire de l'industrie et du commerce en France* (Paris: Alphonse Picard et Fils, 1898)

Fierro, Alfred and Laffont, Robert. *Histoire et Dictionnaire de Paris* (Paris: 1996)

Fremantle, Anne. *Age of Faith* (New York: Time-Life, 1965)

Geirnaert, Noël, and Vandamme, Ludo. *Bruges: Two Thousand Years of History* (Bruges: Stichting Kunstboek, 1996)

Geraud, Hercule. *Paris sous Philippe-le-Bel* (Paris: Crapelet, 1837)

Gies, Frances, and Joseph Gies. *Women in the Middle Ages* (New York: Harper Perennial, 1978)

Gies, Joseph, and Frances Gies. *Life in a Medieval Castle* (New York: Harper Row, 1974)

_____. *Life in a Medieval City* (New York: Harper Row, 1981)

_____. *Cathedral, Forge and Waterwheel* (New York: Harper Collins, 1994)

Gilliat-Smith, Ernest. *The Story of Bruges* (London: J.M. Dent & Co., 1901)

Gimpel, Jean. *The Medieval Machine* (London: Penguin, 1976)

Girouard, Mark. *Cities and People* (New Haven: Yale University Press, 1987)

Goetz, Hans-Werner. *Life in the Middle Ages* (Notre Dame IN: University of Notre Dame Press, 1993)

Gravett, Christopher. *German Medieval Armies 1300–1500* (Oxford: Osprey, 1985)

Bibliography

_____. *Knights at Tournament* (Oxford: Osprey, 1988)

_____. *German Medieval Armies 1000–1300* (Oxford: Osprey, 1997)

Grew, Francis. *Shoes and Patterns* (London: Museum of London, 1996)

Hale, John. *Renaissance* (New York: Time Incorporated, 1965)

_____. *The Civilization of Europe in the Renaissance* (New York: Atheneum, 1994)

Healey, Tim. *History of Costume* (London: MacDonald Educational Ltd., 1997)

Henisch, B. A. *Fast & Feast: Food in Medieval Society* (University Park PA: Pennsylvania State University Press, 1985),

Héron de Villefosse, René. *Histoire de Paris* (Paris: Grasset 1955)

Hillairet, Jacques. *Dictionnaire historique des rues de Paris* (Paris: Editions de Minuit, 1963)

Hills, R. L. *Richard Arkwright and Cotton Spinning* (London: Priory Press, 1973)

Hohenberg, Paul M., and Lees, Lynn. *The Making of Urban Europe, 1000–1950* (Cambridge, MA.: Harvard University Press, 1985)

Hollister, C. Warren. *Medieval Europe: A Short History* (New York: John Wiley & Sons, 1965)

Holmes, George (ed.). *The Oxford History of Medieval Europe* (Oxford: Oxford University Press, 1988)

James, John. *The Traveler's Key to Medieval France* (New York: Knopf, 1986)

Johnstone, Hilda (ed.). *Annales Gandenses: Annals of Ghent* (London: Thomas Nelson & Sons, 1951)

Jordan, William Chester (ed.). *The Middle Ages: An Encyclopedia for Students* Vol. 2. (New York: Charles Scribner's Sons, 1996)

Koch, H. W. *Medieval Warfare* (London: Bison, 1978)

_____. *Middeleeuwen Het Krijgsgebeuren in de Middeleeuwen* (Helmond: 1988)

Laenen, J. *Vlaanderen in het Begin der XIVde Eeuw en de Strijd tegen Philips den Schoone* (Antwerp: De Nederlandsche Boekhandel, 1901)

Langdon, J. *Horses, Oxen, and Technical Innovation* (Cambridge: Cambridge University Press 1986)

Law, Joy. *Fleur de Lys* (New York: McGraw-Hill, 1976)

Le Goff, Jacques. *Medieval Civilization, 400–1500* (London: Blackwell, 1990)

Lepinois, E. de, and Merlet, L. (eds.). *Cartulaire de Notre-Dame de Chartres* (Chartres: Garnier, 1863) Trans. Richard Barton, 1998, Vol. II, pp. 56-62.

Lester, Katherine Morris. *Historic Costume* (Peoria IL: Chas. A. Bennet Co., 1956)

Lloyd, T. H. *The English Wool Trade in the Middle Ages,* (Cambnridge: Cambridge University Press, 1977)

_____. *Alien Merchants in England in the High Middle Ages* (Cambridge: Cambridge University Press, 1982)

Luykx, Theo. *Het Grafelijk Geslacht Dampierre en zijn Strijd tegen Filips de Schone* (Leuven: Davidsfonds, 1952)

217

Bibliography

Maddens, Nicklaas (ed.). *De Geschiedenis van Kortrijk* (Tielt, Belgium: Lannoo, 1990)

van Maerlant, Jacob. *Spiegel Historiael* (Leuven: Davidsfonds-Clauwaert, 1997)

Marechal, J. *Geschiedenis van de Brugse Beurs* (Bruges: 1949)

Märtens, R. *Weltorientierungenund wirtschaftliches Erfolgsstreben Mittelalterlicher Großkaufleute: Das Beispiel Gent im 13 Jahrhundert* (Cologne: Böhlau, 1976)

McClellan, J. E., and Dorn, H. *Science and Technology in World History* (Baltimore: Johns Hopkins University Press, 1999)

McEvedy, Colin. *The New Penguin Atlas of Medieval History* (London: Penguin, 1992)

McKay, John, Hill, Bennett and Buckler, John. *A History of Western Society* (New York: Houghton Mifflin, 1999) 2 vols.

Minois, Georges. *Voluntary Death in the Western World*, trans. Lydia Cochrane (Baltimore: The Johns Hopkins University Press, 1998)

Monier, R. *Institutions centrales du Comté de Flandre du IXe siècle à 1384* (Paris: 1943)

Montgomery of al Alamein. *A History of Warfare* (London: Collins, 1968)

Montross, Lynn. *War through the Ages* (New York: Harper Row, 1960)

Morris, A. J. *A History of Urban Form before the Industrial Revolution* (New York: Addison-Wesley Longman, 1994)

Mumford, L. *The Lewis Mumford Reader* (New York: Pantheon Books, 1986)

Mus, O., and van Houtte, J. A. *Prisma van de Geschiedenis van Ieper* (Ieper: Stadsbestuur, 1974)

Newark, Timothy. *Medieval Warfare* (London: Jupiter, 1979)

Nicholas, David. *Medieval Flanders* (London: Longman, 1992)

Nicolle, David. *Arms & Armour of the Crusading Era 1050–1350* (London: Greenhill, 1988)

_____. *French Medieval Armies 1000–1300* (Oxford: Osprey, 1991)

_____. *Knight of Outremer 1187–1344* (Oxford: Osprey, 1996)

_____. *Italian Militiaman 1260–1392* (Oxford: Osprey, 1999)

Nowé, Henri. *La Bataille des Eperons d'Or* (Paris: La Renaissance du Livre, 1945)

Oakeshott, R. E. *A Knight and His Castle* (Chester Springs PA: Dufour, 1997)

_____. *A Knight and His Weapons* (Chester Springs PA: Dufour, 1997)

_____. *A Knight and his Horse* (Chester Springs PA: Dufour, 1998)

_____. *A Knight in Battle* (Chester Springs PA: Dufour, 1998)

_____. *A Knight and His Armour* (Chester Springs PA: Dufour, 1999)

Oliver, Jane. *Costume Through the Centuries* (London: Oliver & Boyd Ltd., 1963)

Oman, Sir Charles. *A History of the Art of War in the Middle Ages* (London: Greenhill Books, 1989) Volume 2

Painter, Sidney. *Medieval Society* (Ithaca, NY: Cornell University Press, 1951)

Parent-Duchatelet, A. J.-B. *La Prostitution dans la ville de Paris, considérée sous*

Bibliography

le rapport de l'hygiène publique, de la morale et de l'administration; ouvrage appuyé de documents statistiques (Paris, J. -B. Baillière, 1857) 2 vols.

Pirenne, Henri. *Histoire Belgique* (Brussels: Maurice Lamertin, 1922–29) 2 vols.

_____. *Early Democracies in the Low Countries* (New York: Harper Row, 1963)

_____. *Medieval Cities* (Princeton: Princeton University Press, 1969)

Rothero, Christopher. *Medieval Military Dress: 1066 to 1500* (Poole, UK: Blandford, 1983)

_____. *The Scottish and Welsh Wars 1250–1400* (Oxford: Osprey, 1989)

Rodenbach, Georges. *Bruges-la-Morte* (London: Atlas, 1993)

Runciman, Steven. *The Sicilian Vespers* (Cambridge: Cambridge University Press, 1958).

Singer, Charles, et al., *A History of Technology, Vol. II: The Mediterranean Civilization and the Middle Ages* (Oxford: Clarendon Press, 1956)

Strayer, Joseph R. *On the Medieval Origins of the Modern State* (Princeton: Princeton University Press, 1973)

_____ (ed.). *Dictionary of the Middle Ages*, Vol. 6. (New York: Charles Scribner's Sons, 1985)

Tomes, John. *Blue Guide: Belgium and Luxembourg* (New York: Norton, 1989)

Tuchman, Barbara. *A Distant Mirror: The Calamitous Fourteenth Century* (New York: Alfred Knopf, 1978)

Turnbull, Stephen. *The Book of the Medieval Knight* (New York: Crown Publishers 1985)

Velthem, Lodewijk van. *Spiegel Historiael (1248–1316)* ed. H. Vander Linden (Brussels: 1906–38) 3 vols.

Verbruggen, Jan Frans. *De Slag der Gulden Sporen* (Antwerp: Standaard, 1952)

_____. *1302 in Vlaanderen De Guldensporenslag* (Brussels: Koninklijk Legermuseum, 1977)

_____. *Vlaanderen na de Guldensporenslag* (Bruges: Westvlaamse Gidsenkring, 1991)

_____. *The Art of Warfare in Western Europe* (Woodbridge UK: Boydell, 1997)

Villani, Giovanni. *Historie Fiorentine*, in Muratori, L.A. (ed.) *Rerum Italicarum Scriptores*, Vol. 13

Waley, Daniel. *The Italian City Republics* (New York: McGraw-Hill, 1969)

Walker, Paul Robert. *The Italian Renaissance* (New York: Facts on File, 1995)

Warlop, E. *The Flemish Nobility Before 1300*, 4 vols. (Kortrijk: G. Desmet-Huysman, 1975-6)

Werveke, Hans van. *De Gentsche Stadsfinancien in de Middeleeuwen* (Brussels: Paleis der Academiën, 1934)

White, L., Jr. *Medieval Technology And Social Change* (New York: Oxford University Press, 1962)

Wilkinson, Philip. *Building* (New York: Alfred A. Knopf, 1995)

Bibliography

Wise, Terence. *Medieval European Armies* (Oxford: Osprey, 1975)
_____, *Medieval Heraldry* (Oxford: Osprey, 1980)
Wodsak, Felix. *Die Schlacht bei Kortryk* (Berlin: Karl Arnold, 1905)

Articles, Monographs, Pamphlets and Papers

Aspeslag, Pierre. *Chapel of the Holy Blood Bruges* (Oostende: Van Mieghem, 1988)

Bairoch, P. "International Industrialization Levels from 1750 to 1980" *Journal of European Economic History* (Fall 1982)

Barber, Malcolm Charles. "The Trial of the Templars Revisited" The Whichard Lecture, Fall 1999; first published in Nicholson, Helen (ed.) *The Military Orders, Vol. 2, Welfare and Warfare* (Aldershot, 1998)

Beck, H. G. J. (trans.). "William of Hundlehy's Account of the Anagni Outrage" *Catholic Historical Review*, Vol. 32 (1947), pp. 200–1

Begynhof St. Elisabeth Kortrijk (Kortrijk: Committee for Initiative of the Kortrijk Region, undated)

Bennett, Patricia (trans.). *Beguinage "The Vineyard" Brugge* (Oostende: Van Mieghem, 1988)

Berry, Maurice, and Fleury, Michel. *L'Enceinte et le Louvre de Philippe-Auguste* (Paris: Délagation à l'Action Artistique de la Ville de Paris, 1988)

Bland, C. C. Swinton (trans.). *The Autobiography of Guibert, Abbot of Nogent-sous-Coucy* (London: George Routledge & Sons, Ltd., 1925). Abridged and reprinted in L. Barnard and T. B. Hodges *Readings in European History* (New York: Macmillan, 1958), pp. 111–4.

Bovesse, J. "La Régence comtale namuroise en Flandre: juillet 1302–mai 1303," *Liber Buntinx*, pp. 139–65

Brehier, Louis. "Guillaume de Nogaret," *The Catholic Encyclopedia* Vol. XI (New York: Robert Appleton Co., 1911)

Dekker, C. and Kruisheer, J. G. "Een rekening van de abdij Ter Doest over het jaar 1315," *Bulletin de la Commission Royale d'Histoire* Vol. 133 (1967) pp. 273–305

Dendooven, Lucien. *De Abdij Ter Doest te Lissewege-Brugge* (Lissewege: Uitgeverij Groot Ter Doest, 1994–99)

Dewilde B., Pauwels, A., Verbruggen, J. F., and Warlop, E. "De Kist van Oxford," *De Leiegouw* Vol. XXIII (1980) pp.163–256

Diegerick, I. L. A. *Inventaire analytique et chronologique des chartes et documents appartenant aux archives de la Ville d'Ypres* (Bruges: Vandecasteele-Werbrouck, 1853–68) 7 vols.

Espinas, G., and Pirenne, H. (eds.). *Recueil de documents relatifs a l'histoire de l'industrie drapière en Flandre* (Brussels, 1906), p. 648; reprinted in R. C. Cave

Bibliography

and H. H. Coulson. *A Source Book for Medieval Economic History* (Milwaukee: The Bruce Publishing Co., 1936; reprinted, New York: Biblo & Tannen, 1965)

Evans, Martin M. *Ypres in War and Peace* (Andover UK: Pitkin Pictorials, 1992)

Gilmour, B., and Tyers, I. "Courtrai Chest : Relic Or Recent" *Papers of the Medieval Europa Brugge 1997 Conference*, Vol. V, pp. 17–26

Go for a Walk in Kortrijk (Kortrijk: Tourist Information Office, undated)

Godding, P. *Le Droit privé dans les Pays-Bas méridionaux du 12e au 18e siècles* (Brussels: Palais des Académies, 1987) p. 57

Hall E. T. "The Courtrai Chest from New College, Oxford, Re-Examined," *Antiquity*, Vol. 61, no. 231 (March 1987) pp. 104–107

Kortrijk (Kortrijk: Dienst Toerisme, undated)

Laures, Robert. "A Medieval Response to Municipal Pollution" presented to the Mid-America Conference on History (Lawrence KS: The University of Kansas, 17–19 September 1992)

Lissewege (Lissewege: VVV-Lissewege, undated)

Lucas, Henry S. "The Great European Famine of 1315, 1316 and 1317," *Speculum* Vol. V (1930) p. 343–77

Marechal, J. "Het Weezengeld in de Brugge stadfinancien van de middeleeuwen" *Annales de la Société d'Emulation de Bruges* Vol. 82 (1939): pp. 1–41

Marijnissen, R. H., and Van De Voorde, G. "De 'Chest of Courtrai,' een Vervalsing van het Pasticcio-Type" in *Mededelingen van de Koninklijke Academie voor Wetenschappen, Letteren en Schone Kunsten van België*, Klasse Schone Kunsten, Vol. XL (1978), no. 3, pp. 1–17.

le Muisit, Gilles, and Lemaître, H. (ed.). *Chroniques et annales* (Paris: Société de l'Histoire de France, 1905) pp. 67–8

Munro, John. *The Symbiosis of Towns and Textiles: Urban Institutions and the Changing Fortunes of Cloth Manufacturing in the Low Countries and England, 1280–1570* (Toronto: University of Toronto, 18 June 1998) Working Paper Number Ut-Ecipa-Munro5-98-03, Also at: *http://www.chass.utoronto.ca/ecipa/wpa. html*

Prevenier, W. "Motieven voor Leliaardsgezindheid in Vlaanderen in de Periode 1297–1305" *De Leiegouw*, Vol. 19 (1977) pp. 273–88

_____. "La Bourgeoisie en Flandre au XIIIe siècle" *Revue de l'Université de Bruxelles* Vol. 4 (1978) pp. 407–28.

_____, et al. "Tassen Crisis en Welvaart: Sociale Veranderingen, 1300–1482" *Algeme Geschiedenis der Nederlanden* (Utrecht: 1982) Vol. IV

Remy, A. F. J. "Jacob van Maelant" *The Catholic Encyclopedia* Vol. IX (New York: Robert Appleton Co., 1910)

Six, G. "La Bataille de Mons-en-Pévèle" *Annales de l'Est et du Nord* Vol. I (1905) p. 226

Smet, A. de. "De Klacht van de 'ghemeente' van Damme in 1280: Enkele gegevens over politieke en sociale toestanden in een klein vlaamse stad gedurende de tweede helft der XIIIe eeuw," *Bulletin de la Commission Royale d'Histoire* Vol. 115 (1950): pp. 1–15

Smet, J. de. "Brugse Leliaards Gevlucht te Sint-Omaars van 1302 tot 1305" *Annales de la Société d'Emulation de Bruges* Vol. 89 (1957) pp. 146–52.

Vandermaesen, M. "Vlaanderen en Henegouwen onder het Huis van Dampierre 1244–1384" *Algeme Geschiedenis der Nederlanden* (Utrecht: 1982)

Velthem, Lodewijk van (Louis). "Spiegel Historiael" in *Documents Illustrating the History of Belgium* Vol. I (Brussels: Ministry of Foreign Affairs, April 1978) pp. 105–7

Verbruggen, J. F. "De Slag bij de Pevelenberg" *Bijdragen voor de geschiedenis der Nederlanden* Vol. VI (1952) pp. 169–98

_____. "Beschouwingen over 1302" *Annales de la Société d'Emulation de Bruges* Vol. 93 (1956) pp. 38–53

_____. "De Historiografie van de Guldensporenslag" *De Leigouw* Vol. 19 (1977) pp. 245–72

_____. "De 'Chest Of Courtrai,' Een Oorspronkelijk Getuigenis Over 1302" in *Belgisch Tijdschrift voor Militaire Geschiedenis* Vol. XXIII, no. 7 (1980) pp. 585–608.

Visitor's Guide to the Groeningeabdij Kortrijk (Kortrijk: Stedelijke Musea Kortrijk, undated)

Weidenfeld, Katia. *La Police de la petite voirie à Paris à la fin du Moyen-Age* (Paris: L.G.D.J., 1996)

Werveke, H. van. "La Famine de l'an 1316 en Flandre et dans les régions voisines" *Revue du Nord* (1959) p. 5–14

_____. "Bronnenmateriaal uit de Brugse stadsrekeningen betreffende de hongersnood van 1316" *Bulletin de la Commission Royale d'Histoire* Vol. 125 (1959) pp. 431–510.

Wyffels, C. "Nieuwe Gegevens Betreffende een XIIIde Eeuwse 'Democratische' Stedelijke Opstand: De Brugse 'Moelemaye' (1280–81)" *Bulletin de la Commission Royale d'Histoire* Vol. 132 (1966) pp. 37–142.

Electronic Sources

In researching this book, it quickly became apparent that electronic resources were essential. Numerous sources proved useful, while others presented scant or questionable material. The sources below were particularly important in this work and deserve a bit of annotation as well as mention. By far the most useful web site on the topic of the Battle of the Golden Spurs was Joris de Sutter's excellent *De Liebaart* http://home.tiscalinet.be/liebaart/index.htm (2001). Intended for historians and reenactors, this site provides a great deal of well-illustrated material on the battle itself and the political, military, social and economic history surrounding it as well as numerous references.

Numerous medieval sources and gateways to other sites are available on the World Wide Web. *The Medieval Sourcebook* from New York's Fordham University Center for Medieval Studies, includes thousands of medieval resources, including full texts, at *http://www.fordham.edu/halsall/sbook.html*. Particularly useful was Humbert de Romans *On Markets & Fairs http://www.fordham.edu/halsall/source/1270romans.html*. Also the Online Resource Book for Medieval Studies (ORB) *http://orb.rhodes.edu/* provides a wealth of important sources and materials. Michigan State University's excellent online links are at *http://www.msu.edu/~georgem1/history/medieval.htm*. Beau A. C. Harbin's *Netserf* has 1512 links (1995–2001) at *http://www.netserf.org*. Also among the best is Nancy B. Mautz's *Creative Impulse, http://history.evansville.net/medieval.html*. Another is *Cariadoc's Miscellany* by David Friedman and Elizabeth Cook (1988–1992), *http://www.pbm.com/~lindahl/cariadoc/miscellany.html*. Also useful, particularly for the history of daily life, is David Ross's *Britain Express, http://www.britainexpress.com/index.htm*, particularly, *http://www.britainexpress.com/History/medieval-monastery.htm* and *http://www.britainexpress.com/History/Feudalism_and_Medieval_life.htm*.

Online social and economic histories of the medieval period were particularly useful. These include J. Bradford DeLong and Andrei Shleifer's *Princes and Merchants: European City Growth before the Industrial Revolution* (Berkeley: Dept. of Economics, University of California, 7 August 1995), *http://econ158.berkeley.edu/Refereed_Articles/Princes_and_Merchants/Princes.html* and E.L. Knox's, *Medieval Society http://orb.rhodes.edu/textbooks/westciv/medievalsoc.html* (1999). From Yale University, *Topics in Western Civilization: Ideals of Community and the Development of Urban Life, 1250–1700* (1986), at *http://www.cis.yale.edu/ynhtl/curriculum/guides/1986/3/*, has sections on the English guild method of learning; masks, costumes, ceremony life in seventeenth-century France; medieval life: squires, maidens and peasants; the ideas and ideals of man, from the Renaissance to the Reformation; Wooster Square in the context of the Italian renaissance; feasts, fairs and festivals: mirrors of Renaissance society; the vision of the city in the mind's eye, 1250/1700; and the illusion of the Renaissance. *Feudal Life, What Was It Really Like to Live in the Middle Ages*, an Annenberg/CPB Project posted by the Corporation for Public Broadcasting (1997), is available at *http://www.learner.org/exhibits/middleages/feudal.html*. Troy Scheid and Laura Toon's *City of Women* (High School for the Performing and Visual Arts) describes the roles of men and women in a medieval European city. Particularly useful were: *http://library.thinkquest.org/12834/text/visitthecity.html* and *http://library.think quest.org/12834/text/marketplace.html*. The history of guilds is well presented by high school students Bonnie Panagakis, Chris Marszalek and Linda Mazanek of Buffalo Grove, Illinois

Bibliography

(1997) at *http://renaissance.district96.k12.il.us/guildhall/ guilds/guilds.html*. Subsections of this site include The Development of Craft Guilds, Early Guild Regulations, Apprenticeships, Journeymen, Women in the Guilds, Social Services of the Guilds, The Great Weakness of the Guild System, Guild Links Outside of Guild Hall, and References. Guilds are also particularly well-presented by Gloria J. Betcher (Iowa State University, Ames Iowa) in *Date and Composition of The Book of Margery Kempe, http://www.public.iastate.edu/~gbetcher/373/guilds. htm.* Also good on everyday life are *Peasant Houses, http://scholar.chem.nyu.edu/ ~tekpages/peasanthouses.html; The Construction and History of Medieval Timber-Framed Houses in England and Wales, http://wonderful.org.uk/;* and *Windmills, http://scholar.chem.nyu.edu/~tekpages/windmills.html.*

A look at medieval mercenaries is provided by W. F. W. Garcia in *The Golden Falcon* Chap. 5, Winter's Bloom, *http://www.pillagoda.freewire.co.uk/CRECY. htm.* An interesting analysis of crossbows is Brian Jones's "The Crossbow in the Medieval Period" in *The Beckoning, http://www.gci-net.com/~users/W/wolf-soul/medieval/ crossbow/cross_l_v_c.html* (14 April 2001).

Useful among university lectures online is *Medieval Cities, Bruges and Florence* by Rice University's Richard Ingersoll, www.owlnet.rice.edu/~arch343/ lecture9.html (1995). A series of lectures by Gerhard Rempel of Western New England College includes the very useful *Guilds and Commerce, http:// mars.acnet.wnec.edu/~grempel/courses/wcl/lectures/24guilds.html,* as well as *Charlemagne, http://mars.acnet.wnec.edu/~grempel/courses/wcl/lectures/ 18charlemagne.html, Feudalism, http://mars.acnet.wnec.edu/~grempel/courses/ wcl/lectures/19feudalism.html, The Medieval Manor, http://mars.acnet.wnec.edu/ ~grempel/courses/wcl/lectures/22manor.html, Medieval Universities, http://mars. acnet.wnec.edu/~grempel/courses/wcl/lectures/25meduni.html, Gothic Cathedrals, http://mars.acnet.wnec.edu/~grempel/courses/wcl/lectures/26cathedral.html* and *The Black Death, http://mars.acnet.wnec.edu/~grempel/courses/wcl/lectures/ 27blackdeath.html.*

Lynn H. Nelson of the University of Kansas's Department of History posted the following in 1997: *The Rise of Capitalism, http://www.ukans.edu/kansas/ medieval/108/lectures/capitalism.html, The Rise of Feudalism, http://www.ukans. edu/kansas/medieval/108/lectures/feudalism.html, Europe in 1300, http://www. ukans.edu/kansas/medieval/108/lectures/europe_1300.html, Regional Specialization, http://www.ukans.edu/kansas/medieval/108/lectures/eleventh_century_econ-omy.html Five Contributions of the Middle Ages http://kuhttp.cc.ukans.edu/kansas/ medieval/108/lectures/medieval_achievements.html, The Peasants, http://kuhttp.cc. ukans.edu/kansas/medieval/108/lectures/peasants_llc.html, The Medieval Paupers, http://kuhttp.cc.ukans.edu/kansas/medieval/108/lectures/paupers.html.*

One difficulty inherent in using web sources is the fact that many sites become defunct and are lost to researchers (at least in their easily disseminated web form). This has been the case with the excellent *Paris: Urban Sanitation*

224

Bibliography

1200–1789, http://www.op.net/~uarts/krupa/ and a large series of medieval resources at Pennsylvania's Millersville University, which include: Tamara C. Willis, *Feasting and Fasting in Medieval England, http://www.millersv.edu/~english/homepage/duncan/medfem/feast.html* and *Medieval Domestic Life, http://www.millersv.edu/~english/homepage/duncan/medfem/domestic.html*, and Maureen E. Gallagher's *Motive Power, http://www.millersv.edu/~english/homepage/duncan/medfem/peas4.htm.*

Useful sites specific to Flanders include Ivan Sache *Flags in Fourteenth Century Flanders, http://www.crwflags.com/fotw/flags/be-vl-14.html* (April 19, 2001); and W. Simons, "The Beguine Movement in the Southern Low Countries: A Reassessment," *Bulletin de l'Institut Historique Belge de Rome* at Katherine Gill and Lisa Bitel (eds.), *Matrix, http://matrix.divinity.yale.edu/MatrixWebData/Simonsc.txt.* The history of Damme is presented by Raymond Van Meldert in *Damme, boekendorp* at *http://www.ping.be/~pin10181/dammeinform.htm* (October 2, 2000). Laurent Willen's superb site *Cyber-Kortrijk* (1997?) is at *http://www.ccim.be/courtrai/welcome.htm.* An excellent source on Belgian architecture, including numerous medieval structures in Bruges, Damme, Ghent and Lissewege, is maintained by Jeffery Howe of Boston College at *http://www.bc.edu/bc_org/avp/cas/fnart/arch/belgium.html.*

An excellent resource on medieval Paris is Marie-Christine Benveniste, *Paris at the Time of Philippe Auguste* (Paris: Ecole Multimedia, March 1999), *http://www.philippe-auguste.com/uk/index.html.*

Also the following were used for details:

The Belgian Travel Network, http://www.trabel.com/kortrijk/kortrijk-buildingstour.htm; The Linen House (Brussels), *http://www.thelinenhouse.com/learninglinen.asp; The International Museum of the Horse, http://www.imh.org/imh/kyhpl2a.html* (particularly Chapter 2 — "The Legacy of the Horse"); Kateryn de Develyn, *Sausage History, http://www.geocities.com/Athens/Acropolis/4756/sausages.htm;* John Sloan "The Stirrup Controversy," a thread on *medievl-l@ukanvm.cc. ukans.edu* (5 October 1994); and Paul J. Gans, *Medieval Technology Pages, http://scholar.chem.nyu.edu/~tekpages/* (2000), especially for "The Stirrup Controversy" *http://scholar.chem.nyu.edu/~tekpages/texts/strpcont.html* (1999) "The Great Harness Controversy," *http://scholar.chem.nyu.edu/~tekpages/loom.html* (1999) and "The Horizontal Loom," *http://scholar.chem.nyu.edu/~tekpages/loom.html* (1998).

Official (municipal) sites used include Kortrijk, *http://regio.kortrijk.be/index.html.* Ghent, *http://www.gent.be/gent/index.htm.* Bruges, *http://www.brugge.be/toerisme/en/index.htm* and *http://www.brugge.com/. Brugge 2002, http://www.brugge 2002.com/historiek2002/index_en.shtml.* Lissewege, *http://lissewege.gq.nu/.*

A useful directory of Bruges-related web sites is maintained by Lieve D'hont-Mus at *http://users.pandora.be/filip.d.hont/brugge.htm.*

Bibliography

However, the most useful electronic source on Bruges was not a web site, but an excellent multimedia CD-ROM program, *Bruges: More than an Art City* (Bruges: Bryggia/BMG Interactive, 1997). This well illustrated resource features thousands of photos, movie clips, animations and texts describing Bruges's history, geography, art, personalities, legends, etc.

Index

Aachen 50
Aalst 156
Aardenburg 43, 94, 117
abbeys 28, 31, 32, 33, 34, 80, 100, 122, 127, 128, 129, 134, 139, 150, 175, 185, 186
abbots 31, 33, 81, 100, 101, 150
Abelard, Peter 62
accounts 12, 15, 55, 75, 95–97, 117, 121, 125, 127, 140, 163
Ad Clericos 152
The Adoration of the Mystic Lamb (Ghent Altarpiece) 187
Adrianople 48, 82, 189
Aelfrida 104
Aëtius 48
Age of Faith 23, 167, 194
Agincourt 161
Agnes de Bourbon 125
ailettes 88
Albertus Magnus 194
Albigensians *see* Cathars
aldermen 10, 11, 26, 43, 45, 92, 93, 94, 95, 96, 99, 100, 101, 105, 111, 112, 116, 120, 141, 150, 151
Alexander, Prince of Scotland 105
Alfred the Great 104
Alice of Normandy 104
Aljubarrota 190, 192
almonds 41
almoners 33

alms-giving 54
almshouses 7, 22, 26, 35, 80, 178
Alps 3, 9, 17, 59, 179
Althing 194
alum 66
Amandus, Saint 78, 80
amber 16, 115
Amsterdam 43, 179
Anagni 71, 152, 153
Anjou, Angevin 56, 59, 67, 104, 118
Anti-Popes 153
Antwerp 12, 43, 57, 98, 172, 179, 188
apprentices 20–21
Aquitaine 50, 56, 68, 98, 157
Arabs 68
archers 75, 76, 84, 131, 132, 140, 158, 190, 191
Arezzo 61
armies 1, 22, 52, 56, 74–76, 83– 84, 89–92, 108, 109, 117, 121, 125–132, 138–142, 146–148, 156, 158, 160, 162, 165, 166, 189, 190, 194
armor 1, 48, 75, 76, 78, 83, 84, 85, 88, 89, 90, 91, 112, 128, 132, 138, 148, 191
Arnulf 27
Arques 147, 157
Arras 97, 125, 147, 155, 161
arsenals 75
art 23, 34, 79, 104, 115, 170, 179, 180, 181, 182, 187

Index

Artevelde, Jacob van 158, 187
Artevelde, Philip van 160–161, 169
Artevelde, van, family 158, 160–161, 169, 187
artisans 9, 10, 19, 20, 21, 64, 75, 92, 93, 95, 99, 101, 105, 118, 122, 162
Artois, County of 17, 123, 162
Asia Minor 167
Athis-sur-Orge, Peace of 148–149, 151
Atlantic Ocean 16
Attila 48
Aubriot, Hughes 65
Augsburg 12, 18
Augustijnenrei 42
Augustinians 34
Aumale 140
Austria 72, 162, 183, 189, 190
Auvergne 67
auxiliaries 1, 91, 117
Avars 49
Avesnes of Hainault 103, 107, 109, 147, 149
Avignon 153
Avis Dynasty 166
axes 84, 86, 160
Aztecs 167

Babylonian Captivity of the Church 153
bailiffs 11, 50, 93, 100, 151
bakers 21, 39, 95, 165
Baldwin Bras de Fer (Iron Arm) 6, 78
Baldwin II of Flanders 104
Baldwin IV of Flanders 104
Baldwin V of Flanders 104
Baldwin IX of Flanders 98
Ball, John 193
Baltic 13, 163, 166
banks 12, 17, 96–97, 152, 154, 162–163, 179, 183, 184
bannerlords 108, 129
banners 90, 130, 131, 134, 136, 142, 143, 161
Bannockburn 190
Barbavera 158
Bardi 17
barons 52, 140
Baroque style 170, 173, 175
Bar-sur-Aube 13
Basilica of the Holy Blood 24, 180
bathhouses 64
Baudouin, son of Guy of Dampierre 105
Bavon (Bavo or Baaf), Saint 79

Beatrix 104, 105
Beaucaire 69
Beaumont, Alix de 104
beer 41, 53, 96, 97
beeswax 13
beghards 27
beguinages (begijnhofen), beguines 26, 27, 81, 124, 125, 136, 171, 172, 182
belfries 16, 43, 79, 80, 95, 173, 174, 176, 180, 187
Belgian language controversy 181, 188
belts 114
Benedict of Nursia, Saint 29
Benedict XI 153
Benedictines 29, 31, 32, 194
Bernard, Saint 31
Beurs (Beurse) 145, 163, 184
Beursplein 163
Big Margot 161
Bijloke 80
Bishop of Metz 105
Bissegem's Gate 172
Black Death 159, 164, 167
Blanche of Castile 67, 104
bliauds (bliauts) 112, 113
Bocarme, Visart de 181
Bologna 40, 61, 62
bombards 160
Boniface 71, 140, 152, 153
Boniface VII 140
Boniface VIII 71, 152
Borluut, Fulk 100
Borluut, Gerelm 99
Borluut, Jan 99–101, 122, 125, 151
Borluut (family) 99–101, 122, 125, 151
Borluut-van Sinte Baafs feud 99
Boston 146
Boulogne 68, 82, 129, 132
Bourbourg 105
Bourges 161
Bouvines 59, 79, 147
Braamberg district 42
Brabant (Duchy and Province of), Brabantine 12, 17, 39, 47, 57, 79, 98, 100, 104, 106, 125, 126, 128, 129, 131, 138, 140, 142, 143, 146, 158, 162, 170, 180, 188
bracelets 114
braies 76, 87
Brangwyn Museum 182
brassarts 88
Braveheart (film) 2
bread 11, 35, 39, 40, 53, 57, 96

Breidel, Jan 22, 116, 118, 121, 122, 127, 150, 180, 181
Bremen 13
Brétigny, Treaty of 159
Britain 13, 165, 194
Brittany 146, 157, 159
broaches 114
Broel towers 170, 171, 175, 176
broker-hoteliers 162–163
brokers 13, 133, 142
Brothers of the Sack 34
Bruges 3, 5–13, 28, 31, 32, 34–38, 42–45, 59, 64, 67, 74, 75, 76, 80, 92–97, 99, 106, 107, 109, 111, 112, 115–129, 138, 141–143, 145, 149–150, 155–158, 161–164, 166, 169, 176–187
Bruges-la-Morte 179
bucklers 78, 136
Budastraat 172
building 22, 37–38, 42, 57, 59–60, 62–63, 82, 97, 116, 124, 172, 182, 184
Bulgaria 167
Bull Unam Sanctam 71, 152
Bulskamp 109, 110
Burchard of Avesnes 103
Burg 6, 7, 23, 27, 43, 45, 180
burghers 9, 37, 45, 47, 75, 78, 82, 92, 93, 94, 95, 99, 101, 106, 107, 111, 112, 115, 116, 118, 126, 150
Burgundy 48, 104, 159, 161–163, 170, 179–181, 188, 189, 191
Burlats 129, 131, 140
butchers 22, 40, 64, 95, 116, 118, 142, 151, 165, 181
Byzantine Empire, Byzantium 68, 189

Calais 159, 161
calefactory 32
call to arms 83
Calvinists 171
Cambrai 158
Cambridge 61
canals 6, 7, 10, 16, 28, 38, 42, 64, 80, 82, 118, 172, 178, 182, 183, 186, 187
candles 38, 40, 165
canon law 23, 31, 56
Canossa 31
cantors 34
cap-à-pied 88
caparisons 89
capes 76, 113
Capetian kings 51, 55, 56, 59, 84, 157
capitalism 194

cardinals 153
Carmelites 34
Carolingians 23, 49, 51, 55
carpenters 43, 64, 133
carpets 175
carts 5, 15, 16, 17, 43
cash economy 12
Cassel 121, 123, 149, 155, 156, 157, 166, 189
Castille 41
Castle of the Counts 43, 82
castles 6, 43, 57, 60, 78, 82, 116, 120, 121, 124, 125, 126, 129, 136, 137, 169, 170, 173, 187
Catalaunian Fields 48
Catalonia 55
Cathars 56, 59, 68, 69
cathedrals 22–24, 28, 35, 43, 59, 66, 73, 79, 81, 82
Catherine, Saint 67, 173, 175
Catherine of Valois 161
cavalry 48, 75, 77, 82, 84, 90, 91, 128, 132, 133, 142, 147, 189, 190, 191
Celestine V 71
celibacy 31
cellarers 33
cemeteries 22, 63, 173
ceramics 38–40, 175
chain mail *see* mail
chamberlains 49
Champagne 13, 16, 67, 104, 152
Champeaux (Les) 63
chancery 49
chanfrons 89
Chapel of Saint Basil 24
chapels 24, 27, 31, 32, 35, 67, 96, 124, 169, 173, 186
charity 7, 22, 26, 34, 35, 54, 80, 164, 178
Charlemagne 3, 7, 49, 50, 124, 162
Charles I 118
Charles IV 68, 156
Charles VI ("the Mad") 159
Charles VII 161, 162
Charles Martel 49
Charles of Valois 109, 141
Charles the Bald 124
Charles the Bold 162, 181
Charles the Fat 50
Charles the Good 23, 74
charters 10–11, 18–19, 35, 43, 45, 55, 64, 74, 79, 80, 95, 96, 97, 141, 142, 193
Chartres 81
Chateauvilain, Simon de, II 104

229

Index

Châtillon de Saint Pol, Jacques de 110, 111, 116–118, 138, 139
Châtillon-sur-Marne, Hugues de, Count of Blois and Dunois 105
Chaucer, Geoffrey 166
cheese 11, 40, 57
chevalier 88
child-bearing 54
China 12, 145, 167
chivalry 1, 49, 85, 90, 137, 160, 180, 194
choir monks 34
Christ on the Cross 181
chroniclers, chronicles 62, 79, 91, 92, 127, 138, 191
Chroniques de Flandre 138
Chu Yuan-chang 167
church bells 81, 145
Church of Our Lady (Onze Lieve Vrouwkerk), Bruges 24–26, 181
Church of Our Lady (Onze Lieve Vrouwkerk), Damme 35
Church of Our Lady (Onze Lieve Vrouwkerk), Kortrijk,124 140, 171, 173, 176
Church of Our Lady (Onze Lieve Vrouwkerk) Lissewege 28, 30, 150, 185
churches 22–35, 43, 55, 171, 187
Cinque Ports 68, 98
circlets 114
Cistercians 31, 32, 80, 122
citadels 5, 172
Citeaux 31
City Archives (Bruges) 176
City Museums and Public Library (Kortrijk) 176
Claerhout, Jef 185
clays 39
Clement V 153, 154
clergy 31, 34, 54, 57, 71, 86, 105, 141, 145
Clermont 56, 104, 129
clocks 145, 165
clogs 76, 114
cloth 7–13, 17–19, 59, 76, 78, 93–95, 107, 112–114, 124, 151–152, 163–165, 179, 186
Cloth Hall of Bruges 16
Cloth Hall of Damme 35
Cloth Hall of Ghent 187
Cloth Hall of Kortrijk 173–174
clothing 7, 9, 10, 32, 37, 112–115, 165
Clovis 48
Cluny 31
cobblestones 5, 65

coifs 76, 87, 120, 127
coins 52, 106, 107
Cokerulle 95
College of Europe 184
Cologne 5, 15, 16, 18, 32, 166, 180
colombage 37
Colonna, Sciarra 152
Colonna family 71, 152
Comines, Philippe de 170
commerce 3, 5–18, 21–22, 28–29, 56, 59, 63–65, 93–99, 104, 107–108, 111, 146, 151–152, 156, 157, 162–165, 171, 179, 184
commoners 1, 9, 18, 23, 28, 37, 40, 45, 47, 57, 59, 73, 75, 81, 82, 87, 92, 95–99, 105, 106, 108, 111, 112, 115, 116, 118, 119, 121, 122, 126, 128, 129, 142, 143, 150, 191
communio 74
communism 21
Compline 32
Coninck, Pieter de 116–118, 121, 122, 127, 133, 141, 142, 150, 180, 181
coningstavel (*coningstavelryen*) 76
Constable of France 147, 159, 160
constabularies 76
Constantinople 56, 62, 67, 81, 82, 124, 167, 171
construction 22, 37–38, 42, 57, 59–60, 62–63, 82, 97, 116, 124, 172, 182, 184
contracts 12, 19, 21
convents 27, 32, 34, 182
coopers 142
copper 163
Cornwall 29
Cortoriacum 123
cotehardies 112
cotes 112–113
cotton 9, 113
Council of Lyon 70
councils 10, 38, 42, 43, 45, 75, 76, 92, 93, 95, 97, 101, 105, 108, 117, 129, 141, 142, 180
Countess of Blois-Chartres 81
counts 48–51
Count(s) of Flanders 42–45, 47–51, 73, 82, 92, 164
County of Flanders 3, 57, 123, 142, 163, 186, 188
Coupure 183
coursers 89
Courtenay, Mahaut de 104
Courtrai *see* Kortrijk

Index

Courtrai Chest 78, 119, 120, 127, 133, 136, 139, 175
courts 11, 22, 23, 89, 96, 106, 142
couters 88
couvrechefs 114
Coventry 180
cowls 76
craftsmen 9, 10, 19, 20, 21, 64, 75, 92, 93, 95, 99, 101, 105, 118, 122, 162
cranes 7, 183
Crécy 159, 190
Crevecoeur 104
crossbows 74–77, 84, 91, 122, 128, 129, 131–133, 136, 156, 160, 189–190
Crown Flanders 56, 103
Crown of Thorns 67
Crusades 13, 55, 56, 71, 75, 82, 93, 115, 134, 154
cuisses 87, 88
Cultural Capital of Europe, Bruges as 183
Cultuurraad van de Nederlandse Cultuurgemeenschap 188
customs 10, 54, 85, 96, 146
cyclas 112
Czechs 191

daffodils 182
dagges (dagging) 113
Dale, Jan uten 99
Dale, Jozef van 172
damask 113, 115, 124, 175
Damme 6–7, 35–36, 43, 96, 117, 158, 184–185
Dampoort 6, 7, 43, 183
Danes 17, 35, 49, 166, 167
Dante Alighieri 2, 141, 158
Danube 17
daughters 53, 68, 104, 105, 106, 117, 149, 155, 156, 157, 161, 162
debasement 49, 163
debts 105, 107, 149, 154
Dechargeurs, rue des 63
Declaration of Rense 166
Deinze 156
demesne 58
democracy 68, 105
Dendermonde 104, 182
Denmark 17, 35, 49, 166, 167
destriers 88, 89, 91, 134, 191
Devreese, Godfried 176
DeVries, Kelly 190
diamonds 114, 179

Diest 182
Dietrich (Thierry) of Alsace 24, 132
diets 39–41, 57
Dijver 6, 7
Ditmarschen 190
Dominic, Saint 34
Dominicans 34
Dordrecht 98
Dottignies 139
Douai 5, 19, 92, 96, 106, 107, 149
doublets 78
doves, as omens 127
dowries 97
drapers 64, 94, 95, 96, 97, 151
du Guesclin, Bertrand 159
Duiveland 147
Dunkerque Floods 6
Duns Scotus 62
Dutch occupation 172
Dutch Republic 170
dyers 18–19, 66 115
Dyck, Anthony van 175, 181

Earl of Surrey 189
earls 52, 189
earthenware 39, 40
East Flanders 57, 125, 129, 142
economic growth 12, 42, 68, 164
Edward I 68, 70, 93, 98, 104, 106, 108, 109, 110, 190
Edward II 106, 190
Edward III 157–160, 166, 190, 191
Edward, the Black Prince 159
Egypt 29, 62
Eleanor 56, 104
Electors 166
Eligius 5
embargoes 93, 108
enamel 88
England 5, 7, 10, 11, 17, 31, 35, 52, 55, 56, 61, 68–71, 84, 93, 98, 104–108, 110, 119, 146, 151–153, 157–163, 166, 169, 190
English Channel 35, 146, 158–159
English Convent 183
epaulets 88
Erection of the Cross (painting) 175
Eric of Pomerania 167
esprit-de-corps 84
Estates General 159
esterlin 106
Etienne Marcel, rue 60
Eu 140
euro 183

231

Index

European Union 183
Evermardus 31
excommunication 23, 31, 152, 153
Ezelpoort 24, 43, 178

factories 165
failles (falies) 27
falchions 76, 127, 136
families 10, 12, 20, 21, 50, 53, 54, 57, 71, 94, 96, 97, 99, 113, 149, 151, 183
fans 115
fashions 37, 112–115
fasting 41
Faumont 147
feasting 41
Fens 17
Ferdinand of Portugal 79
Ferronerie, rue de la 63
feudal society 9, 55
feudalism 51, 52, 54, 84, 129, 189
fief 3, 53, 94, 103, 107
Fiennes, Jean de 105
fines 65, 83, 97, 103, 151, 157
Finland 13
fire hazards 38
First Crusade 55, 82
First World War *see* World War I
fish 11, 16, 17, 35, 40, 53, 127, 163, 184
fishmongers 142, 151
Fitzalan, English naval commander 158
The Five Great Cities 107, 149
flax 7, 9, 13, 124, 175
Flemish Community 188
Flemish Region 57, 142, 188
Flemish shillings 108
Fleur-de-lys (lilies) 98
Flines 105, 146
Florence, Florentines 5, 12, 17–18, 126, 145, 152, 163, 183
Floris V of Holland 104, 184
Flotte, Pierre 69, 118, 132, 138, 139, 152
Fontainebleau 68, 154
food 11, 13, 16, 20, 34–35, 39–41, 53, 57, 96–97, 163
foot soldiers 1, 2, 74, 76, 78, 84, 90, 91, 108, 120, 126, 131–133, 138, 140, 189, 191
foot treadle 12
Forestiers 173
forests 57
fork 39
fortresses 91

The Foundation of Groeninge Abbey (painting) 175
Franc of Bruges 125
France 26, 27, 31, 48, 50, 55, 56, 59, 61, 67–72, 82, 87, 98, 100, 101, 105–108, 110, 111, 126, 128, 134, 135, 140, 142, 143, 147–149, 151, 152, 153, 154, 158–163, 169, 172, 176, 187, 188, 189, 192, 194
Francis I 65
Francis of Assisi, Saint 34
Franciscans 34, 100
Franks, Frankish kingdom 5, 11, 48, 50, 123, 189
Franzesi, Musciatto de 152
Frederick Barbarossa 189
freedoms 9, 10, 11, 81
friars 34, 67
Friday Market (Ghent) 81
Frisians 17, 27, 35, 147
Fuggers 12
fullers, fulling 7, 12, 18 19, 94, 96, 127, 142, 151, 165
furniture 38
furriers 64, 66
furs 13, 16, 64, 66, 113, 115, 167

Gallican Church 70
gallows 62, 65
gambeson 87
garbage 5, 65
Gascony 56, 68, 98, 106, 157
gates 7, 42, 74, 129, 136, 137, 170, 172, 178
Gaul 5, 48
gauntlets 78, 88
gems 114
Genoa 12, 13, 16, 71, 128, 131, 132, 145, 158, 159, 163, 183
Gentenaars 74, 79, 99, 105, 116, 117, 122, 151, 156, 169
Gentpoort 43, 178
Gentse Feesten 187
George, Saint 183
Germanic peoples 48
Germany 5, 13, 26, 31, 34, 35, 48, 50, 53, 69, 88, 94, 97, 112, 117, 146, 158, 163, 172, 189
Gezelle, Guido 175, 179
Ghent 5, 17, 19, 34, 43, 74, 78–83, 91–93, 97, 99–101, 105–112, 118, 123–126, 141–143, 148, 151, 155–163, 166, 169, 170, 182, 186–187

232

Index

Ghent Altarpiece 187
Ghibellines 71
Ghiselhuus 45
Gistel family 94
gloves 64, 66, 87, 115, 119, 120, 127
Godfrey of Brabant 131, 138, 140
Godwinson, Tostig 104
Goede Vrijdag 118
goedendags 78, 79, 120, 127, 128, 133, 134, 142, 147, 160, 175
gold 59, 88, 90, 105, 111, 114, 115
Golden Bull of 1356 166
Golden Spurs 2, 139, 143, 150, 166, 169, 173, 175, 176, 180, 183, 187, 188, 189, 194
Got, Bertrand de, Archbishop of Lyons 153
Gothic style 24, 26, 28, 32, 33, 67, 80, 124, 170, 180, 186
Gouden Handrei 42
government 10, 18, 19, 45, 49, 51, 52, 92, 93, 95, 97, 112, 116, 120, 122, 142, 159, 160, 163, 164
gowns 37, 112
Grafenburg 6
grand fairs 13, 16, 152
Grand Pont 63
Grande Boucherie 63
Grands Chroniques 70, 110, 135
Graslei 80, 187
Grauzon 146
Gravensteen 43, 82, 83
Great Crane 8
Great Schism 153
Great Yarmouth 98
Greece 51, 194
Gregory VII 31
Grenata, rue 66
Grève, place de 63
Grève market 63
grocer-pharmacists 64
Groene Rei 7, 42
Groeninge Museum 182
Groeninge Abbey 128–129, 175
Groeninge Beek 128, 129, 131, 135, 194
Groeningeabdij Museum 175
Groeningeveld (Groeninge plain) 126, 128, 176, 177, 180, 188, 190–191, 193
Grote Beek 128, 129, 133
Gruuthuse (family and museum) 31, 182
Gueldres 158
Guelphs 71
guild socialism 21
guilds 9–10, 15, 18–23, 64, 75–76, 92–97,

99, 101, 105, 110, 115–118, 121–122, 127–133, 141–142, 149–151, 162–165, 167, 189–190
Guillaume le Breton 63
Guillaume, brother of Guy of Dampierre 93
De Guldensporenslag (painting) front cover, iv, 173
Gulik, William of *see* William of Gulik
gunpowder 162, 178, 190, 191
Guy of Dampierre 43, 68, 93–109, 116, 117, 124–125 130, 132, 143, 149
Guy of Namur 104, 120–121, 125, 128, 130–133, 136, 138, 147

Habsburgs 162
Haec, Wasselin 99, 151
Hainault, County of 103, 107, 109, 111, 124, 128, 138, 146, 149, 155, 158
hair 114
Halles (Les) 63
Hamburg 13
Handelskom 183
handkerchiefs 115
Hanseatic League, Hansa, Hanse 10, 13, 19, 34, 93–95, 163, 166–167, 183, 184
Hapsburg 162, 190
harbors 35, 184
harnesses 17
hats 37, 114, 165
hatters 64
hauberks 87, 120, 127
helmets 83, 84, 86, 88, 91, 119, 120, 128, 133
hemp 13, 77
Hendrik Consciencelaan 178
hennin 114
Henry I 55, 56, 79
Henry II 56, 59
Henry of Bolingbroke 160
Henry of Lontzen 120, 133
Henry the Navigator, Prince of Portugal 166
herbs 41
heresies 56, 154
hériban 83
herring 17, 35, 184
hides 163
Hincmar, Archbishop of Rheims 55
Hoeke 185
Holland 13, 98, 103, 104, 105, 107, 109, 111, 146, 147, 149, 161, 184
Holstein 190

Index

Holy Land 56, 67, 69, 154
Holy Roman Emperor Henry IV 31
Holy Roman Empire, Holy Roman
    Emperors 3, 17, 31, 39, 47, 49, 56, 57,
    71, 79, 103, 106, 153, 166, 188
Holy Saviour's 24
homage 51, 52, 54, 71
honey 13, 41
honeymooners 6, 178, 180
Honorius III 67
Hoogstraat 183
hôpital de la Trinité 66
hôpital de Saint-Christophe 66
Hôpital des Pauvres de Sainte-Oppor-
    tune 67
hôpital Sainte-Catherine 67
horse collars 58
horsemen of the Apocalypse 68
horses 5, 10, 35, 48, 58, 59, 76, 85–91,
    121, 126, 128, 131, 133, 136, 138, 157,
    161, 191
Hospitallers 23
hospitals 22, 26, 66, 67, 80, 176, 181
Hôtel-Dieu 66
houppelandes 113
households 38, 39, 40, 54, 55, 165
houses, housing 22, 37, 62, 182
Hove, Jan uten 99
Hove, Philip uten 99
Hugh Capet 51, 55
Hundred Years War 152, 157–162, 169,
    190, 191
Huns 48
hunting 87, 154
Hus, John 193
husbands 21, 54
Hussite Wars 191

Iceland 194
Iconoclasts 173
Ieper (Ypres) 5, 16, 19, 41, 78, 92–97,
    107, 109, 122, 125, 129, 136–137,
    141–142, 148, 151, 155–158, 163–166,
    172
Imperial Flanders 56, 103, 149, 155
indemnities 95, 97, 148, 161
India 167
indulgences 56
Industrial Revolution 7, 165, 179, 194
industry 12, 17, 18, 21, 34, 66, 93–95,
    124, 163–165, 171, 176, 179
infantry 1, 75, 82, 83, 84, 85, 128, 132,
    133, 142, 147, 189, 190, 191

Inferno 158
inflation 109, 163
Inghelborchtoren 170, 171
inspectors 165
intercropping 58
International Hanseatic Days of Modern
    Times 184
Ireland 29, 160
Isabella of France 157, 160
Isabelle, daughter of Guy of Dampierrre
    105
Isabelle of Aragon 68
Italy 3, 12, 13, 17, 18, 48, 50, 59, 60, 65,
    69, 71, 118, 131, 141, 145–146, 152–153,
    163, 194

Jacquerie 159
Japan 54
Jean II, King of France 159
Jeanne, daughter of Guy of Dampierrre
    105
jewelers 64
jewelry 53, 88, 114, 115, 176
Jews 11, 59, 64, 154
Joan of Arc 161
Joan of Constantinople, Countess of
    Flanders 81, 124, 171
Joan of Navarre, Queen of France 68,
    111, 115
John, King of England 11, 59
John I, Duke of Burgundy 104
John I, King of Portugal 166
John II, Duke of Burgundy 106, 131
John of Avesnes 103, 107, 109
John of Bruges 31
John of Gaunt 160, 166
John of Namur 104, 116–117, 141–142,
    156
John of Renesse 126, 129, 130, 131, 137
journeyman 20, 22
jousts 85
Judith 104
Julian II, Emperor 66
Jülich (Juliers) see William of Gulik
Juliers, Margrave of 158
Julius Caesar 48
Justinian 11, 115
Justinian Code 11

Kalish, Peace of 166
Kerchove, Eustace van den 100, 101
Keyser, Nicaise De 173
kirtles 112

Index

kitchens 34, 39
Klauwaart 98
knights 1, 2, 23, 47, 48, 52, 53, 55, 67, 69, 74–76, 78, 81, 82, 84–91, 101, 108, 109, 111, 112, 117, 118, 120, 125–133, 135–140, 142, 147, 148, 154, 161, 166, 167, 189–191, 194
Knights Templar 23, 130, 154
Koblenz, Treaty of 166
Koksijde 31
Komvest 183
Korenlei 80, 187
Korenmarkt 80
Kortrijk 1, 2, 7, 17, 19, 79, 92, 103, 108, 109, 117, 119, 121–126, 128, 129, 134–137, 140, 141, 142, 146–150, 152, 155–157, 160, 161, 169–179, 182, 184, 187–191
Kossovo 167
Kraanplein 7
Kruispoort 43, 178

La Rochelle 159
Laarne Castle 82
labor unions 18, 165, 194
Lagny-sur-Marne 13
Lambert, Lord of Lissewege 31
lances 77, 84, 86–91, 161
landlords 13, 62, 63
landowners 50, 83
Landry, Saint 66
Lange Rei 7
language controversy 181, 188
Laon 81
Lapscheure 185
Latin Quarter 62
Laupen 190
law 11, 15, 48, 53, 54, 59, 62, 69, 95, 96, 115, 132, 156, 169, 194
leather 1, 13, 64, 76, 84, 88, 98, 114, 163
Left Bank 59
leggings 87
Legnano 189
Leie (Lys) 7, 78, 80, 123, 124, 128, 156, 170, 171
Leliaarts 98, 99, 101, 111, 115–122, 141, 149–151, 155, 156
Lendit market 63
Leopold II 181
Léproserie Saint Lazare 63
letters of exchange 12, 163
Leuven 175, 176, 180, 182, 188
liberties 11

Liebaarts 98, 99, 101, 111, 115, 117, 118, 151, 155
Liège 17, 105, 117
Lier 182
Lier, Treaty of 106
Lieve 24, 25, 30, 78, 172
lilies, as symbols 120
Lille 5, 16, 92, 97, 107, 109, 148, 149, 155, 156, 172
Limburg 57, 106, 188
limestone 28
Limoges 159
linen 7, 9, 32, 37, 76, 77, 87, 88, 112, 113, 114, 124, 175
Lion of Flanders 94, 134, 176
lions, as symbols 98, 120, 130, 131, 134, 142, 143, 176
Lissewege 27, 28, 30, 31, 122, 127, 150, 185, 186
living standards 165
Livre de la Taille of 1292 64
loans 114, 149, 163, 164
Lodi, Henri de 105
Loire 159
Lombard League 189
Lombards 49, 67, 154
London 10, 95, 98, 146, 179
longbows 190
looms 12, 38, 75, 158, 176
Lords of Oudenaarde and Gavre 105
Lorraine 129
Louis of Nevers 156–157
Louis V 51
Louis VI 56, 63
Louis (VI) the Fat 56
Louis VII 56, 66
Louis VIII 67, 103
Louis IX, Saint 67, 69, 70, 84, 103
Louis X 68, 154, 155
Louis XI 162
Louis XIV 172, 176, 184
Louis XIV style 172
Louvain 61
Louvre 60, 65, 152
Low Countries 2, 13, 24, 38, 41, 61, 152, 155, 163, 187
Lübeck 13
Lucca 12
Luke, Saint 193
Lutetia 60
Luxembourg 104, 106, 128, 184
Luxembourg gardens 60
Lys see Leie

Index

Maas River 17, 39, 92
Maastricht 117, 140
Macedonian phalanx 190
maces 74, 84
Machiavelli, Niccolò 194
Maerlant, Jacob van 105, 184
magistrates 10, 97, 111, 116, 155, 170
Magna Carta 11
Magpie Brothers 34
mail 76, 78, 84, 87, 90, 91, 108, 113, 119,
 120, 127
Maine 56, 63
Mainz 117
Maison-Dieu-Sainte-Catherine 67
Male 43, 116, 120, 159, 161, 173
Mali 167
manors 42, 55, 57, 58, 113
manorial system 57, 165
Mansa Musa 167
mansions 10, 37, 38
mantles 113
manufacturing 12, 17, 18, 21, 34, 66, 93–
 95, 124, 163–165, 171, 176, 179
manuscripts 32
Marcel, Etienne 159
Marche, Guillaume de la 62
Marcq 147
Margaret of Cleves 105
Margaret of Constantinople, Countess
 of Flanders 27, 35, 92, 93, 100, 103
Margaret of Lorraine 104
margraves (margravates) 50, 104, 117,
 158
Marguerite 104, 156
Maria Bridge 26
Marie 104, 117
Maristraat 26
Market Square 173
markets 5, 9, 10, 11, 13, 15, 16, 21, 35, 43,
 58, 63, 80, 152, 162–164, 169, 173, 174,
 185
Markt 6, 23, 43
marquis 52
marriage 21, 23, 53, 54, 56, 68, 103–106,
 156, 162
"Marten" and "Kalle" 173
Mary of Burgundy 162, 179
Matilda 104
Matins 32, 103, 118, 119, 120, 122, 125,
 149, 180, 193
Matins of Bruges 118
Maubert, place 62
Maximilian of Austria 162, 179

mayors 10, 45, 49, 92, 120
meals 20, 40–41
Mechelen 98
Medici family 12
medicine 34, 62, 165
melees 85
Melun, Treaty of 107
Memling, Hans 182
men-at-arms 119, 120, 136
mercenary 91, 122, 190
mercers 142
merchants 7, 9–19, 34, 37, 43, 58, 63–64,
 74, 92, 94, 98, 101, 105, 107–108, 122,
 126, 142, 145, 146, 152, 155, 159, 165,
 183
Mercurius 173
Merovech 48
Merovingians 48, 49, 51, 83, 124
Meuse River see Maas
Mexico City 167
Michaelangelo 181
middle class 9, 19
Middle East 145
militias 10–11, 22, 74–79, 85, 93, 101,
 110–111, 120, 127–133, 136–137 141–143,
 146–148, 156–157, 165–166
mills 41–42, 57, 63
Ming Dynasty 167
miniatures 34, 175
mining 31, 65
Minnewater 6, 27, 178
misericorde 88
missi dominici 50
moats 42, 60, 82, 128, 172, 175
Moerkerke 185
Moerlemae 95
Molay, Jacques de 154
monasticism 5, 17, 28–34, 55
Mongols 68, 167
monopoly 10, 18, 19, 23, 35, 57, 64, 95,
 98, 153, 163, 164, 184
Mons-en-Pévèle 147, 148, 157
Montfaucon 65
Montjoie Saint-Denis 134
Montmartre 65
Montpellier 61
Montreuil, Treaty of 93
monuments 176, 177, 185–186
Moors 11, 49, 50, 88
Morat (Murten) 191
Morel 127, 136
Morgarten 190
Morley, English naval commander 158

Index

Moselle 17
Mossenberg 126
Mughal Dynasty 167
museums 170, 172, 173, 175–176, 181, 182
mustard 41, 127
myth 188, 189

Namur 17
Nancy 162, 191
Naples 71, 89
National Flax Museum 175
nationalism 120, 142, 150, 181, 187
nation-state 193, 194
Navarre 55, 68, 111, 115
Neckar 18
Nepomucenus, Saint 170
Nesle 129, 132, 137–140
Netherlands 26, 142, 162, 172, 176, 179, 188
nettle potage 40
Nevele, Walter Van 124
Neville's Cross 190
New College (Oxford) 78, 119
nicolaites 31
nobility 9–12, 33, 51, 55, 57, 65, 67, 69, 81, 85, 86, 98–99, 108, 109, 113–117, 121, 131, 132, 137, 148, 154, 156, 157, 162, 163, 167, 189, 191, 193
Nogaret, Guillaume de 69, 71, 152–154
Noorweegse (Norwegian) Kaai 183
Normans 50–51, 55, 56, 68, 104, 124, 129, 162
Norse 5, 50, 78, 80, 120
North Sea 3, 6, 98, 179
Northern Brabant 142
Northumbria 29
Norway 17, 35, 167
Notre Dame Cathedral (Tournai) 139
Notre Dame Cathedral (Paris) 59, 63
Novgorod 13
novice masters 34
nuns 34, 64

oaths 10, 52–53, 81
oats 121
Onze Lieve Vrouwkerk see Church of Our Lady
Oosterlingenplein 183
Oostkerke 185
opera 118
Orchies 149
Oriflamme 134

The Origin of Our Lady of Groeninge (painting) 175
orphan debt 97
orphan money 97
orphans 22
Orsini 71
Ostend 120, 183
Otto 79
Oudenaarde 105, 129, 156, 182
Oudenburg 123
Our Lady of Hoyen Beguinage 81
ovens 39, 57
Overbeke 172
overpopulation 163
oxen 35, 58
Oxford 61, 78, 119
Oxford (Courtrai) Chest 78, 119–120, 127, 133, 136, 139, 175

pack animals 17
Padua 61
paintings 12, 68, 173
Palatine Court 49
Palermo 118
Palestine 24
palfreys 89
panzers 189
papermaking 66
Parent-Duchatelet, Alexandre 65
parents 20, 23, 54, 55, 69, 124
Paris 5, 47, 50, 51, 59–69, 78, 93, 94, 105, 106–109, 111, 125, 149, 151, 153, 154, 155, 156, 161
parlement de Paris 67, 93, 106, 107, 108, 149
Parliament 166, 194
partible inheritance 50
passage of arms (pas d'armes) 86
Passchendaele 160
Patria Flandrensis 187
paupers 22
paveses, pavises 76–77, 132, 136
Pavia 61
peasants 1, 9, 41–42, 51, 54, 57–58, 66, 74–75, 122, 128–130, 142, 153, 190
Peasants' Revolt of 1381 153
peat 97, 164
Pedro III of Aragon 118
Pelikaan or Pelican House 7
Pepin the Short 49
Perche 63
Persia 189
Pertuis 172

Index

Peter 62, 141, 142, 150, 184
Petrarch 166
petticoats 113
pewter 165
peytral 89
Philip (II) Augustus, King of France 35, 59–66, 69, 75, 79, 81, 84, 106, 158
Philip II of Spain 171
Philip (III) the Bold, King of France 67–68
Philip (IV) the Fair (Philippe le bel) 27, 68–72, 97, 98, 103, 106–116, 125, 128, 130, 141, 142, 143, 146–154, 157, 164
Philip V 68, 155, 156
Philip VI 65, 157–159
Philip of Alsace 11, 32, 35, 79, 82, 95, 97, 124
Philip the Bold, Duke of Burgundy 159, 161
Philippa 105, 106, 149
Philippide 63
Piacenca 61
Picardy 17
pikes 74–77, 84, 90, 91, 127, 128, 133, 147, 160, 190
pilgrimages 24, 27, 28, 32, 35, 66, 154, 169
pirates, piracy 146
Pisa 12
Planckaert, Anna 172
plundering 5, 84
Poitiers 159, 190
Poitou 56
Poland, Poles 13, 166, 179
polders 26, 28
pole weapons 160, 191
poleyns 88
pollution 38
Pontoise, Treaty of 149
Pont-à-Tressin 147
Pont-à-Vendin 147
Poortersloge 7, 9, 145
Poperinge 95
Popes, the Papacy 23, 31, 49, 52, 56, 67, 71, 140, 152, 153, 154, 166
population 3–5, 9, 17–18, 23, 34, 54, 59, 60, 66, 69, 78, 95, 122, 146, 155, 159, 162, 172, 175, 185, 186
Portugal, Portuguese 13, 98, 163, 166, 179, 190
Pottelberg 126, 138
Potterierei 7
pottery 38–40, 175

Pourbus, Pieter 79
Pourceaux square 63
precentors 34
premières écoles 62
privileges 7, 9, 10, 11, 17, 18, 43, 45, 62, 64, 73, 80, 93, 94, 103, 105, 106, 107, 109, 111, 124, 142, 148, 150
Procession of the Holy Blood 24
property tax 107, 124
Protestantism 171, 194
proto-capitalism 165
Provence 67, 146
Provins 13
Purgatory 141
purses 115

quai des Célestins 60
Quiéret, French admiral 158

railways 172, 173
ravens, as omens 127
refectory 32, 34
Reformation 33, 56, 170, 179, 186
Regensburg, Treaty of 172
Regime of the Captains 156
regional fairs 15
Reie River 5, 6
Reinald of Geldren 105
Renaissance 38, 166
Renaud of Boulogne 35
Renaud of Burgundy 104
rents 62, 95–97, 141, 148, 155, 164
Reval 13
Rhine, Rhineland 17–18, 39, 48, 92, 163
Rhône 153
Richard (I) the Lionhearted 59, 84
Richard II 104, 160
Richard II of Normandy 104
Richebourg 104
ridder 88
Riga 13
Right Bank 60
rings 54, 87, 114
ritter 88
Robert II of Flanders 24, 82, 125
Robert of Artois 1, 125–132, 136–138, 140, 141, 169, 173, 188, 189
Robert of Béthune 45, 94, 104, 109, 149, 155–156
Robert of Molesme 31
Robert the Bruce 190
Robrecht "the Fries" 120
Rodenbach, Georges 179

Index

Roeselare Bank 184
Roman forum 173
Roman villas 57
Romanesque 23, 24, 26, 79
Rome 3, 9, 28, 31, 49, 54, 56, 58, 68, 69, 71, 82, 140, 141, 152, 153
roofs 37–38, 60
Rouen 51
royal commissioners 142
royal messengers 50
Rubens, Peter Paul 79
Rudolph of Nesle 132, 137–140
Ruhr 18
Russia 13, 159

Saeftingen, Willem van 34, 122, 127, 136, 150, 180, 185
St. Amand's abbey 124
St. Amandsberg 182
Saint-Clair-sur-Epte, Treaty of 50
St.-Denijs 139
Saint-Denis, rue 66, 67
Saint Donatian's Church 6, 23
Saint Elizabeth Beguinage 124, 136, 182
St-Elooi's church 169
Saint Félix-en-Lauragais 69
Saint-Genevieve Hill 62
Saint George's Guild of Archers 76
Saint-Germain, boulevard 60
Saint-Innocents Cemetery 63
Saint John's Hospital 26
Saint-Laurent Church 63
Saint-Michel, boulevard 60
Saint-Omer 96
Saint-Pol 111, 129–130, 132
Saint-Saviour's Cathedral 24
Saint Walburga's 24
Sainte-Chapelle 67
Salamanca 61
Salerno 61
Salic law 11, 48, 68, 155
salt 41
salt tax 64
saltpeter 66
Samarkand 167
sanitation 64, 65
Santiago de Compostella 28
Saracens 56
Sarges 166
satirical gospel 141
sausages 40
Saussaie 64
Savery, Roelandt 170, 175

Saxons 27, 49, 104, 122
Scheldt 17, 28, 56, 78, 80, 100, 186
Schild en vriendt (shield and friend) 118
Scotland, Scots 29, 56, 68, 105, 109, 146, 153, 157, 163, 184, 189–190, 194
scrinewerkers (chest-makers) 119
scriptorium 32
scutage 53
seals 62, 142, 151
Second World War see World War II
Seine 50, 60, 63, 64, 65, 66
Sempach 190
Serbs 167
serfdom 19, 54, 57, 58
serjeants (sergeants) 76
servants 75, 76, 77, 87, 132
sewers 5, 65, 173
shawls 113
shearers 94, 142, 151
sheep 17, 98, 163
shipbuilders 157
ships 6, 7, 12, 35, 98, 158, 159, 179, 183
shoes 76, 87, 114
shopping centers 165
Shrine of Saint Ursula 182
shrine workers 142
Sicilian Vespers 67, 118–119
Sicily 9, 67, 118–119, 159
siege 50, 74, 75, 79, 84, 120, 153
siege engineers 74
Sigis 175
Sijsele 134, 185
silk 9, 21, 112, 113, 114, 115, 183
Silk Road 13
siltation 7, 35
Sint Andries' chapel 96
Sinte Baafs, Matthew van 99
Sinte Baafs, van, family 99, 100, 101, 122, 151
Sint-Baaf's Abbey 80
Sint Baaf's Cathedral 79, 187
Sint-Baafs-Vijve, Truce of 109
Sint-Jacobs 24
Sint-Jacobspoort 24
Sint-Janhospitaal 35
Sint-Maarten's church 124, 170, 171
Sint-Niklaas Church 80
Sint-Pieter's Abbey 80
skinners 66
sleeves 112
Sluis 7, 35, 109, 158, 159, 184
Smedenpoort 43, 178
smiths 43, 142

Index

social classes 39, 165
socialism 194
socks 114
The Song of Roland 85
Sorbon, Robert de 62
Sorbonne 62
sorcery 154
sorrel 41, 127
Spain 7, 9, 28, 34, 61, 69, 88, 128, 153, 159, 162–163, 171–172, 183, 189
Spaniehof 28
Spanjaardstraat 183
speculation 163
Speculum Historiale 184
Speelmansrei 42
Speyetoren 170, 171
spices 16, 40, 41, 163
Spiegel Historiael (Mirror of History) 184
Spiegelrei 7
Spijker 80
spinning 12, 18, 38, 165
spinning wheel 12
Spinolarei 7, 183
Sporkin, Eustace 122
spurs 2, 88, 89, 90, 94, 138–140, 161, 173, 175, 176
square frames 12
squires 84, 90, 91, 108, 128, 138, 140, 147
Staes, Jan 100, 151
stained glass 22, 170
Statute of Praemunire 166
statues 28, 170, 171, 173, 175, 180, 181, 185, 187
Stedelijke Musea Brugges 8
Stedelijke Musea Kortrijk 79, 140, 175
Steenstraat 23
Stephen of Blois 56
Stettin 13
Stirling Bridge 2, 189
stirrups 48, 58, 77, 89, 136, 189
stock exchange 145, 183, 184
stockings 87
stoneware 39
Stralsund, Peace of 167
Strasbourg 17
streets 5, 15, 38, 65, 66, 82, 118, 155, 172, 173, 175, 178, 183, 184, 188
Sultanate of Delhi 167
Super Solio 153
supermarkets 165
surcotte 76, 88, 113–115, 120, 127, 148
Sweden 13, 35, 167

Switzerland, Swiss 68, 161, 190–194
swords 48, 76, 84–91, 117, 127, 133, 136, 191
Syria 82

tabards 112
taffeta 113
tailors 162
Tamerlane 167
Tancarville 140
taxes 10, 11, 22, 23, 41, 49, 51, 52, 71, 96, 97, 105, 106, 111, 116, 141, 149, 152, 164
Teano, Comte di 104
Templars 23, 130, 154
Tenochtitlan 167
tents 13, 86, 91, 108
Ter Doest 28, 31, 32, 33, 34, 122, 150, 185
Ter Duinen 31, 32
textiles 7–13, 17–19, 59, 76, 78, 93–95, 107, 112–114, 124, 151–152, 163–165, 179, 186
thatched roofs 37, 38
theology 62
Thierry (Dietrich) of Alsace 24, 132
Third Crusade 59
The XXXIX (The Thirty-Nine) 92, 93, 99, 101, 106, 108, 111
Thomas Aquinas, Saint 62, 194
The Three Cities 164
three field rotation 58
timber 13, 41
tin 163
tithe barn 32–33, 185
tolls 11, 52, 142, 164
Tongeren 123
topography 188
Torhout 120
Toulouse 50, 67
Tour de Jean Sans Peur 60
Touraine 56
Tournai 17, 26, 27, 28, 31, 48, 96, 100, 101, 123, 139, 147, 169, 172
tournaments 85–87, 91, 137
town councils 9, 10, 22, 47, 74, 75, 76
town halls 36, 45, 63, 170, 180, 181
townspeople 9, 81, 115, 153
trade 3, 5–18, 21–22, 28–29, 56, 59, 63–65, 93–99, 104, 107–108, 111, 146, 151–152, 156, 157, 162–165, 171, 179, 184
The Transport 164, 166
transportation 5–7, 10, 15–17, 28, 38, 42,

43, 58, 64, 80, 76, 82, 118, 147, 172, 178, 182, 183, 186, 187, 191
treaties 50, 93, 106, 107, 109, 148, 149, 159, 166, 167, 172
trenchers 40
Trie 129, 140
Troyes 13, 161
trumpeters 76, 112, 126
Tuchman, Barbara 190
Tuilleries 65
tunics 37, 76, 78, 112, 113, 115, 136
Turkey, Turks 68, 167, 189

Ullenspiegel, Tijl 184
undersocks 114
underwear 37
Union of Kalmar 167
United Netherlands, Kingdom of the 172
universities 60–62, 67, 78, 175, 176
Urban II 56
Utenbroeke, Philip 184
utensil makers 162

Valenciennes 107, 158
Valladolid 61
Valois 157, 161, 162
Van Eyck brothers (artists) 79, 187
van Velthem, Louis 92, 126, 184
Vandals 48
vassals 9, 47, 52–54, 68, 83, 84, 105, 106, 108
Veaux, place aux 63
vegetables 57
veils 114
velvet 9, 113, 115
venants 86
Venice, Venetians 6, 11, 13, 68, 71, 163, 183
Verbruggen, J.F. 128, 140
Vercelli 61
Verdi, Giuseppe 118
Verdun, Treaty of 50
vervelles 87
Verwersdijk 42
Vespers 32, 67, 118
Veurne 109
Vicenza 61
Vigne, Paul de 180
Vigne-Quyo, Petrus de 187
Vikings 3, 11, 50, 59, 189
Villani, Giovanni 126, 134, 138
Vincent of Beauvais 184

Viollet-le-Duc, Eugène 78
Virgin and Child (statue) 181
Virgin of Flanders 176
viscounts 52
Visigoths 48, 82, 189
Visschere, Pieter de 100, 101
Vitry 146
Vlaendren die Leeu 134, 138
Vlamingstraat 184
voud, vouden 75
Vrijdagmarkt 81, 187

wages 19, 20, 21, 22, 76, 94, 108, 109, 165, 193
wagons 10, 16, 17, 43, 58, 76, 147, 191
Waldensians 56
Wales 29
Wallace, William 189–190
Walloon Brabant 143
Walloons 184, 188
walls 5, 9, 13, 22, 37–38, 42, 57, 60, 73–75, 82, 97, 99, 116, 126, 128, 140, 142, 151, 156, 169, 172–173, 175
war-horses 88–89, 127
Warneton 104
warpers 12
waste disposal 38, 65
water carriers (boatmen) 64
Waterhalle 43
Way of the Cross 170
weavers 7, 12, 18–22, 76, 94, 96, 105, 116, 118, 124, 127, 130, 142, 143, 151, 157, 165, 169, 181, 188
weights and measures 10, 64, 94
Wellington, Duke of 176
West Flanders 129, 136, 185, 188
Westerwald 39
Westhoek 156, 157, 166
Westrozebeke 160, 161, 170, 173, 189, 191
widows 22, 67
wife-beating 54
Wijnendaal (Wijnendaele) 120–121
Wijngaard 27, 182
Wilhelm II 176
Willem's Gate 172
William, King of the United Netherlands 176
William of Boenhem 130, 138, 139
William of Gulik (Jülich) 104, 117, 120, 121, 125, 128, 130, 134, 138, 140, 146, 147, 148
William of Ockham 193
William of Salisbury 35

Index

William the Breton 79
William the Conqueror (of Normandy) 55, 84, 104, 158
wimples 37, 114
windmills 41
wine 11, 17, 31, 35, 40, 41, 53, 64, 81, 92, 96, 100, 127, 152, 163, 184
Woeringen 106
Woesijne, van der, family 94
women 21, 26, 27, 37, 54–55, 64, 67, 95, 112–115, 136, 161, 172, 193
wood 11, 32, 37, 40, 57, 64, 77, 90, 114, 163
wool 7, 9, 10, 12, 17, 18, 31, 32, 37, 43, 47, 93, 95, 97, 98, 108, 112–114, 124, 151, 152, 158, 163, 183
woolen industry 17, 124
World War I 160, 167, 172, 180

World War II 172, 165, 176, 180
Wyclif, John 153, 193

Yolande of Burgundy 104
Yorkshire 160
Ypres 5, 16, 19, 41, 78, 92–97, 107, 109, 122, 125, 129, 136–137, 141–142, 148, 151, 155–158, 163–166, 172

Zannekin, Niklaas 156, 157
Zedelgem 26
Zeebrugge 180, 183
Zeeland 91, 104, 109, 111, 126, 147, 149, 166, 184
Zeger 91
Zierikzee 147, 157
Zwevegem 131, 139
Zwin 6, 35, 158, 179, 180, 184